A SHORT HISTORY OF
AFRICAN PHILOSOPHY

A Short History of African Philosophy

SECOND EDITION

Barry Hallen

Indiana University Press
Bloomington and Indianapolis

This book is a publication of

Indiana University Press
601 North Morton Street
Bloomington, IN 47404-3797 USA

www.iupress.indiana.edu

Telephone orders   800-842-6796
Fax orders   812-855-7931
Orders by e-mail   iuporder@indiana.edu

Library of Congress Cataloging-in-Publication Data

Hallen, B.
A short history of African philosophy / Barry Hallen. — 2nd ed.
p.   cm.
Includes bibliographical references (p.   ) and index.
ISBN 978-0-253-35364-1 (cloth : alk. paper) — ISBN 978-0-253-22123-0
(pbk. : alk. paper) 1. Philosophy, African—History. I. Title.
B5305.H35   2009
199'.6—dc22
2009017093

1 2 3 4 5 14 13 12 11 10 09

Contents

A SHORT HISTORY OF
AFRICAN PHILOSOPHY

Introduction

To potential readers, who perhaps are not familiar with the subject matter of African philosophy, I will say that this second edition has been revised—certainly in part—with you still in mind. Philosophy in any cultural context is not likely to be the easiest subject in the world. But its presentation can make it seem excessively technical and obscure in nature (at least in this author's opinion), and can frustrate or deter understanding unnecessarily. On the other hand, it would do the discipline a disservice to reduce it to banal and trivial generalizations that virtually no one would find of interest. I hope this revised text continues to strike some form of balance between these extremes by using rhetoric and a format that are suitable for a general audience and still give fair representation to the work of those colleagues whose ideas are discussed.

There have been any number of important developments in African philosophy since the first edition of this book was published in 2002. For example, the chapter on the early history of philosophy in the African context demanded expansion, given recent reconsiderations about those who deserve to be regarded as canonical figures. In addition, contemporary philosophers in and of Africa have continued to articulate and develop their ideas in new publications (which has also required extensive additions to the bibliography at the end of this book). These involve continuing discussions surrounding the issue of the philosophical heritage of Africa's precolonial and indigenous cultures, and how this should relate to contemporary African philosophy. Arising in part from those discussions, an increasing number of African philosophers are endorsing the preservation and enhancement of the communal character of Africa's indigenous cultures. This is seen as a healthier alternative to Western emphases on self-interest, excessive individual "freedoms," and a family that is only "nuclear" in character—all seen by some African philosophers as questionable contributions to human welfare if it is to be promoted in a social context. African philosophers have also progressed further in their criticisms of Western feminism and associated Western social values, and are now advocating distinctively non-Western formulations of gender issues that are drawn directly from and relevant to the African context. These are a few highlights from the revisions to this new edition.

The manner in which the contemporary material has been subdivided into chapter headings (rationalism, relativism, phenomenology, Marxism, etc.) has been deemed controversial by some reviewers of the first edition, who argue that this imposes an essentially Western taxonomy on African thought. But, as a number of the new additions to this text also indicate, the appropriate relationship between Western and African philosophy, with regard to methodologies especially, continues to be a subject of vigorous debate, and a consensus seems to be emerging that certain commonalities shared between them may be more than merely superficial. I do, however, fully appreciate the fact that if one were to take into account the entire corpus of writings of some of the philosophers whose work is discussed in only one chapter, they might well qualify for inclusion in two, or even three, different chapters. The explanation I can offer is that this is meant to be a *short* history of African philosophy and, as such, it pays particular attention to a select or limited number of themes or topics that have been deliberately extracted from their broader contexts, in order to facilitate the relevant comparisons.

I again feel it necessary to say something to those colleagues who find their ideas represented in this text. It can be a very disheartening, even maddening, experience to find your ideas misconstrued in a secondary source. But it becomes even worse when that secondary source takes on vestiges of being received as a more authoritative or "correct" rendition of those ideas than your own originals. Those who feel they have been somehow victimized by the way they are treated in what follows should please communicate their thoughts to the author.

Finally, a number of other people deserve special thanks for their help in bringing this new edition to fruition. Those who come to mind are D. A. Masolo, Nkiru Nzegwu, Tsenay Serequeberhan, Olufemi Taiwo, and, in particular, Kwasi Wiredu. My two institutional affiliations again have been instrumental to its completion. Here I am thinking of the W. E. B. Du Bois Institute for African and African American Research at Harvard University, where I have been privileged to be a Fellow or Associate since 1995; in particular its Director, Henry Louis Gates Jr., and the Fellows Officer, Vera Grant. Thanks to Harvard's superb bibliographic resources and research facilities, I have been able to undertake a number of research projects relevant to African philosophy while associated with the Du Bois Institute. As well, I express thanks to my colleagues in the Department of Philosophy and Religion at Morehouse College, Atlanta, Georgia, USA, to the Morehouse College administration that has helped to support my travels to and from Africa, and most importantly to the students at Morehouse who have been subjected to my courses in African and African American philosophy. Dee Mortensen, my editor at Indiana University Press, has been enthusiastic and supportive about the project from the very beginning, and June Silay, my project editor at the Press, has made a number of constructive contributions. Kate Babbitt, my copy editor, deserves thanks for her helpful comments and suggestions.

1

The Historical Perspective

The characterization of Africa's precolonial indigenous cultures as significantly ahistorical in character has been dismissed as patently false. The significance of the word "primitive," as originally used by *non*-Africans to type Africa's cultures, was that those cultures could serve as contemporary exemplars of how human beings had lived in primeval and pristine times, "before" recorded history (Kuper 1988; Mudimbe 1994).

This false ahistorical stereotype had profound consequences for Africa's status vis-à-vis philosophy as an international enterprise. "Early" human societies anywhere in the world were not thought to have developed the capacity for the intellectual reflection definitive of this supposedly sophisticated discipline. Therefore Africa's indigenous cultures were, in both principle and fact, disqualified from occupying a place in the philosophical arena.

The response on the part of many African philosophers, scholars, and intellectuals to this falsely ahistorical, as well as deeply offensive, typing of the cognitive significance of their civilizations has been sustained and vigorous. The fact that these efforts have only recently begun to have recognizable consequences in and on the Western academy would probably be cited by those same individuals as further evidence of how profound the influence of this demeaning caricature of Africa's cultures was on the rest of the world and, in some cases, on Africans themselves.

In this introductory chapter, attention will focus upon a variety of significant sources of philosophical thinking from the African historical context that predate the so-called modern era: Egyptian texts that date back as early as 3000 BCE;[1] the philosophical and theological writings of some of

1. I use the alternative abbreviations BCE ("Before the Common Era") and CE ("Common Era") for designating years, rather than BC and AD, with the inherent references to Jesus Christ that they contain.

the earliest African (Christian) Church Fathers, which were instrumental in forming what was (and, in some cases, was not) to become doctrinal ortho-doxy; a selection of texts by African Islamic philosophers from the sixteenth through nineteenth centuries that contain important but long-neglected African contributions to and viewpoints on the multicultural philosophical traditions of the Islamic world; a collection of treatises from Abyssinia (a country that consisted essentially of what is today Ethiopia and Eritrea) that began to be produced during the seventeenth century CE; and the remarkable successes and striking argumentation of the Ghanaian philosopher Anton Wilhelm Amo, in eighteenth-century European academia.

The claim that examples of philosophical texts existed in ancient Egypt is sometimes misleadingly overidentified with the school of thought that has come to be known as Afrocentrism. And Afrocentrism itself is sometimes unfairly and one-dimensionally typed as an attempt to inflate the interna-tional importance and influence of ancient Egyptian culture totally out of proportion to the "scientific" evidence for it. But from both a historical and a cultural point of view, the reaffirmation of ancient Egypt as an integral part of the African continent constitutes a rejection by African[2] scholars of those who have used the Saharan and Nubian deserts as a kind of "iron curtain" between the "black" African cultures to their south and the "non-black" (but somehow also "non-white") peoples to their north (Obenga 1992, 2004). At worst, the qualitatively different characteristics of the civilizations thereafter attributed to these two groups are said to have transposed racism from the modern to the ancient world. At best, they are said to disregard the history of the commercial and cultural exchanges that always took place between the peoples of north, west, east, central, and south Africa.

It is impossible to characterize all of the literature currently associated with Afrocentrism with a set of simplified generalizations. Afrocentrism is probably best known in Western scholarship for its arguments that both the form and content of ancient Greek (and, hence, eventually European/ Western) philosophy and science were derived directly from Egyptian civili-zation (Ben-Jochannan 1994; Diop 1974; James 1954; Obenga 1995). This in turn has generated a concerted response from Western classicists (aca-demics who specialize in Greek and Roman civilization) that the charac-ter of Greek thought and civilization was, in these respects, fundamentally different and distinctive from that of their Egyptian counterparts and that consequently no such fundamental linkage or crossover can be established. (Basically, the Greeks are distinguished by their "abstract" and "reasoned"

2. The term "African" will be used to refer to scholarship that is specifically concerned with the African continent and its cultures. "Africana" is a more inclusive term for scholarship related to both Africa and the diaspora.

thought, while Egyptian thought is characterized as "regimented" and "practical" [Lefkowitz 1996; Lefkowitz and Rogers 1996]). Somewhere on the stormy seas that contain these contending forces also lies the work of the American scholar Martin Bernal, whose three-volume *Black Athena* (1987, 1991, 2006) aims at presenting sufficient empirical evidence to establish the importance of ancient intellectual interactions between Greek, Semitic Mediterranean, and African peoples once and for all on an acceptably scientific basis.

Although it would be noteworthy poetic justice for a discipline —philosophy—that was once denied to Africa to have in fact originated there, this book will not concentrate on the debate over whether Egyptian culture was the progenitor of Western philosophy. Here I will emphasize the element of historical continuity and development that, for example, the reintegration of Egyptian, Christian, Islamic, and Abyssinian thought into Africa's intellectual history provides. This point will also be discussed in chapter 8, in relation to the Nigerian anthropologist Ifi Amadiume's critical evaluation and adaptation of Cheikh Anta Diop's theories relevant to the historical issue of gendering in the African cultural context.

In an attempt to bracket any underlying ethnocentric biases, on purely technical or scholarly grounds why has it been maintained that Egyptian thought *in general* should be typed as pre- or non-philosophical?

> I use the term *philosophy* in the more specialized, modern sense, to mean *the study of causes and laws underlying reality*[3] or *a system of inquiry designed specifically to study those laws and causes.* The ancient Egyptians and Babylonians were learned and had what we would now call advanced civilizations; they could have developed *an abstract terminology* for discovering causes and principles had they chosen to do so. But they did not *study and analyze the nature of reality in abstract, nontheological language.* This specialized notion of philosophy was invented, so far as anyone knows, by the ancient Greeks. (Lefkowitz 1996, 188–89; my italics)

One fundamental objection that contemporary Africana scholars raise against this definition is that it is factually false and ignores the *abstract* intellectual merit of some of the literature that has been inherited from Egyptian culture. Also, because of the definition's blatant metaphysical or ontological bias, it ignores disciplines such as ethics or moral philosophy as elements of legitimate philosophical enterprise. And one reason for this is that the point of view this definition represents is too narrow and culturally specific,

---

3. Surely those "causes and laws" could constitute as well as underlie "reality."

based essentially upon a paradigm that once was embraced, most notably, by Western philosophy.

The Congolese Egyptologist and philosopher Theophile Obenga (1936–) argues that this mistaken stereotype ("non-abstract," "regimented," "practical") arises in part from an erroneous appreciation of the powers of Egyptian hieroglyphics (rather than the "written" word) to express theoretical ideas:

> Egyptian thinking was graphic and abstract at the same time. Pictures were used as symbols of thought. . . . The Egyptians did develop a kind of semiology by studying the relationship between signs and pictures, using material objects to represent something invisible or abstract. This is not to say that the Egyptian philosophers thought in graphic and concrete terms. They made use of graphic and concrete forms to think abstractions. This may seem quaint for the modern mind, because of the alphabetical system of writing. In fact, semiotic structures in hieroglyphic signs were a fine equipment for precise abstract thinking. (2004, 34)

It therefore makes sense to consider the hard evidence that is relevant to this controversy. The specific text to be considered here is included in many anthologies of Egyptian and/or African literature and is frequently referred to as "The Moral Teachings of Ptah-hotep."[4] Various versions of the text exist, but scholars seem to agree that Ptah-hotep was an official of the Old Kingdom (Fifth Dynasty) who lived c. 2400 BCE.

The heart of Ptah-hotep's manuscript consists of thirty-seven principles (for lack of a better word) that define and, more importantly, justify certain forms of behavior as being moral (*Maat*). A complication in assessing the text's philosophical significance is that it has been translated into English using a variety of formats—as poetic verse (Asante 2000), as imperative maxims (Gunn 1909), and as an essay (Hilliard 1987). For purposes of the present discussion the essay format is preferable because a sentential rendering highlights the underlying reasoning more clearly.

Many different forms of behavior are discussed—some are discouraged, some are commended—and I encourage readers to refer to the original text itself (Hilliard 1987) for a more comprehensive statement of them. One scholar has summarized the forms of behavior that are commended as "respect for proper speech, respect for elders and leaders, ritual remembrance, good behavior, absence of arrogance, lack of threats, absence of gossip, submission to authority, pursuit of truth, attainment of justice, generosity, self-control, impartiality, avoidance of hasty speech, masking one's inner feelings, and good listening skills" (C. Lehman as quoted in Asante 2000, 41). For most of the thirty-seven principles Ptah-hotep also provides reasons, often in the

---

4. Why not "The Moral *Philosophy* of Ptah-hotep"?

form of potentially adverse or positive consequences, why a particular form of behavior is to be discouraged or commended, as in the following:

> 25. If you are mighty and powerful then gain respect through knowledge and through your gentleness of speech. Don't order things except as it is fitting. The one who provokes others gets into trouble. Don't be haughty lest you be humbled. But also don't be mute lest you be chided. When you answer one who is fuming, turn your face and control yourself. The flame of the hot-hearted sweeps across everything. But he who steps gently, his path is a paved road. He who is agitated all day has no happy moments, but he who amuses himself all day can't keep his fortune. (Hilliard as quoted in Hord and Lee 1995, 28)

What is intriguing is the repeated emphasis Ptah-hotep gives to a more select set of values that have also been outlined in the work on Yoruba moral epistemology done by Hallen and Sodipo.[5] Again and again, Ptah-hotep stresses the importance of "good speech," which is defined as (a) accurately recording/reporting what one personally has seen or heard ("Listen carefully" [Hord and Lee 1995, 27]; "Just keep to the truth. Do not exceed it" [26]; "Give the message exactly" [26]). And (b), when contributing new ideas to a discussion, expressing oneself in a thoughtful and perceptive manner ("The trusted man is one who does not speak the first thing that comes to mind" [26]; "Speak when you know that you have a solution" [28]; "Be deliberate when you speak so as to say things that count" [31]). Again and again, Ptah-hotep stresses the importance of self-control, internal as well as external ("Self-control will be the match for . . . evil utterances" [25]; "Gain respect through knowledge and through your gentleness of speech. . . . When you answer one who is fuming, turn your face and control yourself " [28]).

These values are enunciated in no less than fifteen of the thirty-seven principles, as well as in the introductory and concluding passages that accompany them. The accompanying text makes it clear that Ptah-hotep affirms them as moral values because they promote truth, and therefore they have epistemological consequences as well. A person whose word(s) can be relied upon is a moral person, and vice versa. A person who maintains self-control is in an optimal state to be an objective observer of his or her surroundings and, hence, to correctly understand, record, report, and offer advice (if needed) about what is going on.

> The fool who does not *hear* [listen, observe, and speak with care and forethought], he can do nothing at all. He looks at ignorance and

5. The Yoruba are an ethnic group inhabiting present-day West Africa, mainly southwestern Nigeria, whose distinctive culture has attracted the attention of many scholars. See chapter 4 for discussion of the Hallen-Sodipo approach to philosophy in the African context.

sees knowledge. He looks at harmfulness and sees usefulness. He does everything that one detests and is blamed for it every day. He lives on the thing by which one dies. His food is evil speech [things that are not true]. His sort is known to the officials who say, "There goes a living death every day." One ignores the things that he does because of his many daily troubles. (Hilliard 1987, 30; my italics)

Though these similarities between Ptah-hotep's ethics and Yoruba moral epistemology are striking, that does not necessarily mean that a process of direct philosophical transmission or exchange between these two cultures took place. This is an issue that would require much more in-depth research. For the moment, what it may indicate is the extent to which Ptah-hotep's society was also an oral (as well as literate) culture, and hence—as in Yoruba—the spoken word was deliberately assigned a heightened moral status because of the manner in which its truth-value reflected a speaker's moral character.

Discussions of African philosophy that focus exclusively on the cultures of *sub*-Saharan Africa are virtually devoid of any reference to philosophical scholarship in *North* Africa (with the exception of *ancient* Egypt) or the prosperous Sahelian emporiums and centers of learning, such as Timbuktu (in present day Mali). One justification seems to be that these regions were so heavily affected and influenced by Arab/Islamic culture that any truly autochthonous philosophical thinking was overwhelmed. Interestingly, the empirical basis on which this historical presumption is based (and the geographical, cultural, and intellectual bifurcations that resulted) is today increasingly being challenged by a number of African philosophers who are reexamining those regions' hitherto comparatively neglected oral and written philosophical sources that have survived, created and/or written by Africans.

The underlying issue—of what should be regarded as authentic sources for and of African philosophy—has been a subject of outright controversy in contemporary African philosophy for decades. Kwame Nkrumah (1909–1972), both politician and philosopher, for example, explicitly recognizes the undeniably tripartite character (traditional, Islamic, Christian) of Africa's intellectual heritage in his well-known *Consciencism* (1964/1970). But it also seems to be the case that a substantive number of contemporary philosophers in and of Africa continue to shy away from incorporating overtly Islamic or Christian themes in their accounts of African thought, and therefore intentionally concentrate on the so-called traditional—on identifying and working with elements of supposedly *pre*-Christian and *pre*-Islamic thought—as a basis and even central focus for their work.

To a point this strategy is understandable. For decades Africans had to suffer both cultural and intellectual humiliation at the hands of a Western imperialism whose scholars presumed to understand more about Africans and their cultures than the Africans themselves. With political liberation from Western colonialism and the exhilarating intellectual liberation that ensued, it is understandable that African philosophers made it a priority to determine precisely what the beliefs, practices, and intellectual characters of their native cultures were *pre*-Islam, *pre*-Christianity, and *pre*–European occupation. It is difficult to believe that anyone in African studies generally today could deny that this impetus has had profound consequences for the general character of work in that field—as, for example, is evidenced by the radical realignment of relationships between Western researchers and African populations (whose members are no longer referred to as "informants" or, as Kwasi Wiredu puts it, "informational servants" [2004, 7]).

How this realignment, of what is and is not entitled to be included under the rubric of African philosophy, will work itself out is a phenomenon that will continue to be of considerable interest as time passes. But, for our historical purposes, perhaps a more expansive view is justified. For if someone such as the Ghanaian Anton Wilhelm Amo (c. 1703–1758), whose work will be discussed below, is lauded for his mastery of Western philosophy during his lifetime, why should not other Africans associated, for example, with either early Christian or Islamic theology and philosophy (at that time the division between the two disciplines was sometimes hard to draw) deserve equal recognition?

Some of the most famous names associated with the group that has come to be known as the "Early Church Fathers" are Origen (CE 185–253), Tertullian (c. CE 155–240), and Aurelius (better known as "Saint") Augustine (CE 354–430). But how often are their origins and identities as native Africans similarly highlighted? The Kenyan philosopher D. A. Masolo has written a provocative synopsis (2004a) of their intellectual contributions to early Church doctrines that highlights their status as African intellectuals whose original and influential contributions to Christian philosophy are responsible for their elevated/illustrious status.

Origen was born in Alexandria, Egypt, and was commonly referred to during his lifetime (as were Tertullian and Augustine) as "the African" (Masolo 2004a, 53). Masolo speculates that he was therefore likely of Berber or Punic origin. Interestingly, he was convinced that "philosophy occupied a special place in history," particularly as an instrument for conversion (2004a, 53). But what is of special interest to Masolo are the various apparently syncretic elements of his theology, probably adopted or adapted from classic Egyptian as well as indigenous North African sources, that eventually led to his being deposed from his post in the Alexandrian Church for heresy. Among them are the belief that a basic spiritual and divine component of the human being (in addition to the soul) is the *pneuma,* which seems similar to the "vital force" ontology which we shall see below (chapter 2) that Tempels attributes to the Bantu of sub-Saharan Africa; the enhanced importance he assigns to resurrection and immortality, which at the time were most prominently associated with the Egyptian god Osiris; and the precise composition of the doctrine of the Trinity, again as influenced by classic Egyptian beliefs arising from a hierarchy of deities (2004a, 55). This in part leads Masolo to suggest that "the theological systematization of the doctrine of the Trinity was done by [these] African pioneer" converts to Christianity (2004a, 56). Origen is distinctive because of his determination to systematize the diverse doctrinal elements that sometimes led to sectarian controversy in the early Church. For this reason Masolo concludes that "Origen is arguably the most influential theologian of the early Church and the most important theologian of the entire Church before Augustine" (2004a, 52).

Tertullian was born and lived his life in the North African city of Carthage (located in what is today Tunisia). "Tertullian's African descent is discerned by historians from both his literary style and his hatred for anything Greek" (2004a, 57). The latter possibly also helps to explain his hostility (unlike Origen's positive viewpoint) toward philosophy (as a potent source of heresy), his commitment to faith as the exclusive basis for religion, and therefore his coining of the famous phrase, contra reason, to justify that faith (later to be repeated by the Danish philosopher Kierkegaard in the nineteenth century): *"credo quia absurdum"* (I believe that which is absurd) (2004a, 58).

Aurelius (St.) Augustine was a Berber who is deservedly famous for his autobiographical *Confessions,* in which he famously describes the incident that led to his conversion to Christianity. Although he too appreciated the importance of faith as a foundation for Christian belief, Augustine also maintained that "truth is not created but only discovered by reason; and it exists in itself prior to such discovery" (2004a, 61). In his *City of God* he demonstrates the rigor of his thinking when he proposes the following somewhat convoluted line of reasoning (anticipating Descartes's more famous proof of the *cogito* arising from the "I think, therefore I am" argument): "If I am mistaken, I am. For, if one does not exist, he can by no means be mistaken. Therefore, I am, if I am mistaken. Because, therefore, I am, if I am mistaken, how can I be mistaken that I am, since it is certain that I am, if I am mistaken (2004a, 61)?"[6]

The passage, preservation, and elaboration of many of the classic Greek philosophical texts in the Islamic world is a story too well-known to be repeated here.[7] Suffice it to say that Al Ma'mun, the caliph of Baghdad, authorized the creation of an institution for the translation of the Greek texts into Arabic in the year CE 832. That philosophy (or *philosophia*) was assigned a prominent place in this new body of literature is attested to by the Arabic coining of the term *falsafa* to represent it.

6. As quoted by Masolo from *The City of God (De civitate Dei, XI, 26).*

7. Another neglected potential source of ancient Greek and Roman philosophical manuscripts is the Byzantine Empire (c. CE 330–1453). See, for example, K. Ierodiakonou, *Byzantine Philosophy and Its Ancient Sources* (2004).

The Senegalese philosopher Souleymane Bachir Diagne (1955–) has written an intriguing exploratory account of the influence and effects of this body of literature on Africa as a whole (2004a). He begins this account be rearticulating the protest noted above against the attitude that "what is 'authentically' African is simply assumed to be what remains once you have removed all the deposits [e.g., Islam] that history has left on the continent" (2004a, 66). Various forms of philosophical thinking, via Islam, first began to be introduced into the African context more than one thousand years ago, and if that is not enough time to establish their pedigree as "authentically" African, "one ends up thinking that identity exists *in spite of* history, instead of *in* and *by* history" (2004a, 66).

This is not to say that the new forms of argumentation and thinking promulgated by *falsafa* were received with unreserved admiration. From the beginning there was an opposing faction in Islamic culture "according to which all true sciences have to be exclusively rooted in the very letter of the Revealed Text [the Qu'ran]" (2004a, 68). Nevertheless this foster child of Greek origin was to have profound influence in at least parts of the Islamic "world," Africa included.

One of its earliest and most celebrated African exponents was Ahmad Baba (1556–1627), an *ulama* (learned scholar) from Timbuktu who was therefore identified by Islamic sources as coming from the *Bilad as-Sudan* (translated by Diagne as "the Black people's land") (2004a, 69). Ahmad Baba so intrigued the *ulama* of Morocco and the sultan of the Songhay empire in North Africa that he was taken to the city of Marrakesh (Morocco), where he was detained but allowed to give public lectures for fourteen years. Although many of his lectures were on jurisprudence—philosophy of law in the Islamic cultural context—Diagne suggests that Baba was deliberately demonstrating, via the erudite content of his lectures, that the peoples of the Sudan (the "Blacks") had as much intellectual[8] and moral integrity, and therefore claim to independence, as the population of any segment of the Islamic world (2004a, 69).

Another interesting feature, noted by Diagne, of *falsafa* in the *Bilad as-Sudan* was, because of the scarcity of books, its transformation into oral literature.[9] But this is not to deny the creation of original *written* texts in the *Bilad as-Sudan,* sometimes in local languages transliterated into Arabic characters, that qualified as *falsafa* as well. Diagne mentions several famous

8. "To take an example from the field of logic (*mantiq*), Ahmad Baba's *grandfather,* Ahmad 'Umar Muhammad Aqit (d. 1583), wrote a commentary on al-Maghili's [d. c. 1505] poem on logic" (2004, 72; my italics).

9. Note the word "poem" in the preceding footnote. This should be of interest to those trained in the Western tradition to accept, as one of the prerequisites to the origins of Greek philosophy, that what had been oral literature began to be written down.

books on Islamic theology and philosophy that were written in the Hausa language using Arabic script in the fifteenth and seventeenth centuries that had widespread influence in the greater Islamic world (2004a, 71).

> Scarcity of books also explains the incredible role played by memorization[10] in the study of Islamic sciences. And this is true not only of the Quranic text, but also of more "secular" disciplines like logic. In fact, in order to help the memorizing, the authors themselves will, very often, write their theoretical works in poetry. For instance, the most celebrated treatises that were used in the study of Aristotelian logic were written in verses, such as the *Rajaz* of al-Maghili [d. c. 1505] or the *Sullam al Murwnaq* by Abd ar-Rahman al-Akhdari (1514–46). The latter is said to have been a celebrated textbook in Aristotelian logic taught in different mosques and other madrasas (schools) throughout North Africa as well as at the sub-Saharan African intellectual centers [e.g., Timbuktu in Mali; Kano in Nigeria]. (2004a, 70)

Finally, Diagne is concerned to point out that this tradition of elaborating upon theological and logical themes central to *falsafa* continued in the Sudan unabated up through the nineteenth century. It is evidenced in the writings of Uthman dan Fodio (d. 1817), celebrated leader of the *jihad* in northern Nigeria that gave rise to the so-called Sokoto Caliphate: "The *jihad* he fought is quite famous but should not overshadow his intellectual contribution to African philosophy in Arabic as well as in some African languages" (2004a, 73). And it is also evidenced in the until recently neglected work of Abd al-Qadir b. al-Mustafa al-Turudu (d. 1864), "the author of *Kulliyat al-alam al-sitta,* about 'universals' in philosophy" (2004a, 73).

The most prominent Abyssinian philosopher of the seventeenth century was a man named Zar'a Ya'aqob (1599–1692). The remarkable text he produced during his lifetime has as its English-language title *The Treatise of Zar'a Ya'aqob.* In the original Ge'ez language, it is known as the *Hatata.* This term, *hatata,* will deserve careful consideration because of its methodological implications.

Zar'a Ya'aqob was a religious man who had been educated in the Coptic Christian faith but, as his manuscript indicates, was also familiar with other Christian sects (Catholicism), Islam, Judaism, and Indian religion (Hinduism, Buddhism?). Indeed, it was the dilemma of choosing between these conflicting faiths, all meant to worship God, that appears to have been one of the motivating factors in his decision to rely upon his own powers of reasoning

10. Following upon the preceding footnote, this leads one to wonder, was the process for the recording of thought that is genuinely "philosophical" in character, from oral to written, in these instances reversed?

or understanding to promote his own personal nonsectarian relationship with that God:

> All men are equal in the presence of God, and all are intelligent, since they are his creatures; he did not assign one people for life, another for death, one for mercy, another for judgment. Our *reason* teaches us that this kind of discrimination cannot exist in the sight of God. . . . But Moses was sent to teach only the Jews. . . . Why did God reveal his law to one nation, withhold it from another? At this very time Christians say: "God's doctrine is only found with us"; similarly with the Jews, the Mohammedans, the Indians and the others. Moreover the Christians do not agree among themselves: the *Frang* [Europeans, Catholics] tell us: "God's doctrine is not with you, but with us." (Sumner 1976, 12; my italics in part)

Consequently, Zar'a Ya'aqob tells us, "People took me for a Christian when I was dealing with them; but in my heart I did not believe in anything except in God who created all and conserves all, as he had taught me" (Sumner 1976, 24).

What is philosophically remarkable about this text is the prominence, indeed primacy, it assigns to the analytic powers of human reason or understanding as the arbiter, or agency, responsible for what a person decides to accept as true:

> But truth is one. While thinking over this matter, I said: "O my creator, wise among the wise and just among the just, who created me with an *intelligence,* help me to *understand,* for men lack wisdom and truthfulness." (Sumner 1976, 7; my italics)
>
> God indeed has illuminated the heart of man with *understanding* by which he can see the good and evil, *recognize* the licit [right] and illicit [wrong], *distinguish* truth from error. (Sumner 1976, 10; my italics)
>
> Man aspires to know truth and the hidden things of nature, but this endeavour is difficult and can only be attained with great labour and patience, as Solomon said: "With the help of wisdom I have been at pains to study all that is done under heaven; oh what a weary task God has given mankind to labour at!" Hence people hastily accept what they have heard from their fathers and shy from any [critical] examination. (Sumner 1976, 8; Sumner's brackets)
>
> I have learnt more while living alone in a cave than when I was living with scholars. (Sumner 1976, 17)
>
> Behold, I have begun an inquiry such as has not been attempted before. You can complete what I have begun so that the people of our country will become wise with the help of God and arrive at

the science of truth, lest they believe in falsehood, trust in depravity, go from vanity to vanity, that they know the truth and love their brother, lest they quarrel about their empty faith as they have been doing till now. (Sumner 1976, 24–25; my italics)

In the course of his reflections upon the torturous process of critical reflection itself, Zar'a Ya'aqob also evaluates a number of more worldly issues: fasting, celibacy, scholarship, solitude, equality of husbands and wives, and justice, to name a few. But what is of greater philosophical interest is the critical methodology that underlies all of these reflections, the methodology that has come to be identified with the Ge'ez word *hatata.*

As Claude Sumner, the philosopher who has undertaken extensive translation, study, and commentary upon the work of Zar'a Ya'aqob, puts it: "Now the root . . . *hatata,* originally signified 'to reduce to small portions by rubbing, to grind.' Its meaning has progressively passed from the physical reality to the figurative application of: 'to question bit by bit, piecemeal; to search into or through, to investigate accurately; to examine; to inspect'" (Sumner 1978, 95). It is tempting to assign meaning to the obvious similarity between these root meanings and the contemporary academic philosophical approach that has come to be known as "analysis" or as "analytic philosophy," but that temptation should be moderated lest one underrate the originality of Zar'a Ya'aqob's thought by summarily reducing it to nothing more than a curiosity insofar as it becomes an anticipation of mainstream twentieth-century academic philosophy.[11]

Zar'a Ya'aqob himself uses the term *hatata* no fewer than twenty-one times in his treatise (Sumner 1978, 94). And the human faculty primarily responsible for its activation or application is designated by the word *amr,* which, Sumner tells us, "usually has the meaning of 'reason'; and, in a descending ratio, of 'intelligence,' 'understanding,' 'knowledge,' 'science,' 'thoughts' and 'doctrine(s).' In Zar'a Ya'aqob, reason is presented as a light which sheds clarity on the object it focuses upon. It is God-given, and belongs to all men. It enables them to distinguish truth from falsehood" (Sumner 1978, 107). Sumner characterizes the role of reason in the *hatata* overall:

Inquiry and reason are linked up as activity or process together with the intellectual power which is at their source. "The light of reason" . . . is purely philosophical and positive. It is the very means or

11. Although Verharen, in a review of the first edition of this book (2003), does suggest that it would be appropriate to note the similarities between Ya'aqob's methodological emphases upon systematic doubting and the "light of reason" with René Descartes's adoption of methodological doubt and "the natural light" of reason. He also points out that the two were near contemporaries, even if unknown to one another: Ya'aqob (1599–1692), Descartes (1596–1650).

condition for the application of the inquiry to any specific problem. The *hatata* presupposes the power of comprehending and inferring, an intellectual activity, the due exercise of the reasoning faculty or of right thinking. Such an activity acquires a vital importance in the philosophy of Zar'a Ya'aqob . . . since it permits the discrimination between the results of independent thinking and the lies which are perpetuated among those who accept indiscriminately what has been transmitted to them by the social environment in which they were brought up. It is the light which dispels the darkness that blocks those who are intellectually blind. (Sumner 1978, 104–105)

Yet another African figure of historical importance is the Ghanaian philosopher Anton Wilhelm Amo (c. 1703–1758). Although the circumstances through which he arrived in Europe are not clear,[12] it is a matter of record that he was "on October 10, 1730, granted the degree of Master of Philosophy and the Liberal Arts, renamed Doctor of Philosophy, a few years later, enabling him to lecture in Wittenberg from 1730 to 1734" (Abraham 2004, 93). Amo became quite well known in European academic circles of the time, and after finishing his formal education he taught in several German universities before returning to his native Ghana.

In eighteenth-century Europe, the discipline of philosophy still included a wide range of subjects (sciences as well as humanities) under its umbrella heading. Still, the specific topics to which Amo addressed himself are a matter of record and are of special interest in at least one respect for the manner in which they relate to and express his Africanity. This is especially the case with his first dissertation, which would have secured him a degree in both public and private law. Its theme, if not its title, is "On the Rights of Black Africans in Europe." Although the original manuscript has so far not been located, the contemporary Ghanaian philosopher William Abraham has used secondhand historical records to reconstruct Amo's basic argument.

This amounted to a critique of slavery, more specifically of the African slave trade. Drawing upon Europe's proud heritage of the Roman Empire, Amo seems to have argued that Rome was justly famous for eventually awarding all of her population—domestic and "foreign"—Roman citizenship. In principle, this made the entire population free and equal citizens of Rome, including those who lived in Africa. Therefore, Amo argued, Europeans were violating their own cultural heritage by enslaving human

12. William Abraham's "The Life and Times of Wilhelm Amo, the First African (Black) Philosopher in Europe," in *African Intellectual Heritage: A Book of Sources,* ed. M. K. Asante and A. S. Abarry (Philadelphia: Temple University Press, 1996), and his subsequent "Anton Wilhelm Amo" (in Wiredu 2004) provide excellent accounts of Amo's life and work. They have also served as my basic references for this segment of the text.

beings whom their own culture, as both Roman and Christian, had once recognized as free and equal and no different from themselves.

Amo's second (doctoral) dissertation, which is now to be found in the libraries of a number of universities, was a severe critique of the "modern" French philosopher René Descartes (1596–1650). Descartes is probably best known for his thesis of dualism—that the human being is a composite of a material substance (the body) and an immaterial substance (the mind). Descartes also maintained (which plain commonsense would say is obvious) that the (immaterial) mind experiences physical (bodily) sensations (pain, etc.). Amo suggested this was somehow problematic, inconsistent, or even a contradiction in terms. And, indeed, how two fundamentally different substances could interact became one of the more celebrated weak points of Cartesian philosophy, underscored by Descartes' having recourse to the lowly pineal gland as the point at which immaterial mind and material body somehow intercommunicated.[13]

A passage from an address made by Gotthelf Loescher, the professor who chaired Amo's successful defense of this second dissertation in April 1734 gives some idea of the high regard in which he was held:

> We proclaim Africa and its region of Guinea, separated by a very great distance from us, and formerly the Gold Coast, so called by Europeans on account of its abundant and copious yield of gold, but known by us as your fatherland, in which you first saw the light of day, the mother not only of many good things and treasures of nature but also of the most auspicious minds: we proclaim her quite deservedly! Among these auspicious minds, your genius stands out particularly, most noble and distinguished Sir, seeing that you have excellently demonstrated felicity and superiority of genius, solidity and refinement of learning and teaching, in countless examples before now, and even in this our University, with great honor in all worthy things, and now also in your present dissertation.
>
> I return to you still intact, and absolutely unchanged in any respect, that which you have conscientiously and with elegance worked out [his dissertation], supported by your erudition, in order that the power of your intellect may shine forth henceforth all the more strongly.
>
> It now only remains for me to congratulate you wholeheartedly on this singular example of your refined scholarship, and with a more abundant feeling of heart than words can convey. I solicit for you good fortune; and to the Divine Grace and also to the Highest and Most Noble Prince Ludwig Rudolph,[14] for whose health and

13. For a more detailed analysis of Amo's dissertation see Wiredu 2004a.

14. Presumably the Duke of Brunswick-Wolfenbüttel, the family that seems to have been Amo's benefactors throughout his stay in Germany.

safety I shall never tire of worshipping the Divine Majesty, I commend you. (Abraham 2004, 194–95)

There is yet another dimension to the history of philosophy in Africa—the virtual mountain of historical texts, still incompletely catalogued, that have been indiscriminately labeled African "oral literature."[15] For it certainly is the case that academic philosophers were for long predisposed to turn up their noses at the suggestion that an anonymous corpus of writings that included myths, legends, poetry, song, and proverbs was truly worthy of the title "philosophy."

This is an issue that will be discussed at greater length in the succeeding chapters. For the moment it is sufficient to suggest that most African philosophers, as well, would have reservations about labeling the whole of their continent's oral literature, literally, "philosophy." But that is not to say that it would be justifiable to reject the whole of that amorphous corpus as philosophy, either. One thing upon which Africana scholars and intellectuals largely agree is that the criteria used to define what is and what is not philosophy in the world today are unfairly biased by and for "philosophy" as presently construed by Western culture. There may have to be *some* common ground if the word "philosophy" is to continue to have cross-cultural significance. But Africa, in particular, has not received just consideration in that regard. In fact, as was pointed out at the beginning, initially Africa was not said to have produced any philosophers or philosophy at all.

That cultures which were significantly oral in character, or somehow different in other respects, produced forms of literature which are not conventional in present-day Western culture need not mean that they are lacking in philosophical content or substance. In so many respects, it seems, Africa's cultures have not benefited from the kinds of exhaustive and empathic scholarship that are being lavished upon other parts of the world. The oral literature of the African continent, therefore, has not even begun to receive the attention it merits. Elements of that corpus such as Ifa divination literature (Abimbola 1975, 1976, 1977; Taiwo 2004b), *The Ozidi Saga* (Clark-Bekederemo 1991), *The Myth of the Bagre* (Goody 1972), the *Song of Lawino* (p'Bitek 1966), and Samuel O. Imbo's *Oral Traditions as Philosophy* (2002) are just five random selections out of the literally thousands of monumental expressions of ideas that deserve careful consideration and analysis before they can be dismissed (as has effectively been the case) as quintessentially "religious," as quintessentially "mystical" or "mythical," as quintessentially *non*-philosophical.

Before this chapter comes to a close, three points remain to be made.

15. Kenyan writer Ngugi wa Thiong'o recommends replacing this term with "orature" to affirm that it represents as significant an intellectual accomplishment as so-called literature (1998, chapter 4).

What is becoming increasingly clear, as more and more meaningful research is done on precolonial Africa, is that philosophy in the African *historical* context does have a voluminous, rich, distinctive, original, and multicultural heritage. The days when one had to appeal only to the beliefs and practices of ancient or classic Egypt to evoke some sort of African philosophical heritage are long gone. More and more rediscoveries of texts and traditions that were meant to be deliberately philosophical in character are being made. Slowly but surely the chronological "gaps" that implied nothing of philosophical importance was taking place are being filled in. The authentic *history* of philosophy in Africa, therefore, is becoming as exciting and dynamic a field as whatever is taking place in the present day.

A second point relates to the importance African scholars themselves attach to the reintegration of Egyptian civilization with Africa's overall cultural heritage. African scholars who specialize in Africa south of the Sahara, so-called black Africa, would be deeply offended by any intimation that the intellectual reclamation of Egypt is an attempt to bolster, to upgrade, the cultural sophistication of their own indigenous cultures by associating them with "mighty" and "glorious" Egypt. In fact, those "other" African cultures or civilizations have their own integrity and have no need of an Egyptian connection to elevate the status of their civilizations. What they do need is for that integrity to be recognized and appreciated by scholarship and the world generally. To paraphrase V. Y. Mudimbe (1988), much of Africa still waits to speak for itself, but who is ready to listen?

A third and final concern is to provide some form of transition to the next set of chapters (2–7), which is devoted primarily to contemporary (twenty-first century) academic (university-based) philosophy in a select number of African countries. European colonialism as well as genuine intellectual curiosity have exposed and attracted a number of African scholars to Western philosophy. In addition, a much smaller number of Western academic philosophers have taken a special interest in philosophy in the African context. As the two major colonial powers in Africa were Britain and France, it has become conventional to refer to the countries on the African continent that have had to, in some measure, come to terms with these two European languages and the cultures they represented as "Anglophone" and "Francophone" respectively. (Chapters 2–7 will pay more attention to the history of academic philosophy in Anglophone Africa.) Readers particularly interested in the Francophone tradition are referred to Irele 1995. How African and expatriate philosophers have come to terms with relating to Western philosophical traditions, which some defend as universal and others challenge as culturally relative, is another important dimension to the ongoing story of what "philosophy" is and will be in the African context.

2

Twentieth-Century Origins

Academic philosophy in Anglophone Africa arose in a conservative yet turbulent intellectual climate. Conservative because philosophical paradigms in the English-language academy derived principally from the analytic tradition, which provided for a comparatively more narrow conception of the discipline than its European Continental counterparts. Turbulent because of the competing claims about what could constitute the sources of African philosophy as advocated by Africanists and African intellectuals from a diverse variety of disciplinary and vocational backgrounds—social anthropology, missionary and religious scholarship, and academic philosophy.

Placide Tempels's *Bantu Philosophy* was originally published in French (1949) and was intended for a Francophone readership. But these are not sufficient reasons to overlook the effects on an Anglophone African readership of its later publication (1959) in English-language translation. That Africans of a Bantu origin were said to explain and perceive the world as expressions of "vital forces" was found to be, at least initially, a satisfactorily radical alternative to Western mechanism. This "vital force" approach was shortly thereafter popularized in a fashionably lyrical, artistic, and best-selling English-language translation of *Muntu* (1961), written by the German scholar Janheinz Jahn. To adapt this more specifically aesthetic dimension to the "vital force" approach, Jahn also drew heavily upon the theory of Negritude as expressed and propounded by Aimé Césaire (1972) and Léopold Sédar Senghor (1971). But Tempels and Jahn share a view of the African intellect that, once it was better appreciated for its negative consequences, particularly where philosophy is concerned, has been enough to cause many African intellectuals to reject it as ethnocentric and even derogatory of the African mentality generally. For Africans themselves are said, by Tempels, for example, to be incapable of articulating the "views" reported by these studies, views on the basis of which Africans purportedly perceive and understand the world.[1]

Africans are said to live in a world that is fundamentally *symbolic* and *ritualized* in character. These two terribly overworked terms are meant to convey the point that Africa's indigenous peoples express their beliefs and values most directly by means of symbolic and ritualized behavior (so-called rites, rituals, masquerades) rather than with discursive verbal statements. The closest such cultures come to any sort of systematic verbalization is said to be found in their myths and proverbs. More often than not, of course, this makes the participation of the alien academic fieldworker, who is professionally trained to decode (interpolate the meanings of) such behavior (symbolic and ritual), myths, and proverbs indispensable to any scholarly intercultural exercise; without their active participation there could be no studies of the African mentality written in the systematic, reflective, critical, and discursive manner that is taken to be conventional by Western paradigms of scholarship.

Perhaps the most positive enduring heritage of these studies is their rudimentary efforts to link their theses to key concepts in the Bantu languages said to be fundamentally expressive of this culture's worldview.[2] This characterization of African peoples as having only limited verbal articulateness was dramatically challenged in 1965 by the English-language translation of yet another widely read (and still enduringly popular) text of Francophone origin, *Conversations with Ogotemmeli,* as recorded and edited by the anthropologist Marcel Griaule. This book purports to report a series of discussions with a Dogon elder in which he comprehensively and systematically decodes, in a clear and discursive manner, much of Dogon symbolism, ritual, and myth!

With regard to the development of African philosophy generally as an independent discipline, one important and enduring consequence of Griaule's *Ogotemmeli* is that it did *not* provide a Dogon replication of Tempels's "vital force" ontology. The hierarchical, yet unified and somehow uniform, metaphysical structure to the universe—as well as its organizing principles— Ogotemmeli outlined argues in a convincing manner for the diversity of Africa's indigenous systems of thought. That Ogotemmeli, without any for-

1. The English-language technical/specialized vocabulary/terminology dating from this period used by foreign scholars to characterize things related to the African intellect has for long been a subject meriting more detailed study in its own right.

2. African philosopher Alexis Kagame's much more detailed and thorough study (1956) of Bantu language(s) has never had the impact on Anglophone African philosophy it merits because, lamentably, it has yet to be translated from French into English.

mal training in the conventional Western sense (indeed, he had undergone no modern education and spoke no Western language), is able to do this in so compelling a manner so went against the grain of previous studies in and of African thought that there were published insinuations that these "conversations" were, in fact, fabrications by members of a Griaule research team in search of international fame and fortune.

Two seminal works of Anglophone African origin are W. E. Abraham's *The Mind of Africa* (1962) and John Mbiti's *African Religions and Philosophy* (1970a). Interestingly, both contain reasonably extensive assessments of the work of Tempels and Jahn, while the opposite is not the case.[3] Abraham is generally scathing in his assessments of Western scholarship regarding Africa. But the simple facts that he is African and that he was formally trained in academic philosophy had very positive consequences for the viewpoints he advocates about the philosophical dimensions of Africa's indigenous cultures. In doing so, he chooses an essentialist interpretation of African culture, in the sense that all of the subcontinent's cultures are said to share certain fundamental beliefs and values. He then chooses to analyze his own Akan culture (which is located in present-day Ghana) as an exemplar of how those beliefs and values function in a particular context.

Here, for the first time, one finds extensive discussion of such specifically (and thorny!) distinctively philosophical issues as whether there must be "African philosophers" in the conventional (Western academic) sense in order for there to be "African philosophy" (Abraham 1962, 104). He also discusses the sources one might turn to in Africa's indigenous cultures that would be relevant to epistemology or the theory of knowledge, with specific reference, for example, to the form of conceptual analysis undertaken by British philosopher Gilbert Ryle. Abraham also exhibits such prescient insights as the following with regard to the African context: "The resort of linguistic philosophers to what we say or do is not, therefore, shortsighted. This is where relativism might affect philosophy" (Abraham 1962, 105).

Despite his analytically orthodox philosophical training, overall Abraham might be said to advocate a methodologically pluralistic approach to the study of the philosophical in Africa's indigenous cultures. There is a place for language analysis, but there is also a place for the study and interpolation of oral literature and the beliefs and values enshrined in African social institutions (religious, political, legal, etc.). At the same time, Abraham insists that African philosophy not become obsessed exclusively with the

3. This difference in references to each other's works indicates the one-way traffic between translations of Francophone and Anglophone African scholarship, but the different times at which the original manuscripts were crafted is obviously also an important factor. Jahn does make the briefest of references to Mbiti as "the young story-teller" (1961, 212).

Africa that existed prior to European imperialism and colonialism. If Africa's cultural heritage is to come to terms with the latter-day problems of modern nation-states in a globally international community, then African social, political, and economic demands upon and priorities within that community also have to be enunciated and addressed.

Mbiti, coming by contrast from a theological background, sees African philosophy as subordinate to African religion (another thorny issue, as we shall discover). As did Abraham, Mbiti effectively adopts an essentialist rendering of "African philosophy," in that he argues that it consists of certain beliefs and values all African peoples share (Mbiti 1970a, 2).[4] This makes his approach to African philosophy much less technical in both character and content, more in line with the popular expression that every culture must have some sort of "philosophy of life" or "worldview." The greater proportion of his book is devoted to discussions of conventional African views about God, creation, and the afterlife rather than of technically philosophical problems or topics.

Perhaps it is because of this more ethnographic approach to philosophy and its deceptively straightforward title (*African Religions and Philosophy*; note the singular, *Philosophy*) that this book became and remains so popular, virtually a best-seller; it was also the text used in most introductory university courses taught during the 1970s in African thought, religion, or philosophy. The book is perhaps best known for the maxim Mbiti coined to express the importance of communal life in the African context: "I am because we are" (Mbiti 1970a, 141). However, gradually the book's limitations came to outweigh its merit, at least as a work of technical philosophical significance. This eventually was recognized, and the book was challenged by a growing number of professional philosophers in Africa.

For example, in a chapter that is addressed to a topic of specifically philosophical importance—the notion of "time" expressed by Africa's indigenous languages[5]—Mbiti makes the remarkable claim that Africans generally have no expression for or conception of the distant (as contrasted with the "immediate") future. The apparent evolutionary implications of this claim, that Africans have yet to develop such a notion, and its clear falsity with regard to any number of African languages, has led to numerous published critiques of this aspect of his work by African philosophers.[6] The salutary

4. "We shall use the singular, 'philosophy,' to refer to the philosophical understanding of African peoples concerning different issues of life" (Mbiti 1970a, 2).

5. Mbiti bases his more general claims on his more specific studies of the Kikamba and Gikuyu languages (both classified as Bantu).

6. See, for example, Gyekye 1975a and Masolo 1994, 111–19.

benefits to African philosophy that arose from this debate are threefold. First, it has led to extensive discussions of notions of "time" by philosophers in a variety of African cultural contexts. Second, it again focuses attention on the usefulness of African languages as a basis for philosophizing. And third, it forces African philosophers to come to terms with the overriding issue of whether it should be taken for granted that all of Africa's cultures share certain core concepts, values, and beliefs.

At this point, the two disciplines with which African academic philosophy inevitably had to come to terms in order to establish itself as an independent subject of substance were religious studies and social anthropology. In important as well as strategic respects, the interests and claims of these two fields undermine and even contradict the notion of an African philosophy arising from the subcontinent's indigenous cultures. Take for example the thesis that Africa's indigenous cultures are essentially "traditional" in character. By this is meant that virtually every major element of African society and culture was inherited from a distant past, is preserved relatively unchanged in the present, and will be passed on as normative to the future. This is interpreted to mean that if Africans are asked to explain *why* they hold a certain belief or practice a certain form of behavior, their response will essentially be an appeal to tradition ("because this is what we inherited from the forefathers"). All of this fits very nicely with the idea of a people who, when persuaded or compelled, explain their culture primarily on the basis of a kind of trust or faith in the value of inherited traditions. Consequently, for years, the departments in many African universities entrusted with teaching African students about "African traditional thought" were departments of religious studies.

Anglophone (essentially British) social anthropology in Africa began by concentrating primarily on appropriately social elements such as kinship and social institutions. But when anthropologists became interested in such things as beliefs and values as objects of interest in their own right, the approach that predominated was once again that of symbolism and ritual. Africans do not so much articulate their beliefs as they live them, social anthropologists argued. They also maintained that because Africans are preliterate peoples who are relatively inarticulate when it comes to reflecting on (much less criticizing) why they do what they do, observing their behavior (the old "fly on the wall" technique) and then inferring its rationale are the most reliable methodological keys to an anthropologically correct understanding of the reasons why they do what they do.

As such, social anthropology and religious studies were one in claiming that Africa's cultures are essentially traditional (often with a capital "T") in character, and that when it comes to characterizing the African intellect, mentality, or modes of thought, the most appropriate terms are "precritical," "prereflective," "protorational," "prescientific," "emotive," "expressive," "poetic," and so forth. Of course, all of this did not do much for the early proponents of African academic philosophy. Indeed, as the discipline defined by the Western canon as preeminently reflective, critical, and rational (as contrasted with "emotive," etc.), African modes of thought seemed diametrically opposed to those most clearly valued and enunciated by philosophy as an intellectual exercise.

In 1967, Robin Horton's two-part essay "African Traditional Thought and Western Science" appeared in the interdisciplinary journal *Africa*. With formal training in philosophy, science, and social anthropology, Horton, in a controversial theoretical comparison and critique of elements of African and Western systems of thought, provided a catalyst that, for a number of philosophers in the African context, led to a more deliberate development of African philosophy as an independent academic discipline.

Because of the vigorous critical responses it has eventually evoked from African philosophers, some may not fully appreciate the fact that Horton's position vis-à-vis African systems of thought is equally controversial within British anthropological circles. Horton rejected the claim that the African mentality is most fundamentally symbolic and/or ritualistic in character. Regarding himself a descendant of the "Intellectualist" anthropological tradition, as epitomized by E. E. Evans-Pritchard and Daryll Forde, Horton argued that indigenous African religions are better approached as genuinely theoretical systems whose purpose is to provide members of the relevant cultures with models of explanation, prediction, and control that will allow them to link events in the world of everyday life with causal forces that either transcend or underlie that world. It is this fundamental claim or insight that entitled him to compare them with the theories formulated and proposed by (Western) science.

If Horton had stopped there, his comparative analysis probably would have received general acclaim within African academia. However, in the second part of his two-part essay he proceeded to identify a number of logically or empirically erroneous types of reasoning, which he also claims are characteristic of African systems of thought, that limit the integrity of these systems as intellectual statements. Many African scholars (philosophers included, of course) challenged this portion of Horton's essay as both methodologically flawed and empirically false.

To be fair to Horton, it is important to stress that the basis for his comparisons between African and Western systems of thought was meant to be at the level of what he described as the "theoretical," those comparatively abstract elements or forces that are said to be responsible for what happens on the level of the everyday or ordinary life (gravity as responsible for an object's falling; a person's destiny as responsible for a specific incident during their lifetime). However, Africans are said to have yet to develop a notion of objective truth, of theories as independent of any special interests or values. Theory in their cultures is said to be fundamentally linked with whatever happens to be the local worldview (or religion).

Africans are therefore said to be reluctant to imagine or experiment with alternatives to that worldview—precisely the kind of theoretical alternatives that would promote the development of a notion of objective truth. They are said to be less able to reflect upon and distance themselves from their theoretical or religious beliefs as possibly true or possibly false or to imagine what it might mean to envision, much less to embrace, alternative beliefs and therefore to identify the nature of the logical and empirical criteria and testing that would need to be used to facilitate serious consideration of such alternatives (Horton 1967, no. 2, 155–67). Subsequently Horton recast his position on this issue by suggesting that "a single theoretical framework is subject to a more or less continuous series of innovations in response to the flow of novel experience" (1982, 222); that "'traditionalistic' thinking as it emerges from recent monographic studies in Africa, . . . despite its conservatism . . . has an essentially 'open' character" (1982, 223–24); and finally that "beliefs are accepted, not just because they are seen as age-old, but because they are seen as time tested" (1982, 240).

3

Rationality as Culturally Universal

The debate about the nature of the African intellect marked a kind of watershed in the history of Anglophone African philosophy. It incited the scholarly momentum, the motivation, that led to a coalescing of philosophical discussions, debates, and endeavors in Africa that would result in an autochthonous, independently minded analytic tradition. Many philosophers in the African context felt that religious studies and anthropology were exceeding their disciplinary limits if and when they claimed the right to define "rationality" in the African cultural context. "Rationality," as both concept and capacity, constitutes part of the core of philosophy as a discipline, and it was certainly not the case that scholars in these other two disciplines were dependably philosophically literate. In a sense, then, African philosophers were reclaiming their own territory when by both deed and word they reasserted the prerogative of their discipline to define the "rational" in any culture.

The most frequently footnoted critique of Horton's essay by an African philosopher is Kwasi Wiredu's "How Not to Compare African Traditional Thought with Western Thought" (1976f). In it Wiredu implies, most importantly, that Horton's basis for comparison between Africa and the West is problematic. For example, one fundamental issue on which he challenges Horton is the legitimacy of comparing (African) religion with (Western) science, particularly in terms of their respective objectivity—the importance attached to criticism, verification, falsification, and the revision of theories designed to explain, predict, or control human experience. Wiredu and others argue that a more realistic basis for comparison would be to contrast the role(s) and evidential and argumentative bases for religion between the two cultures (Olupona 1991).[1]

1. See, for example, Bodunrin 1975a; Emmet 1972; Pratt 1972; and Skorupski 1967.

Wiredu continues by pointing out that science constitutes a very specialized enterprise. Its methods and theories are not things with which the ordinary man in the street is conversant. Yet the majority of African beliefs (which Horton had to reclassify as "theories" in order to justify the basis for his comparison) that Horton chose to compare with scientific theories *are* things with which the ordinary African is conversant. And it is unrealistic to expect such commonplace beliefs to be the product of or be subject to the rigors of scientific testing and verification. If anything, the species of African beliefs Horton discussed are of a universal ethnographic order that, Wiredu suggests, is better regarded as "folk" philosophy. These are the sorts of things that anthropologists refer to as the customs and mores of a society. Western culture certainly has its own customs and mores, and these would provide a more suitable basis for a comparison of this type. As generalized, this remains the single, most important, methodological legacy of Wiredu's contention—that a prerequisite for judicious comparison(s) between African and Western cultures is that the materials selected share sufficient attributes in common to constitute a legitimate basis for comparison.

In addition to this methodological critique, Wiredu has more recently challenged Horton's contention that African worldviews generally employ personal rather than impersonal models of causal explanation because of the greater senses of order and security supposedly attributed to the human community compared to the wilderness synonymous with nature, or "the bush" (Wiredu 1995k). He does so on the basis of a cosmological verse from Akan oral literature in which the Creator is said to have created the following in sequence: (1) Order, (2) Knowledge, (3) Death, and so forth, the point being that the Order created was not limited to the domain of the human community but applied to all aspects of creation—animate and inanimate, and that this Order includes a fundamental causal determinism.

Another critique of Horton's position that seems to have had lasting consequences is my "Robin Horton on Critical Philosophy and Traditional Thought" (Hallen 1977). In this essay, I argue that Horton's assessment of African systems of thought as "closed," as resistant to change or revision on the basis of critical or reflective thought, is exaggerated. The article provides firsthand evidence of individuals within Yoruba society who do seem to regard fundamental beliefs with a degree of reflective objectivity.[2]

Other published articles contributed to the debate concerning the nature of African "traditional" thought.[3] But what becomes of importance for the independent development of *analytic* philosophy in the African context is

2. Horton makes important additions to his original position in Horton 1982. I published revised versions of my essay in English and Kalumba 1996 (Hallen 1996a) and in Hallen 2006.

3. Two frequently footnoted anthologies are Wilson 1974 and Horton and Finnegan 1973.

that African philosophers now bring the techniques of that approach to bear in a more systematic and comprehensive manner on a subject matter that had heretofore primarily been the domain of religious studies and/or social anthropology. The late Peter Bodunrin,[4] a Nigerian philosopher, is thought of by some as having been hostile to the possibility that African philosophy could be based upon the beliefs and values of Africa's indigenous cultures. This is said to be because he contends that philosophy, as a scholarly enterprise, is quintessentially critical, argumentative, and reflective in character (Momoh 1985, 82). The implicit and unresolved issue that demands resolution here, again, is what, in fact, is the true nature of the indigenous African intellect.

It is not clear from his published writings that Bodunrin ever answers this question to his own complete satisfaction.[5] What is clear is his consistent demand that philosophy of any stripe or color be distinctively reflective and critical in order to be worthy of the name. But this insistence does not necessarily exclude Africa's indigenous cultural heritage. Where that heritage contains critical and reflective elements, they could be directly incorporated into the philosophical mainstream. Where it does not, African philosophy still has an important role to play insofar as such elements can be (and should be) subject to critical analysis and reflective evaluation of the evidence and reasoning underlying their development and application. Bodunrin would have agreed that if and when these two forms of philosophical endeavor can be combined, there can be a basis for a philosophy that is at the same time reflective and critical in cross-cultural terms and of distinctively African (cultural) orientation.

Coming to terms with Ghanaian philosopher Kwasi Wiredu's corpus of work is a formidable task. His publications extend over most of the philosophical spectrum—epistemology, ethics, logic, metaphysics, social and political philosophy—and are interrelated in a subtle but systematic manner. In this chapter, I shall discuss and assess only three of the important themes to which Wiredu addresses himself: (1) the proper relationship between academic or professional philosophy and Africa's indigenous cultural heritage; (2) the problem of truth; (3) the problem of cultural universals. In "On an African Orientation in Philosophy" (Wiredu 1972c), published in the Nigerian journal *Second Order*,[6] Wiredu outlines a number of themes that he has continued to develop over the years with regard to the philosophical "prepossession(s),"

4. Regrettably, Peter Bodunrin died in April 1997.

5. Compare, for example, Bodunrin 1981 with Bodunrin 1992.

6. *Second Order: An African Journal of Philosophy,* principally under the editorship of the late J. Olubi Sodipo of the University of Ife, Nigeria, provided a vital and remarkably effective forum for the discussion of many viewpoints and issues relevant to philosophy in the African context.

as he likes to put it, of indigenous African cultures. It is in this article that, to my knowledge, he first discusses the notion of folk philosophy.

Wiredu suggests that we take a closer (philosophical) look at the different kinds of beliefs Africans actually do have as well as the languages with which they are expressed. Here Wiredu is out to knock down the fences that have been erected to intellectually segregate the African mentality as somehow idiosyncratic—as protorational, precritical, and so forth. He has always been fundamentally committed to the notion that all of humanity shares certain basic rational attributes and that the exploration of the consequences of these attributes for human understanding should be assigned the highest priority for those committed (as Wiredu certainly is) to a vision of philosophy that truly crosses cultures. Hence the importance of his underlying reasons for classifying a host of relatively unsystematized beliefs in all human cultures as elements of folk philosophy.

Then what of Wiredu's position concerning theoretical, technical, or academic philosophy in the African cultural context? This is where his work with regard to the role of Africa's indigenous languages in African philosophy becomes of crucial importance. Africans cannot undo the past and erase the cultural consequences of European colonialism. But they certainly can come to terms with them. First, they need to remind themselves that a very limited number of Europeans became fluent in an African language and that this ignorance had profound consequences (which also affected Western scholarship about Africa) for communication with and hence comprehension and appreciation of the African intellect. Second, they need to recognize the intrinsic instrumental value of *some* of the more technical varieties of information and methods of reflection, such as scientific method, that the colonial experience has put at their disposal. Third, such relatively culturally neutral and instrumentally useful elements can be adapted by Africans and used to develop their own interests.

Wiredu further elaborates his views on the question of rationality as a universal in an article entitled "Can Philosophy Be Intercultural" (1998). His response again is emphatically in the affirmative. In this essay he addresses at least one bothersome criticism that has repeatedly been made of African philosophy. This is the argument that any importation into the African context of problems, issues, and methodological techniques from Western philosophy for the exposition and analysis of philosophical material presumed to derive directly from Africa's indigenous cultures amounts to a form of Western philosophical interference that must inevitably distort the philosophical identity of Africa.

His first point is that African philosophy has no choice but to be intercultural insofar as African philosophers are, at least for the time being, compelled to express their work in non-African languages (e.g., English, French, etc.). If the resulting translations of African ideas are regarded as expressively valid, then there must be substantive, shared foundational semantic and logical canons between these different natural languages (1998, 148) that provide additional evidence for the possibility of "intercultural dialogue in philosophy" (1998, 147). Otherwise African philosophy becomes a specious species of fictional creations that are the result of translations arising from two or more languages that are semantically incompatible.

Secondly, as far as the critique of the use of methodological techniques derived from Western philosophy in the African context is concerned, Wiredu argues that rather than merely objecting to this practice in a carte blanche manner, one must provide cogent reasons against the legitimacy of instances of this practice, which, by the way, could also be invoked against any illegitimate importation of African techniques and issues into Western philosophy. Also for him (1997b) this procedure is, theoretically, as applicable to the use of, for instance, phenomenological methods in African philosophy as it is to the use of analytic methods. And, of course, for any such critique to make sense and be relevant to African *and* Western philosophy, it would have to transcend the basic semantics of both—further evidence of the intercultural character of philosophy and of substantive universal rationality.

Of course, cross-cultural adaptation of methodological techniques can be done in an insufficiently reflective and therefore improper manner. This is why care must be taken, that is, good reasons must be given in the process so that both the techniques and terminologies employed do actually promote the philosophical treatment of the ideas in their original meanings. As Wiredu puts it at one point: "for Africa the remedy does not lie in abjuring [philosophical] interculturalism but in cultivating it with eyes more widely open" (1998, 153).

Wiredu's philosophical scholarship has always had two dimensions. He addresses some purely technical philosophical problems, in the treatment of which factors such as national affiliation and cultural background are to all intents and purposes irrelevant or, at most, happenstance.[7] In other instances, he explores the philosophical "prepossessions" of select concepts or aspects of the language and culture of the Akans that happen to constitute his African heritage. In some cases, as with his ruminations about "truth," the two dimensions are combined and interrelated, but always on a common basis of analytical rigor.

With reference to the first dimension, he has, for example, tried to develop a cogent, technical, philosophical theory of truth. Wiredu argues that whatever is called the truth is always *someone's* truth. For a piece of information

7. His numerous published papers on formal logic are, presumably, the clearest examples of this.

to be awarded the appellation "true," it must be discovered by, known by, and defended by human beings somewhere, sometime. Furthermore, as past experience has clearly demonstrated, what human beings defend as "true" can prove to be false from an alternative point of view. Therefore whatever is called "truth" is more starkly described as *opinion*.

Wiredu's interpretation of truth as opinion means that he rejects what in technical philosophical circles is referred to as the objectivist theory of truth.[8] This is a theory that posits truth as an independent property of time-less eternal information located in some transcendent realm that we humans must ceaselessly endeavor to reach if we are to know it (*the* truth). The truth about virtually everything is more or less there and always has been there, waiting for us to discover it or, better, decipher it. Wiredu suggests that such an objectivist theory of truth implies that truth is categorically distinct from opinion. But this, in effect, would make truth "as a matter of logical principle, unknowable," because every claim to truth would then be reduced to only an opinion advanced from a particular point of view and therefore "categorically distinct from truth" (Wiredu 1980b, 115).

Wiredu argues that truth in fact arises from human endeavor and effort—from perception and rational inquiry—rather than deriving from some tran-scendent reality: "We must recognise the *cognitive* element of point of view as intrinsic to the concept of truth" (Wiredu 1980, 115; my italics). That "truth" arises from human agency does not mean knowledge will degener-ate into the merely subjective or relative: "What I mean by opinion is a firm rather than an uncertain thought. I mean what is called a considered opin-ion" (1980, 115–16).[9] This notion of the considered opinion is of fundamen-tal importance to Wiredu's overall theory of truth. In other contexts he links it to the notion of "warrant" arising from the American philosopher John Dewey's pragmatism (Wiredu 1980b, 216–32; 1993; 1995c; 1996b, chapters 2–4), although he insists it is not identical. "Something is warranted [well-considered] not because it is true, but true because it is warranted; better, it is true if and only if it is warranted."[10] Truth as opinion must, of course, always be entertained from some point of view. But that opinion becomes

8. Wiredu characterizes the objectivist theory as maintaining that "once a proposition is true, it is true in itself and for ever. Truth, in other words, is time-less, eternal" (1980b, 114).

9. The differences between 'objective truth' and 'cognitive truth' are more than rhetorical. The first claims that truth must be determined by an indepen-dent, transcendent reality to which human knowledge can be shown to corre-spond. The second, as expounded by Wiredu, argues that human beings have no direct access to such a 'reality' and that truth can therefore only be determined by rigorous, careful reasoning and experimentation—cognition.

10. K. Wiredu, personal correspondence with the author.

considered or warranted when it arises in a genuinely intersubjective context where it is grounded upon shared canons of rational inquiry. In his view, such intersubjectivity becomes a sine qua non to truth and is responsible for his enduring opposition to both subjectivity and relativism.

In his discussions of Akan discourse relating to the notion of truth, Wiredu is concerned to elucidate the phrase that he renders into English as something's being "so" (*Nea ete saa;* Wiredu 1996b, chapter 8): "To say that something is true, the Akan simply say that it is so, and truth is rendered as what is so.[11] No undue sophistication is required to understand that although the Akan do not have a single word for truth, they do have the concept of truth" (Wiredu 1985a, 46). He then goes on to suggest that the notion that something is so is the same as the notion that something is a fact. But if this means that in Akan truth amounts to correspondence with fact, this is nothing more than a restatement of elementary correspondence theory (of truth) and, as such, less than enlightening.

In order to be more clear about the philosophical prepossessions of Akan discourse about the "truth," more information about ordinary usage would be required. And in the end, the most frustrating limitation to Wiredu's (Twi) analyses is that he does not aim to offer a complete explanation of what is meant by saying (in Akan) that something is so.[12] What the *it* that is *so* might correspond to or cohere with are left as speculative possibilities. This is not a criticism of his analyses, by the way. It is rather a consequence of the fact that there are some questions that ordinary discourse and usage do not answer—they do not resolve some issues because there is no need for human beings to be so technically specific about such matters at the level of ordinary everyday discourse. However, in the other dimension of his philosophical scholarship—that devoted to purely technical philosophical problems—Wiredu has gone on to explore in further detail what might be required for something to be so. This occurs in the course of a critical evaluation of the three standard theories of truth (correspondence, coherence, and pragmatic) and as a consequence of the suggestion that being so may, broadly speaking, again be interpreted as being warrantably assertible (Wiredu 1980b, chapter 10, section III; 1985a; 1996b, chapter 8).[13]

We have seen how Wiredu levels the intellectual cross-cultural playing field with regard to folk philosophy so that it becomes a universal human

11. The *Concise Oxford Dictionary* records this form of usage in the English language for the word "so" as: "In that state or condition, actually the case" and cites as one example "God said 'Let there be light' and it was so." The equivalence Wiredu himself favors is that 'p is so' means 'p is true.'

12. The epistemological significance of the "so" in 'it/that is so' and 'what is so.'

13. K. Wiredu, personal correspondence with the author.

attribute. An analogous process of leveling may now be seen to be taking place with regard to every culture's standing as contributor to technical philosophical debate. "Truth," as a construct of the considered opinions of human beings in *any* culture, when coupled with (as we shall soon see) a concern to demonstrate that certain rational principles are universal to *all* cultures, effectively makes reasoned debate a prerogative of every culture in the world (Africa's cultures included, of course).

It is perhaps because of his coining of the term "folk philosophy" to characterize unreasoned African (and Western) beliefs that Wiredu is sometimes misinterpreted as overtly hostile to Africa's "traditional" cultural heritage.[14] In fact, his position has always been that the elements of that heritage must be continuously reevaluated with a view to gauging their negative, positive, or neutral consequences when they are retained as priorities of contemporary African societies. For example, several "traditional" values and practices that he recommends should be carried over in order to be made of fundamental importance to the contemporary African polity are the emphases traditionally placed upon *consensus* and *reconciliation* (note the analogies between these terms and "considered opinion" and "warrantably assertible") as a basis for governing and government. This is an idea he first introduces in 1977[15] but develops in detail in two essays specifically devoted to the issue of democracy in Africa (Wiredu 1996b, chapters 13 and 14).

Wiredu is leery of the conventional (Western) multi-party system and the form of majority rule it entails. In the African context, it seems to favor political parties that are structured and divided along ethnic lines, thereby heightening social tensions. It can therefore lead to elected governments that fail to represent a substantial portion of the population, further exacerbating social tensions. He argues that affirming and reformulating the African tradition of government on the basis of consensus, negotiation, and reconciliation (in effect, a non-party form of democracy) would better foster an impression of the entire electorate's participation in the institutions of government, and this would contain the divisiveness that has too often become a characteristic of politics in the modern African nation-state.

Wiredu has always been concerned with what he has come to describe as "the possibility of universal canons of thought and action" (Wiredu 1996b, 1). In a series of recent articles, he argues that certain logical and ethical concerns are necessarily common to all human cultures simply by virtue of the fact that they are human.[16] Exemplary logical universals to which

14. This is also why he has sometimes been unfairly labeled an extreme 'positivist.' See, for example, Owomoyela 1987.

15. Wiredu 1980a (revised and reprinted as chapter 1 of Wiredu 1980b).

16. In 1996b (chapters 2 and 4), he goes so far as to suggest that their universality is ultimately of (human) genetic origin.

he makes specific reference are the principles of non-contradiction ("that a proposition cannot be true and false at the same time") and induction ("the capacity to learn from experience" [1996b, 27]). As for the ethical, the priority assigned to "the harmonization of the interests of the individual with the interests of society" (1996b, 64), when it is formulated as a principle, also becomes a candidate for cultural universality. (A more detailed discussion of Wiredu's position on the relationship between the individual and his or her community will be found in chapter 8. There his position on this issue will be compared with that of his Ghanaian colleague Kwame Gyekye and that of his South African colleague Mogobe Ramose.)

Perhaps some commentators will see these more recent steps in his philosophical development as inevitable given his long-term determined commitment to a universal rationalism, a commitment which consistently persuades him to reject relativism as a productive philosophical alternative. But it is also possible to see his commitment to a (universal) rationalism as motivated by an even more fundamental commitment to a form of humanism that was evident in even his earliest publications. It rejects the possibility that some cultures may be of intrinsically greater merit than others because the people who founded them are, as human beings, somehow intrinsically better intellectually endowed than other human beings. It is with this in mind that he also challenges and rejects moves by some elements of Western culture to hegemonize its customs and mores (components of its "folk" philosophy) as things that should be adopted by all the cultures of the world on pain of eternal damnation. For Wiredu this is a superficial, false, and unphilosophical form of cultural universalization, nothing more than a manifestation of (Western) cultural ethnocentrism.[17]

In a subtle but perfectly deliberate fashion, one of Wiredu's aims from the beginning is to provide empirical evidence (predominantly linguistic) and a reasoned basis (universal rationalism) for Africa's liberation from pejorative cultural stereotypes. Cultures can and do differ from one another, but on a more fundamental level, as expressions of a common humanity, they manifest and share important common principles such as those listed above. It is on this basis that Wiredu can argue that no cultures merit second-rate status as somehow intrinsically rationally deficient or defective. It is on this basis that he can argue that despite our apparent (and real) differences, it is this common humanity with all it may entail which cannot fail to unite and thereby benefit all humankind, once it is recognized and acknowledged (ignorance is our greatest common enemy).

17. See, for example, Wiredu 1996b, chapter 6 ("Custom and Morality: A Comparative Analysis of Some African and Western Conceptions of Morals"), 61–77.

Standard expositions of the analytic approach to philosophy are grounded upon the thesis that philosophical questions are primarily questions of language. The main tasks of the philosopher therefore become clarification ("analysis" in the narrowest sense) of the meanings of the words/language with which our beliefs are expressed and justification—in the sense of identifying and assessing the arguments and evidence with which those beliefs are justified. As such, orthodox analytic philosophy does not create or invent the beliefs it targets. They are received as preexisting elements of whatever language culture happens to be its target of interest. This means that it is often relatively passive with regard to advancing alternative theses (beliefs) that might prove to be of greater truth value.

But this passive (or non-reformist) attitude toward analysis is something with which Wiredu fundamentally disagrees. He believes change is something philosophers should encourage; he exemplifies change in his own work via the pragmatic perspective that he adapts from John Dewey. For, as we have seen, he conceives of philosophy as a dynamic endeavor whose aim is to encourage the introduction of novel, warrantedly assertible truths about the origins of our beliefs, as well as to reevaluate, revise, or discard old beliefs and to introduce new ideas that might possibly achieve the status of truth. He argues that the better humankind understands the world in which it finds itself (human nature included, of course), the more likely it becomes that it can procure satisfaction from it.[18] This dynamic approach to philosophizing is further demonstrated by some of his essays that speculate on the genetic impetus for human knowledge.[19]

Kwame Gyekye[20] is another Ghanaian philosopher whose recent publications cover a broad and important range of topics. His *An Essay on African Philosophical Thought: The Akan Conceptual Scheme* (1995) uses an analytical approach that is meant to set a precedent for how material of philosophical substance can be identified in and derived from Africa's indigenous cultures. Although Gyekye's claims about the philosophical dimension of Africa's cultures may appear to be rhetorically more forceful and direct (he does not use the "prepossession" word, for example), the

---

18. "I would concede, or even insist, that philosophy is ultimately political, for the understanding of reality that we seek is for the betterment of human existence" (Wiredu 1996b, 148).

19. See, for example, "A Philosophical Perspective on the Concept of Human Communication" (Wiredu 1996b, 13–20).

20. Pronounced phonetically as "Je-che," with the two "e's" as in the English-language "met."

differences between his approach and that of Kwasi Wiredu to their culture seem more those of emphasis than of substance.[21]

Gyekye's presentation makes a clear distinction between the methodology he embraces and the results of that methodology when applied to elements of Akan culture. The forthright phrasing of the opening statement of this book, meant to summarize its aims, is characteristic:

> [1] to stress the fact of the universal character of the intellectual activity called philosophy—of the propensity of some individuals in all human cultures to reflect deeply and critically about fundamental questions of human experience; [2] to point out that philosophy is essentially a cultural phenomenon; [3] to argue the legitimacy or appropriateness of the idea of African philosophy and attempt a definition of (modern) African philosophy; [4] and to demonstrate that there were sages or thinkers in Africa's cultural past who gave reflective attention to matters of human existence at the fundamental level, and, as part of the demonstration, to critically explore the philosophical ideas of the Akan traditional thinkers. (of Ghana [1997a, ix])

Gyekye's approach to Akan philosophy is significantly conceptual. He identifies terminology in Akan (Twi) discourse that is of philosophical significance. But he also emphasizes the intellectual importance of proverbs in that culture as analogous to philosophical nuggets that contain highly condensed judicious insights and wisdom, a characteristic of an oral culture that could not have recourse to extensive written tracts.[22] At the same time, he categorically rejects a purely technically philosophical, linguistic, or conceptualist approach to these materials (Gyekye 1995, 64–65). This is because their function, most importantly, is not merely to express or to record wisdom— they also serve as *practical* guides to life and human experience.

To research their practical consequences[23] in Akan culture, Gyekye has

21. Perhaps the most pronounced difference between the two is that Gyekye does not make as clear a distinction between philosophy as purely technical (universal) and philosophy as cultural (distinctively culturally relative). For him, all philosophy is somehow culturally related, even if human being (and all that implies) is indisputably universal.

22. "Akan proverbs are the wise sayings of individuals with acute speculative intellects. They become philosophically interesting when one sees them as attempts to raise and answer questions relating to the assumptions underlying commonly held beliefs and to make a synthetic interpretation of human experience" (Gyekye 1995, 21). Though Gyekye chooses to concentrate primarily on concepts and proverbs, he does not exclude aphorisms, myths, "stories," and other forms of oral literature as potentially philosophically significant.

23. Gyekye therefore characterizes Akan morality as "consequentialistic" (1995, 139).

undertaken what he unabashedly refers to as "fieldwork"—seeking out "sages" in traditional Ghanaian society who can explain this aspect of the concepts and proverbs he finds of interest (in effect, they illuminate the relationship between theory and practice). But rather than remain with sets of random concepts and proverbs and the isolated individuated meanings or insights they express, Gyekye sets out to weave them together (Gyekye 1995, 16) so that they can then be seen to express more systematic philosophical viewpoints on such topics as God, causality, free will, and ethics, or morality.

Gyekye further maintains that this philosophical substratum of Akan proverbs will turn out in many cases to replicate the proverbial wisdom of other African cultures. He explores this thesis in greater detail in a later book, *African Cultural Values* (1996).[24] For example, in a chapter on "Moral Values," he favorably compares specific humanistic values expressed by the Akan with similar virtues affirmed by the Yoruba ethnic group of Nigeria in West Africa and the Swahili language and culture of East Africa. Yet at the same time, he wants to maintain that it would be a serious error to infer from this that there is such a thing as a *unique*—in the sense that it contains *ideas not found anywhere else* in the world—African (traditional) philosophy shared by all the subcontinent's peoples (Gyekye 1995, xvi). He is equally reluctant to argue that there is a unique Akan cultural philosophy. What one does find in every culture in the world are certain common philosophical concerns and questions,[25] to which different answers (destiny versus free will, for example) in different formats (proverbs versus deductive arguments, for example) have been proposed (Gyekye 2003). The particular combination or interrelation of formats and answers to these concerns or questions found in a particular culture may somehow be distinctive, but this is of a very different order from being literally unique to that culture.

Gyekye argues that philosophy is a historical as well as a cultural

24. "There is of course no pretense made that the moral values of various African societies are the same across the board, but there are some values that can be said to be shared in their essentials by all African societies" (1996, 55–56). Such shared beliefs and values are said to fall under the following headings: (1) metaphysics (ontology, causation, the concept of person, fate/destiny, the problem of evil); (2) epistemology (including the paranormal as well as the rational/empirical); (3) morality (as established and maintained on a secular rather than religious foundation); (4) communalism (the idea that self-interest must be reconciled with communal interests) (1995, 195–210).

25. "I argue that philosophy is a universal intellectual activity that has been pursued by peoples of all cultures and that the propensity to raise fundamental questions about human experience can be found in peoples belonging to different cultures, even though the answers may be different, despite our common humanity, and may not all be equally compelling" (Gyekye 1995, xiv).

enterprise. By this he means that the issues which concerned African philosophers in precolonial or "traditional" times may not be the same as those that concern African philosophers in modern or contemporary times (Gyekye 1995, xi–xii). But this does not imply that there should be no connection between the two. He is prepared to be flexible about what exactly that connection should be. From the standpoint of the history of philosophy in Africa, all viewpoints relevant to "traditional" philosophy would become important. But since the philosophical priorities and concerns of every society change over time, this would mean that, from the standpoint of modern or contemporary African philosophy, some "traditional" themes may prove of less interest or relevance than others.[26]

When it comes to specific examples of Akan philosophical thought as derived from that culture's concepts and proverbs, obviously there is a wide range of topics from which to choose. The one that will be selected here as exemplary of Gyekye's approach is the ultimate basis for morality in Akan "traditional" culture and the consequences of this tenet for the relationship between individuals and their community. A misleading stereotype of "traditional" Africa, as we have already seen in the case of Mbiti, is that every important element of such cultures, morality included, is inextricably bound up with religion. For example, the prominent role assigned by some Africanists to a notion such as "taboo,"[27] whereby violating such injunctions leads to disastrous consequences that emanate from the level of the divine or spiritual for those concerned. For Gyekye, this is too simplistic, and he emphatically rejects so prominent a role for divine intervention by saying: "I reject the view that religion constitutes the basis of Akan morality" (Gyekye 1995, 131). Gyekye's more fundamental point is that the values that define moral or immoral conduct or practice in Akan culture are not, ultimately, of supernatural or divine origin.[28] What he proposes as an alternative philosophical and more factually correct way of interpreting morality in Akan culture is to treat it as a form of humanism ("what constitutes the good is determined not by spiritual beings but by human beings" [1995,

26. "By 'connection to the traditional,' I was only calling for some analytic attention to be paid *also* to the traditional thought categories, values, outlooks, and so on, as a way of affirming an existing African philosophical tradition, some features or elements of which may be considered worthy of further philosophical pursuit" (Gyekye 1995, xi–xii).

27. Defined by the *Concise Oxford Dictionary* as a system or act "of setting apart persons or things as accursed or sacred." Gyekye rejects religion as the basis for taboos in Africa and reinterprets its force as morally normative: "It is the humanistic, nonsupernaturalistic outlook of Akan morality that in fact underpins the reasons offered by Akan thinkers for considering some things as morally taboo" (Gyekye 1995, 134).

28. Gyekye relates this to the fact that traditional African religion is not a

133]). "In Akan moral thought the sole criterion of goodness is the welfare or well-being of the community" (1995, 132). This is not to say that the Akan believe God and religion have absolutely nothing to do with the moral. Certain events that take place may be linked to supernatural approval or disapproval of an individual's or group's conduct (Gyekye 1996, 17–18). But the individual and communal practical consequences of different kinds of behavior have more to do with why certain moral values are honored and observed by members of that culture (1996, 57).

Gyekye then proceeds to give a list of terms or concepts prominently associated with being moral in Akan culture, whose importance, as elaborated by the sages and as systematized by himself, is illustrative of this humanism: "kindness (generosity: *ayamyie*), faithfulness (honesty, truthfulness: *ahohoye, adoe*), that which brings peace, happiness, dignity, and respect (*nea ede asomdwee, ahomeka, anuonyam ne obuo ba*)" (Gyekye 1995, 132). He also offers examples of proverbs that imply a similarly humanistic provenance: (1) "When a person descends from heaven, he [or she] descends into a human society" (Gyekye 1996, 36); (2) "A man must depend for his well-being on his fellow man" (1996, 45); (3) The person who helps you carry your load does not develop a hump" (1996, 49); (4) "'Given a choice between disgrace and death, one had better choose death' (*aniwu ne owu, na efanim owu*)" (Gyekye 1995, 139).

As for the optimal relationship between individuals and their community,[29] the Akan ideal is that both should benefit on a reciprocal, still essentially humanistic, basis: "The good is identical with the welfare of the society, which is expected to include the welfare of the individual" (Gyekye 1995, 132). Gyekye acknowledges that in some circumstances, individuals will be torn between favoring their own (self-) interests and those of the community (1995, 154–62). But he also points out that the possibility of such conflicts of interest is acknowledged and to a certain degree accommodated by Akan morality, since it retains an element of flexibility on this issue: "Akan social thought attempts to establish a delicate balance between the concepts of communality and individuality. Whether it succeeds in doing so in practice is of course another question" (1995, 161).

Gyekye's *Tradition and Modernity: Philosophical Reflections on the African Experience* (Gyekye 1997a), presents thoughtful and comprehensive reflections on how one might reconcile some of the more admirable qualities of "traditional" Africa with the policies, priorities, and problems of the modern nation-states that now configure the subcontinent. Much of this

---

revealed religion, the product "of a prophet claiming to have heard and received a divine message directly from God for use as a guide to the spiritual and moral life either of a specific group of people or of all humanity" (1996, 6).

29. Wiredu also suggests this as a universal ethical priority. See p. 38 above.

volume is devoted to topics that are conventionally regarded as social and political philosophy, but, as Gyekye explains in the preface, this is because today they constitute some of the most important problems with which contemporary African philosophers need to come to terms (1997a, ix–xi).

Several themes from Gyekye's earlier work carry over and serve as basic structural elements. He frequently refers to the "thought and practice of the Akan society of Ghana" as a basis for African cultural extrapolation (Gyekye 1997a, x). Furthermore, to deal with such compelling contemporary African problems as how to integrate the "traditional" with the "modern" in the nation-state or how to overcome ethnic rivalries or how to achieve political stability or how to eliminate political corruption and combat increasing public immorality, he falls back upon humanism and a humanistic ethic as one of the most powerful remedies that the African philosopher can proffer. But with this generalization I do not mean to oversimplify his approach to these problems, for he offers important new insights into the meanings of ethnicity, the traditional, modernity, and morality.

For example, Gyekye criticizes the notion of ethnicity ("tribalism") in Africa as a dangerous invention and tool of political ideologues and argues that it must be supplanted by notions of group identity comparable with those found in contemporary multicultural societies. As for the "traditional" and the "modern," he argues that the time has passed when these words can be used to type whole societies or cultures. Traditions, or conventions inherited from the past, also play a role in so-called modern societies. The most satisfactory basis on which they can be justified, always, is that they serve a useful, positive purpose. Gyekye's vision of modern African society, therefore, becomes one which incorporates and interrelates the best elements of other cultures in the world[30] with those elements of Africa's cultural heritage that deserve to be similarly valued.[31] The transcendent (and universal) criterion on the basis of which the positive contribution of any of these elements can be rated is again humanistic: "bringing about the kinds of progressive changes in the entire aspects of human culture necessary for the enhancement and fulfillment of human life" (Gyekye 1997a, 280).

It is tempting to speculate about possible intellectual interchanges and influences that might have taken place among these three Ghanaian philosophers (Abraham, Wiredu, and Gyekye). Certainly there is at least one important common theme in their work, first expressed by Abraham and

30. He makes specific reference to a "developed economy, technological and industrial advancement, [and] the installation of democratic politics" (Gyekye 1997a, 279).

31. He makes numerous references to the greater emphasis placed upon the importance of the community or group as opposed to individualistic self-interest (Gyekye 1997a, 278).

later not only taken up but developed in a hybrid manner by Wiredu and Gyekye. Wiredu summarizes it as follows:

> It comes out clearly, for example, in Professor Abraham's *The Mind of Africa* . . . that in theoretical sweep and practical bearing traditional African philosophies concede nothing to the world views of European philosophy. Why, then, should the African philosophy student not be steeped in his own heritage of philosophy before looking elsewhere? (Wiredu 1980b, 28)

That this would involve demonstrating the presence and importance of the rational in "traditional" African thought by philosophers in Africa is a point that has already been stressed. That the forms in which it was expressed (proverbs, for example) might be different, even distinctive, also seems to have been convincingly established.

This chapter has been entitled "Rationality as Culturally Universal" because each of the philosophers considered argues for a model or paradigm of cognition or understanding that is universal to every human culture. That view is also consistent with the topical and methodological priorities of the Nigerian, 'Segun Gbadegesin.[32] Gbadegesin's *African Philosophy: Traditional Yoruba Philosophy and Contemporary African Realities* (1991a) employs conceptual analysis and the critical evaluation of the argumentation and evidence underlying so-called traditional beliefs and practices as fundamental methodological techniques (1991a, 4). He argues that there always has been an individualistic, reflective, and critical dimension to the formation and reformation of such beliefs and practices in African cultures (1991a, 5). As for the character of African rationality, he states without qualification in a discussion about the work of Robin Horton: "If we grant such thought systems are 'eminently logical,' what else is required to demonstrate their philosophical nature?" (1991a, 18). But this is also an intensively "hands-on" text, in that its author is most deeply concerned to demonstrate that philosophy can be of practical value for solving some of Africa's current social, cultural, economic, and political problems.[33]

But, Gbadegesin argues, Africans cannot be in a strategic position to solve current problems and plan for a better future unless they are fully informed about their cultural past, about where they're coming from (Gbadegesin 1991a, 216). With this in mind, he devotes the first half of

32. An adequate English-language phonetic rendering would be "Shay-gun Bah-deh [with the 'deh' pronounced as if the 'de' in "destroy"]-gay-shin."

33. This is a theme that has already been introduced by Abraham (1962), Wiredu (1980, 1996), and Gyekye (1995, 1997). Certainly the latter's *Tradition and Modernity* has precisely this as its central aim. For Kwame Anthony Appiah's more guarded viewpoint on humanism in the African context, see 1992a, 155.

his text to clarifying select beliefs and practices fundamental to his native Yoruba culture. Although he explicitly refuses to promote "traditional" Yoruba beliefs, customs, and values as providing a paradigm or model for all of Africa's cultures, at the same time he admits to a conviction that there are common cultural priorities of African-ness that need to be more clearly identified; a fundamental priority is the importance attached to the common good, or communal welfare (1991a, 104). Gbadegesin too will conclude that the moral values that distinguish "traditional" Yoruba and, by implication, African culture delimit a form of humanism: cooperation, a healthy sense of community, generosity, and respect for others.

He begins by exploring a carefully chosen set of Yoruba "traditional" beliefs and values relating to (1) the nature of personhood (the physical and spiritual components of a human being, the powers it has at its disposal, and the forces to which it may be subjected while in the world); (2) the nature of the dialectic between individual and communal interests and priorities and how they may be reconciled so as to benefit both (here Gbadegesin defends a secularist view of Yoruba moral values or virtues, very much along the lines of Gyekye's 'consequentialism'); (3) the ways certain beliefs fundamental to Yoruba traditional religion differ fundamentally from both Christianity and Islam but appear to be more compatible in practice as well as theory with the humanitarian values he finds distinctive of Yoruba culture; (4) the ideas that the comparatively absolute Western dichotomy between the natural and supernatural does not fit the Yoruba worldview and that various beliefs and practices relating to the supernatural that might appear exotic or bizarre to Westerners become eminently reasonable when sited within that worldview.

Having outlined these basic elements of Yoruba culture, Gbadegesin then proceeds to identify (in certain instances to denounce) and (more importantly) to propose solutions to a cluster of contemporary social and cultural problems that are literally bedeviling Yoruba society today. It would be too simplistic to say that he sees these problems as consequences of modernity. "Modernity" itself is an ambiguous term that must combine, at least in the African context, European (economic and cultural) imperialism, colonialism, and the varieties of neocolonialism that are local manifestations of the global competition between capitalism and socialism (in all of their various forms as well, needless to say).

In the second half of his text, where he addresses these problems, Gbadegesin sets out to demonstrate that the philosopher too can contribute to their solution. He provides numerous examples of how Christianity and Islam have become culturally irrelevant and socially corrupt and recommends that Yoruba traditional religion be reaffirmed as most compatible with that culture's positive moral priorities. He denounces the negative connotations that have become associated with the idea of doing "work," especially manual labor (Gbadegesin 1991a, 215), and suggests measures and programs that need to be supported by government if Africa's notoriously low productivity is to be raised. He insists that the focus upon that ubiquitous term "development" in Africa must be upon economic development (1991a, 256), but economic development can be assured only if there is political stability. Finally, if there must be a choice between capitalism and socialism, the latter in its democratic forms appears to be more compatible with the humanitarian values definitive of Africa's "communitarian" societies.

The combined impact of these philosophers, who defend the thesis of rationalism as a cultural universal, upon African philosophy has been profound. Their defense of this thesis is anything but simplistic, for they all also allow for distinctive African cultural heritages and orientations as long as they are grounded or founded upon patterns of reasoning and cognitive systems that share essential and defining characteristics in common with what it means to be "rational" in other human societies, in particular the so-called paradigm of the "rational" as propounded by the Western philosophical establishment.

However, there is another school of thought on this subject among philosophers in and of Africa that queries whether African cognitive systems can be done analytic justice if they are typed as essentially universal, as somehow the same as their Western equivalent(s). The point is that perhaps African conceptual and cognitive systems may, in certain distinctive respects, deserve to be regarded as genuinely alternative pathways to the "truth." In academic philosophy, the differences between these two points of view relate most directly to the old and ongoing debate between universalism and relativism.

4

Rationality as Culturally Relative

A number of philosophers in and of Africa contend that there are elements to African cognition that are sufficiently unique or distinctive to somehow set it apart. Their major complaint against the so-called universalists is that when undue emphasis is placed upon the supposedly common or universal elements of African cognition, these uncommon features are underrated and fail to receive the recognition they deserve and the credibility they merit as alternative pathways to understanding.

Pride of place in this chapter must go to Léopold Sédar Senghor (1906–2001), the philosopher, poet, and statesman who became the first president of an independent Senegal in 1960 and remained so until his retirement in 1980. As an African philosopher Senghor is most prominently identified with the philosophy or movement that has come to be known as Negritude. Though this theory came to include a wide range of interests, including aesthetics and social and political philosophy, given the orientation of this chapter attention will focus on Senghor's portrait of the African intellect, of African understanding of the self and the world of which it is a part.

In developing his theory, in part, Senghor was aggressively responding to Western-generated denigrating anthropological accounts of the African intellect as essentially poetic and symbolic in character—fabricating rituals and worldviews, based prominently on spiritual or supernatural entities and forces, that provided Africa's peoples with emotional comfort and reassurance because such beliefs enabled them to feel they had an understanding of why things happen as they do. At the same time Senghor was less than enamored with the Western emphasis on analytic reason as the primary basis for true understanding, to the virtual exclusion of human emotion or feeling (with its invented goal of being 'objective') from any form of true understanding. Drawing upon his firsthand knowledge of the cultures of Africa, he therefore promoted the theory of Negritude as an original but empirically representative and accurate portrait of African cognition and the indigenous African intellect (Senghor 1963).

African understanding does not make the rigid distinction between reason and emotion that has become conventional in the Western world. Understanding in the African cultural context is therefore as much involved with emotion or feeling as it is with reason.

> The African . . . does not begin by distinguishing himself from the object, the tree or stone, the man or animal or social event. He does not keep it at a distance. He does not analyse it. Once he has come under its influence, he takes it like a blind man, still living, into his hands. He does not fix or kill it. He turns it over and over in his supple hands, he fingers it, he feels it. The African is . . . a pure sensory field. Subjectively, at the end of his antennae, like an insect, he discovers the Other. (Senghor 1965, 29–30)

Such a humanly involved form of understanding is understandably more comfortable with things like symbols and intuition, thereby expressing itself as well via music, poetry, myth, ritual, proverbs, and the like, because such expressive forms do not artificially hide the human dimension to understanding that, in all honesty, cannot be eliminated or ignored.

> Young African intellectuals . . . who are still not altogether cured of the inferiority complex given them by the [European] colonizers, criticize me for having reduced the African mode of knowledge to pure emotion, for having denied that there was an African "rationality" and an African technology. . . . It is a fact that there is a white European civilization and a black African civilization. The question is to explain their differences and the reasons for these differences, which my opponents have not yet done. (Senghor 1965, 33)

Senghor insisted that his theory continued to provide an important role for reason, but it was a form of rationality that ignored the artificial Western distinction between (knowing) subject and (alien) object. Understanding in the African context is felt as much as thought. Therefore any process of cross-cultural scholarship that begins from the presumption that Western paradigms of reason and objectivity set the standards by which any other culture should be judged is bound to miss the truths enshrined in African forms of cognition. For Senghor's point throughout is that African forms of cognition have just as much integrity as those of any culture in the world.

The collaboration between myself and the late J. Olubi Sodipo when we were colleagues at the Obafemi Awolowo University (formerly University of Ife), Nigeria, is one such case in point. The two major schools of philosophical thought then dominant in the Anglophone Western academy were phenomenology and analytic philosophy. Phenomenology, in part due to its association with the European continent and with existentialism, was associated with the avant-garde, with something other than the mainstream, and thereby probably appeared more open to new fields of endeavor. Analytic philosophy was identified with the mainstream academic conservative Western philosophical establishment, which would be less likely to be open to the potentially deviant field of endeavor to which the term "African philosophy" might refer. Indeed, as we shall see, the analytic approach has since come to be increasingly criticized as the cultural by-product of a West that ethnocentrically flaunts that culture's philosophical priorities as things that should be universal.

The more immediate appeal of phenomenology to philosophers in and of Africa, who of course also insisted on purely instrumental grounds that its methodology was more viable for the African context, will be discussed in a succeeding chapter. As for early evidence of the analytic approach in the African context, any number of papers were published by African philosophers with titles that are a variation on "The So-and-So's Concept of 'X.'" For "So-and-So" substitute the name of any African ethnic group. For "X" substitute a concept such as "beauty," "truth," "person," and so forth. In this kind of article, which uses source material derived primarily from oral traditions—proverbs, parables, myths, stories, and so forth—African philosophers set out to analyze the meaning of a concept that occurred in an African language and that they believed to be of philosophical prepossession and interest. But this class of papers was effectively ignored by the Western analytic establishment. One explanation is that Western philosophers were not inclined to treat the philosophical analysis of a single concept extrapolated from an African language seriously when they had already been persuaded by anthropology that the conceptual network, the entire language of which it was a product, was created and used by a people whose mentality, whose rationality, was typed as prelogical and precritical.

The fact that the (Western) analytic establishment took virtually no notice of these African conceptual studies was a major obstacle to gaining recognition of analytic African philosophy as a scholarly endeavor that de jure was as qualified as more established traditions to claim its place within the larger discipline of philosophy. Therefore, as far as the Hallen-Sodipo approach is concerned, the basic motive for experimenting with an analytic style that would be suited to the African context is strategic rather than the result of any deeper allegiance to analytic philosophy as the "correct" way to do philosophy. In too many respects to be excused as unintentional, the Western analytic establishment had taken on the trappings of a culturally exclusive sect in whose shrine or temple true rationality reposed. And African philosophy, already prejudged as some form of deviant tradition, was being denied entry.

The most obvious resolution to this situation was to find ideas and techniques within the mainstream analytic tradition itself that could be redirected, rechanneled, reformulated so as to work in an African context. One such idea was suggested by the work of American philosopher W. V. O. Quine. Quine had already forcefully challenged the ontological-epistemological status of meanings (of words, actions, etc.) as entities that could somehow be explored and analyzed independently of the real-life situations in which human beings say what they say and do what they do (behaviorism).[1] This also meant that he could challenge the notion or presumption that meanings are universal to all human cultures or societies—that the word or sound in Chinese, Arabic, or Zulu may be different from the word in English, but the underlying meaning will be the same. To the contrary, Quine suggests, since we have no direct experience of such universal meanings, the possibility arises that, to a significant degree, each natural human language is a unique creation that has its unique conceptual elements—ontological, epistemological, aesthetic, and so on—that are a product of the human creative genius in that particular culture or society.

When Quine thereafter turned his attention to the status of (presumably) non-Western languages, he introduced his Indeterminacy Thesis of Radical Translation via an imaginary encounter between a trained Western linguist-anthropologist and a native speaker of a non-Western language that has never before been encountered and therefore has never been translated into Western terminology. On the basis of his previous arguments against universal propositions (meanings) and the physical and intellectual constraints (behaviorism) such a hypothetical situation would impose upon precise understanding or expression of the alien meanings in translation, Quine was able to draw a cluster of consequences that can be incorporated into a strategy favorable to a rigorous program of philosophical analysis of non-Western, in particular African, languages.

Quine's consequences included that, since we do not have direct access to the consciousness of others, the most the linguist can have access to are alien sounds coming out of an alien mouth. This means that the assignment of meanings to those sounds by the linguist is always open to a degree of indeterminacy, inaccuracy, and interpretation; the degree of indeterminacy, of guesswork, increases with the degree of abstraction of the terms involved

---

1. The well-known dialogue, debates, and even polemics between Quine and philosopher-linguist Noam Chomsky, who defends the idea of a universal semantics, are one consequence of this.

(compare "tree" with "freedom"). Consequently, translation on the abstract level is much more difficult to verify and thereby make determinate. All of this would mean that any supposed rendering of African meanings (abstract meanings in particular) in translation, especially one meant to demonstrate a precritical or prelogical mentality, would be established on a much more fragile and thereby vulnerable basis than we might suppose. In fact, any extended translation exercise between two languages that historically have had no reason to share a single cognate in common becomes an elaborate network of innumerable hypotheses that stipulate, for example, that the meanings of specific English-language terms are literally the same as specific alien-language words. But if each rendering of an alien meaning is, in effect, an interpretation or interpolation rather than a precise translation, the approximate nature of the entire exercise is revealed (Quine 1960, chapter 2).

Once again, all of the above means that a prelogical mentality could be the creation of a prelogical translation. For example, one would have reason to be suspicious of a translation of an African language that assigned contradictory meanings to the same term(s) (as proof of prelogicality). Given the cumulative effects of the indeterminacy of translation between radically different languages, an alternative explanation for such inconsistencies could be that translators have recourse to contradiction because they, perhaps unwittingly, have not been able to arrive at a determinate or precise translation. In effect, then, the translator makes the alien culture responsible for his or her confusion(s) when in fact the real culprit is the translation.

Even the possibility that Quine's Indeterminacy Thesis could be of some practical consequence was enough to warrant a much more systematic and rigorous philosophical reappraisal of African meanings as expressed by African languages. And, as linguistic analysis was a virtual trademark of the analytic approach, the next step was to choose which specific tools or techniques developed by that approach would be best suited to the African context. In this regard, our approach to the use of 'Western' analytic techniques in African philosophy deliberately seeks to comply with the precautionary attitude recommended by Kwasi Wiredu on pp. 33–34.

To begin with, there was an obvious need for some foundational data, by which is meant a special effort devoted to the collection, prior to the analysis and systematization, of African-language usage by scholars with specifically philosophical sensitivities. After careful consideration of the possibilities, what has come to be known as the Hallen-Sodipo approach arose from an adaptation of the philosophical tradition conventionally known as Ordinary Language Analysis.

This involves concentrating upon certain fields of discourse in the language under study because of their potential philosophical relevance and interest (the vocabulary used for rating information as more or less reliable, for instance, because of its relevance to epistemology) rather than on single concepts. But, just as important, the level on which to approach those meanings is the situations in which this terminology is used by ordinary people in everyday discourse. The linguistic philosopher sets out to collect information about both paradigm cases, in which the relevant terminology is used in a correct manner, and examples of wrong usage, where the term or terms should not have been applied. All of this helps identify the criteria governing a term's usage and the interrelations between terms within the same field of discourse.

The first concrete result of the Hallen-Sodipo adaptation of ordinary language analysis to African philosophy was *Knowledge, Belief, and Witchcraft: Analytic Experiments in African Philosophy* (1997). The overall aim of this text is to argue, on the basis of ordinary language analysis, that the meanings of the presumed equivalents of three English-language terms ("knowledge," "belief," and "witchcraft") in the language of the Yoruba of southwestern Nigeria were in fact *not* the same. When and if Yoruba discourse was translated into English as if their meanings were the same, the Yoruba were made to appear hopelessly confused about certain issues and thereby prelogical and precritical. But the real reason for this was that, with specific reference to the distinction between "knowledge" and "belief," the Yoruba criteria for evaluating information as more or less reliable were eminently consistent and coherent in their own right but not the same as those employed in English-language discourse.

For example, in Yoruba discourse, "knowledge" and "truth" or "certainty" can arise most importantly from firsthand experience. Information that is obtained on the basis of secondhand sources, such as other persons, the media, and so forth, usually qualifies as "belief" and as possibly true or possibly false. If an individual is able to test a piece of this secondhand information in a firsthand manner and thereby verify it, then it can be upgraded to "knowledge" that is "true." If it remains untested and unverified, merely as secondhand information that an individual has at his or her disposal, then it must remain a "belief" that is possibly true or possibly false.

For those accustomed to think in English-language terms, the differences between the two cultures about the reliability of secondhand information should be apparent. The overwhelming proportion of the knowledge a person in Western culture is instructed to regard as "true," whether it be scientific, historical, factual, and so forth, is received by the Yoruba as secondhand and therefore would, from their point of view, have to be reclassified as "belief." If English-language speakers were to persist in their claims that this information (which the overwhelming majority have never tested and will never be able to test) is knowledge, the Yoruba would likely view them as naive and ignorant.

Some might view this apparent difference as an interesting cultural curiosity but then question whether it is of any real philosophical significance. In fact, (Western) epistemology has long agonized over the truth status of so-called "propositional knowledge," an issue which directly involves the reliability of information obtained on the basis of secondhand sources. This is the same issue underlying the definition of such "knowledge" as "justified, true belief" and the controversy generated by the so-called Gettier counterexamples (Gettier 1963). Yet, given the Yoruba criteria for distinguishing "knowledge" from "belief," it appears that two of the Western criteria used to define knowledge (belief and justification, insofar as it involves secondhand evidence) would no longer need to apply. In Yoruba discourse it would not make sense to say that one has secondhand "belief" about something one already "knows" firsthand. And firsthand experience of something implies its own justification. Therefore there would be no need to turn to secondary sources.

In a sequel to this text, *The Good, the Bad, and the Beautiful: Discourse about Values in Yoruba Culture* (Hallen 2000b), I went on to explore the interrelations between these Yoruba epistemological criteria and specific moral and aesthetic values that are acknowledged as priorities by Yoruba discourse. How does one come to know or to believe that another person is moral or immoral? How does one come to know or to believe that someone or something is beautiful?

Because Yoruba society is still significantly oral in orientation, the most obvious source of secondhand information must be other people. Apparently to encourage individuals to be reliable sources of such information, they are explicitly encouraged to be forthright about the basis upon which they themselves came by it (firsthand, secondhand, fabrication), to be attentive listeners (to have heightened powers of attention and observation), to be good speakers (to make perceptive contributions to a discussion), and to be patient and maintain self-control (which is thought to be favorable to optimum application of the intellect and powers of observation).

The consequences of this interrelation between ethics and epistemology are that persons who are reliable sources of information tend to be identified as having good moral character. Those whose behavior evidences compliance with or adherence to these values would tend to be regarded as reliable sources of information. This would mean that these fairly specific ethical values are perhaps better characterized as epistemological virtues.

Aesthetic values and concerns become interrelated because of a popular aphorism in Yoruba discourse to the effect that "True beauty is a good moral character." In other words, when human beings are concerned, physical or bodily beauty is purely external and therefore of relatively superficial consequence. What matters most in rating a person as attractive or unattractive is the inner beauty that may be manifested by their moral character. This means that a person who, physically, is decidedly unattractive can still be referred to in discourse as extremely beautiful, in fact a virtual paradigm or model of "beauty."

One of the persistent and frustrating responses to these publications has been a tendency on the part of commentators and critics to label them examples of ethnophilosophy. What ethnophilosophy is, or is said to be, will be the subject of the next chapter. Suffice it to say, at this point, that because our chosen sources for information about ordinary Yoruba language usage were *oníṣègùn*[2] (traditional healers or masters of medicine), it is sometimes presumed that we were targeting meanings and/or information that went far beyond that possessed by the ordinary person. There were a few exceptional exchanges with the *oníṣègùn* in which they did make reference to professional matters. But most of our discussions were devoted exclusively to determining the correct usage of a selection of terms in Yoruba deemed to be of philosophical prepossession and interest on the basis of ordinary, everyday discourse.[3]

Why turn to the *oníṣègùn* for such information, then? Because the consensus of the local population where this research was concentrated at the time was that they were more knowledgeable about Yoruba culture generally, and therefore the most obvious sources of such information. In any case, one of the more positive attributes to an ordinary language approach is that results should be comparatively easier to confirm or contest.[4]

To further and more firmly distance our analytic approach from ethnophilosophy, I published a text specifically addressing this issue in 2006: *African Philosophy: The Analytic Approach*. In it I attempt, in part, to emphasize or underline the differences between ethnophilosophy and ordinary language philosophy. I also severely criticize the work of the American philosopher Richard Rorty. Although he is taken by some to be a fan of multiculturalism and therefore non-Western philosophy, a closer reading of his work reveals his firm conviction that philosophy is exclusively a Western cultural phenomenon.

Subsequent subsections of the book are devoted to critical analyses of purported expositions of morality or ethics and aesthetics in the African context, along with further elaborations of Yoruba moral and aesthetic

2. Phonetic pronunciation: "oh-knee-shay-gune" (this last syllable to rhyme with the English-language "dune").

3. In his foreword to the 1997 edition of *Knowledge, Belief, and Witchcraft*, the American philosopher W. V. O. Quine explicitly links our methodology to ordinary language philosophy.

4. See Bello 1988, 2003 for his critical evaluations of some of our findings.

discourse. Presumably readers will find that many of these Yoruba epistemic, moral, and aesthetic priorities represent fundamentally different viewpoints on knowledge, on morality, and on beauty when contrasted with their conventional Western counterparts. The question may still be asked, of course, whether these differences are enough to justify the conclusion that they support philosophical relativism, but the Hallen-Sodipo response to this has so far been in the affirmative.

Godwin Sogolo, formerly professor of philosophy at the University of Ibadan, Nigeria, is another African philosopher of relativistic persuasion, insofar as he argues that there are certain dimensions to African "form(s) of life" that are unique and cannot be adequately or fairly treated or understood using the techniques of a Western philosophy that has originated from Western "form(s) of life." In other words, for Sogolo, philosophical methodologies, as well as theories and paradigms, are culturally relative. Africa will therefore receive accurate and unbiased representation by this discipline only when philosophers in and of Africa begin to develop methodologies for the study of their societies that are uniquely suited to the African cultural context(s). Sogolo's most comprehensive statement of this position is to be found in his book *Foundations of African Philosophy: A Definitive Analysis of Conceptual Issues in African Thought* (1993).

Those who are familiar with Sogolo's published work may be surprised to find him being classified here as a relativist. There are passages in his work where he sounds as "universal" as any universalist:

> There are certain universals which cut across all human cultures. Indeed, to say that man is a rational being is to imply that mankind as a whole shares in common certain features whose absence in a given group raises the question as to whether such a group is human by definition. Pre-eminent among these universal traits of humans is the ability for self-reflection and rational thought governed essentially by certain principles of reasoning. (Sogolo 1993, xv)

But this apparently uncompromising claim is followed immediately by:

> It is important to add that this unique human quality, like others, has its own local colour and peculiar mode of manifestation, all depending on the contingencies of the intervening culture. (Sogolo 1993, xv)

At another point, one finds the following apparently universalist statement:

> The point to be emphasized is that the structure of the human mind is essentially alike and men reason alike in all cultures. (Sogolo 1993, xv)

This, again, is qualified by what immediately follows upon it:

> There are, however, cultural factors that condition the forms in which this reasoning is manifested. Its peculiar form in any culture cannot, therefore, be seen as a deficiency or worse still taken as a mark of irrationality. (Sogolo 1993, xv–xvi)

Perhaps it would be more fair to Sogolo to say that there is a certain ambivalence to his thinking about what should constitute universality and what should constitute relativity. Nevertheless, it is clear that he feels universalist philosophers, such as Wiredu, have embraced a paradigm of cross-cultural rationality that is too extreme and too Western in orientation and therefore unfairly discriminates against the rationality of certain African modes of thought and beliefs:

> There is a contradiction Wiredu does not seem to notice. On the one hand, he holds (as any universalist would do) that "philosophical truth can, indeed, be disentangled from cultural contingencies"; on the other hand he insists that contemporary African philosophy can only be built on the "resources" of traditional African philosophy. It is not clear how these "cultural contingencies" are distinct from the "resources" Wiredu refers to. It seems clear that Wiredu is rejecting the contextual necessities of African philosophy in one breath only to admit them in another. (Sogolo 1993, 5)

What "forms of life" or modes of thought does Sogolo find distinctive of Africa, and what sort of philosophical treatment does he feel they would need to receive in order to do them justice? Let's begin by trying to answer the second part of this question first. Sogolo argues that in any single culture there are likely to be irreconcilable "universes of discourse" when compared on the basis of their "conception of reality and criteria of rationality" (Sogolo 1993, 73). Two such different universes of discourse might be the religious and the scientific.[5] It would be ridiculous and wrong to evaluate scientific beliefs on the basis of religious criteria or to evaluate religious beliefs on the basis of scientific criteria. Yet, says Sogolo, this is precisely what has been happening in the case of Africa (refer back to the discussion of Robin Horton and Kwasi Wiredu's critique of same), and, as a result, Africans have too often been made out to be an ignorant and naive "folk" whose essential

---

5. In his more radical moments, Sogolo (1993, chapter 3) seems to suggest that notions of "knowledge" (as contrasted with "belief ") and of what is considered to be "logical" (as contrasted with what is "illogical") also may depend upon the particular culture concerned and the different universes of discourse within that culture. (Of course the same would therefore hold for intercultural comparisons as well.) "Hollis' claim about the universality of logical rules and modes of reasoning seems to be the relic of the traditional efforts by rationalists to justify faith in what they believe to be the supremacy of reason" (1993, 76).

modes of being and understanding are to live in a form of life and universe of discourse overflowing with witches, spirits, and incantations. In fact, in African societies too there are multiple universes of discourse, such as the commonsensical, the scientific, and the religious. For the most part, Africans have the good sense not to mix them up or confuse them, as is also the case with the peoples of other cultures in the world.

As for the first part of the question—what types of philosophical analysis would be more properly suited to African "form(s) of life"—this is a project Sogolo evidently feels philosophers in and of Africa need to undertake and to bring to fruition:

> The mind of the African is not structurally different from that of the Westerner. Also, the contextual contrast between Western thought and traditional African thought, which considers only the former as a suitable material for philosophical reflection, rests on false premises. The truth is that both are similarly marked by the same basic features of the human species. The difference lies in the ways the two societies conceive of reality and explain objects and events. This is so because they live different forms of life. And it is for this reason alone that an intelligible analysis of African thought demands the application of its own universe of discourse, *its own logic and its own criteria of rationality*. The primary task of the African philosopher is to fashion out these unique working tools with which to unearth the complexities of the social form that confronts him. (Sogolo 1993, 74; my italics)

African cognition is somehow fundamentally the same as in other human cultures and somehow fundamentally different. This is a refrain that recurs again and again in Sogolo's writings, and it is undeniably one of the most important and fundamental topics with which African philosophers have still to contend. But, and this is a very important but, Sogolo also advises philosophers in and of Africa that they have much homework to do before they will be in a position to have profound understandings of their respective cultures' forms of life and universes of discourse.

The universality or relativity of rationality is not the only issue that Sogolo deals with in this text. Other important chapters are devoted to explanatory models (in particular, what it means to characterize a form of explanation as "scientific"), to morality in "traditional" Africa (with an interesting discussion of what it may mean to type a society as "traditional"), to the possibly genetic basis of social mores and human society, and to social and political philosophy in the African context (noteworthy for its discussion and critique of Senghor's [1971] theory of Negritude). In relation to each of these topics, Sogolo continues to be concerned to defend the integrity of modes of thought, conventions, and institutions that he finds unique to and definitive of Africa's indigenous cultures.

M. Akin Makinde is former professor of philosophy at the Obafemi Awolowo University (formerly University of Ife), Nigeria. His most well-known publication is the book *African Philosophy, Culture, and Traditional Medicine* (1988a). This text mounts a more forthright and radical claim that African systems of thought, including especially systems of divination, may contain and constitute alternative but legitimate approaches to, and methodologies for understanding, the nature of reality. Though Makinde focuses on the Yoruba of southwestern Nigeria, he means for his claims to be more broadly based and to apply, in principle, to all African cultures. Divination, for example, may not be based upon the same methodology as science. But this need not mean that the conclusions it comes to about the nature of reality and the prescriptions it recommends for coming to terms with that reality are false or untrue. In a sense, the world awaits the birth of a mastermind who will someday be able to interrelate and thereby confirm the truths of these two apparently diverse and sometimes contradictory fields of endeavor in a syncretic manner (1988a, chapter 1).

In his discussion of the nature of philosophy (chapter 3), Makinde argues that the (Western) academic analytic tradition has promoted itself to a point where it now maintains an intellectual monopoly over the discipline. As a result, the modes of thought and beliefs of thinkers and cultures that do not satisfy its paradigm(s) are relegated to the non- or unphilosophical. In fact, Makinde argues, the spirit of the discipline has always been more open to a multiplicity of avenues of thought. This alone should be enough to secure a position within philosophy for the thought systems of non-Western, in particular African, cultures. Philosophy is defined by speculation (most prominently with regard to metaphysics) as much as it is by critical analysis,[6] and this issue in particular is a field in which Africa's cultures offer rich and fruitful intellectual harvests (Makinde 1988a, 45). Makinde therefore proposes that one fertile ground for making comparisons between African and Western thought within a truly international discipline of philosophy would be with regard to their respective speculations (metaphysics) about topics such as the existence of God, the concept of the "person," the immortality of the soul, human destiny, and so forth.

Perhaps the chapter of his text that has attracted the most interest is the

---

6. On the issue of the relationships between a "universal" rationality and a "universal" logic, Makinde appears to express more than one view: (1) "It cannot be shown that there are any systems of human thought anywhere in the world in which the principles of logic (noncontradiction, identity, and excluded middle) are never employed in reasoning, either consciously or unconsciously" (Makinde 1988a, 41); (2) "Logic is either universal in all thought or it is relative to different thought systems. So, in neither case can we deny logic in the thought systems of others" (1988a, 43).

one in which he seeks to relate African "traditional" medicine to (African) philosophy.[7] "We hope to show that African traditional medical assertions occur already in an epistemologically constituted universe" (Makinde 1988a, 87). He then sets out, in accordance with the approach to African philosophy previously affirmed, to site or to situate the framework and techniques of Yoruba traditional medicine within the broader context of Yoruba metaphysics. He also suggests, in an analogy to the hoped-for reconciliation between divination and science, that further research may defuse the controversy that has arisen over the apparent inconsistencies between the magical and medicinal elements of traditional medicine, as typed and at times belittled by Western researchers.

In 2007 Makinde published a collection of essays published over the course of his career, supplemented by several new pieces, entitled *African Philosophy: The Demise of a Controversy*. The title is meant to refer to the fact that African philosophy now exists as a legitimate discipline and can no longer be dismissed as a form of oxymoron. The chapters in this volume span virtually the entire philosophical spectrum, and it is therefore difficult if not impossible to do it justice with some kind of summary statement. But, as far as African philosophy is concerned, he has at least the following things to say: (1) any form of ethnophilosophy or folk philosophy relative to the African context should not qualify as genuine philosophy insofar as it consists of nothing more than *descriptions* of peoples' beliefs or ideas (hence no critical content [2007, 509–14]); (2) philosophy is an undertaking that must be pursued by individual thinkers (2007, 512); (3) the way African philosophy should be done is "the way it [philosophy] is understood by all philosophers, whether in Africa, Asia, Europe or America" (2007, 516); (4) by subjecting material derived from Africa's traditional cultures to critical philosophical analysis, theories of genuine philosophical significance may be produced (2007, 517); (5) the results of such critical analyses may very well result "in different philosophical opinion . . . and the difference, if any, between the underlying assumptions and issues in African and Western philosophies may be discovered" (2007, 517).

The appearance of V. Y. Mudimbe's *The Invention of Africa: Gnosis, Philosophy and the Order of Knowledge* (1988a) marks a turning point in the overall development of African philosophy. Mudimbe, sometime professor of anthropology, language(s), and literature at Duke and Stanford Universities, who is originally of Zairean (now Democratic Republic of the Congo) origin, would justifiably protest at being typed simply a "philoso-

---

7. The book also contains a useful chapter on the social and political thought, frequently characterized as "African socialism," of Chief Obafemi Awolowo.

pher." This is because he also approaches philosophy as an historian of ideas and literature and therefore writes about it from outside its confines more than he does from within.

By adapting select techniques of the French historian of ideas and sciences Michel Foucault and combining them with insights into the "nature of culture" (a phrase he might find amusing), as an African and Africanist scholar immersed first in his native culture, next in the Continental (European) academic tradition, and then in the Anglo-American (avowedly analytic and empirical) academic tradition, Mudimbe achieves a breadth and depth in his writings about these subjects that many readers find remarkable. And when this is further combined with critical elements derived from the deconstructive and postmodern movement(s)—perhaps as most notably exemplified by the work of philosophers Jacques Derrida, Michel Foucault, and the sociologist Pierre Bourdieu—the power of his carefully crafted critiques of Western intellectual history and the Western intellectual "establishment" are at many points as devastating as they are, in the end, constructive.

The central theme of *The Invention of Africa* is that whatever field of (Western) scholarship one looks to—whether anthropology, history, literature or, in particular, philosophy—the portrait of Africa that emerges (no matter how supposedly "scientific" the approach is) is as much a product of Western cultural priorities and prejudices as it is of anything African. Much of the power of Mudimbe's critically architectonic analyses derives from the fact that he shows how these accounts of Africa tell us as much, or more, about their authors' Western cultural orientations as they do about anything African.[8]

The result is that African academic philosophy is reduced to an extension of various Western philosophical traditions—the analytic, the Marxist, the phenomenological, and so forth—into the African context. This does not necessarily mean it is bad philosophy, but it does allow Mudimbe to question whether it should then be regarded as authentically African. Of course, this critique extends to African scholars who have imbibed and employ these (Western) approaches to knowledge as well. It is culture rather than birthright that determines the identity of an individual's scholarship.

The effects of this challenge on the African Studies establishment generally have been profound. It has led to much soul-searching about the supposed objectivity of the methodologies of the disciplines involved (philosophy

---

8. Mudimbe's detailed critical analyses of individual philosophers in and of Africa are of more positive value than this very broad synopsis might indicate. For example, his exegesis of the work of Placide Tempels (see pp. 23–24 above) and the cultural and historical context in which it occurred, provides important insights into the roots of Tempels' *Bantu Philosophy* (1959).

included, of course) and of the human beings who employ them. This is a process that is best described as ongoing. In this particular text, Mudimbe himself proposes no resolution other than to suggest that Africa still waits to be discovered, to speak, to be understood:

> *Gnosis* is by definition a kind of secret knowledge. The changes of motives, the succession of theses about foundation, and the differences of scale in interpretations that I have tried to bring to light about African *gnosis* witness to the vigour of a knowledge which is sometimes African by virtue of its authors and promoters, but which extends to a Western epistemological territory. The task accomplished so far is certainly impressive. On the other hand, one wonders whether the discourses of African *gnosis* do not obscure a fundamental reality, their own *chose du texte,* the primordial African discourse in its variety and multiplicity. Is not this reality distorted in the expression of African modalities in non-African languages? Is it not inverted, modified by anthropological and philosophical categories used by specialists of dominant discourses? Does the question of how to relate in a more faithful way to *la chose du texte* necessarily imply another epistemological shift? Is it possible to consider this shift outside of the very epistemological field which makes my question both possible and thinkable? (Mudimbe 1988a, 186)

In a subsequent text that includes an important chapter on the development of academic philosophy in a particular region of Francophone Africa, *Parables and Fables: Exegesis, Textuality, and Politics in Central Africa* (1991a), Mudimbe, at some points as immanent and sometimes transcendent expositor, takes us through the origins of Western-inspired accounts of the philosophies of the peoples of Zaire. As was the case in other African colonies, 'African' philosophy began as the discourse of anthropologists who were writing about the beliefs of people seen as situated at the lower end of the evolutionary intellectual scale. It was in this historical context that Tempels' *Bantu Philosophy* appeared as revolutionary (1991, 34; see pp. 23–24 above), in that it maintained that indigenous African peoples had already formulated their own sophisticated worldviews, even if fundamentally different and therefore understandably overlooked or misinterpreted by even the trained Western anthropologist. What this resulted in, at least for a new generation of scholars, was a shift in paradigms in that a new fashion for writing about Africa became to discover African philosophies that were distinctively exotic and bizarre, yet somehow reasonable in their own right, to anything taken as conventional by the Western philosophical establishment.

Of course the issue or question of the truth of either alternative becomes pertinent at some point. But it is Mudimbe's deliberate reticence to embrace any alternative as truly objective, as representing anything more than a new trend in writing or storytelling about a subject, which makes his work enduringly thought-provoking, controversial, and frustrating. Nevertheless, leaving it at that would be to overlook his conviction that the history of human understanding is the invention, adoption, application, and eventual rejection of successive different taxonomies (instruments, tools, and models of understanding) applied to the same subject matter. As he says in the "Introduction" to this book: "My own text might be only a fable or a parable about other fables. In effect, a fable is a fictitious story that claims to teach a lesson, and a parable is also a story that pretends to illustrate a normative lesson. Cannot we reduce interpretations in any culture to these two simple basic lines" (1991, xxi)?

Kwame Anthony Appiah is the son of the late Ghanaian patriot, lawyer, and intellectual Joe Appiah; he is professor of philosophy at Princeton University. He would probably not object to being characterized as an analytic philosopher in his own right, and there is clear evidence in his published works of his commitment to a form of universal rationalism. For that reason I have always had reservations about situating him in a chapter devoted to relativism in African philosophy. Yet I continue to do so because, when it comes to the issue of philosophers and philosophy in the African context generally, he steps outside his own philosophical convictions and vigorously defends the rights of African intellectuals to formulate original forms of philosophical thought, as long as they attempt to do so on reasonable grounds. This is generous of him, and probably positive for academic philosophy in the African context since, as we have seen, it has suffered from so many demeaning and damaging constraints over the course of its brief lifetime.

In his published works he at times invokes an element of postmodernism[9] that also implies a vigorous defense of a multicultural approach to philosophy. That the Western world has chosen to embrace analytic philosophy is all well and good, but this is no reason for it to deny other cultures in the world an equal right to develop their own ways of doing and expressing their ideas about what philosophy is and should be. He repeatedly encourages philosophers in and of Africa to claim, aggressively if need be, a legitimate place for their possibly divergent views in the international academic marketplace (Appiah 1992a, 143, 145, 149):

> Postmodernism can be seen, then, as a new way of understanding the multiplication of distinctions that flows from the need to clear oneself a space; the need that drives the underlying dynamic of cultural modernity. Modernism saw the economization of the world as the triumph of reason; postmodernism rejects that claim, allowing

9. See, for example, chapter 7 in Appiah 1992a ("The Postcolonial and the Postmodern").

> in the realm of theory the same multiplication of distinctions we see
> in the cultures it seeks to understand. (Appiah 1992a, 145–46)

His *In My Father's House: Africa in the Philosophy of Culture* (1992a) is one of the few books devoted to the subject of African philosophy that have also attracted a general readership. As was the case with Mudimbe, Appiah is important because of his disciplinary breadth as much as for his disciplinary depth. In addition to an astute grounding in technical philosophy, this collection of essays exemplifies a talent for interdisciplinary exegesis involving such diverse fields as literature, art, and science.

As might be expected, a text that sets out to address a number of different issues and hot topics in diverse disciplines has given rise to considerable controversy. Perhaps the most controversy has been generated by Appiah's discussion of the concept "race" (Appiah 1992a, chapters 1–3). His claim that this is a notion that has been proven false on both scientific (genetics) and cultural grounds and therefore should be banished from halls of debate and the vocabularies of languages has provoked both strong protests and wide-ranging intellectual discussion.[10] Since it is culture and not race that should define any people's identity, Appiah is also suspicious of those who claim there is some form of philosophy common to all of Africa's peoples (as he must also therefore be about claims to some common African culture) (1992a, Chapter 4; 2004a). But he insists that for something to qualify as philosophy in the academic sense, it must amount to something more than a mere catalogue, or mapping, of beliefs, concepts, and meanings. There also must be some evidence of efforts to determine whether what is believed and what is meant is also true (1992a, 96–98). If this is what some commentators have in mind when they refer to "critical" or to "reflective" thought, then so be it.

There is an important underlying qualification to this discussion that demands clarification. By making this assertion, is Appiah closing the philosophical door to those African philosophers who would insist that the beliefs, proverbs, and customs of their cultures do amount to a form of philosophy? Probably not.[11] He would advocate that the door be open to

10. See, for example, Lewis Gordon, "In a Black Antiblack Philosophy," chapter 6 in his *Her Majesty's Other Children* (New York: Rowman and Littlefield, 1997), 115–38; or Tsenay Serequeberhan, "Africa and Identity: Kwame Anthony Appiah and the Politics of Philosophy," chapter 4 in his *Our Heritage: The Past in the Present of African-American and African Existence* (New York and Oxford: Rowman and Littlefield, 2000), 35–45. See also Appiah's responses to his critics as evidenced, for example, by *Color Conscious: the Political Morality of Race* (with Amy Gutman, Princeton, N.J.: Princeton University Press, 1996).

11. Especially since he himself recently co-authored a volume on Akan proverbs: *Bu Me Be: Proverbs of the Akans* (Banbury, Oxon, UK: Ayebia Clarke Publishing, 2008).

them as well, but once they are inside, he, as an African philosopher in his own right, would side with someone like Kwasi Wiredu in saying that what also is advisable is that these elements of a people's folk philosophy then be subjected to critical analysis and evaluation.

In another text concerned with contemporary African philosophy per se, Appiah devotes considerable time and energy to the issue of what may or may not be distinctive about "traditional" African cognition insofar as this element of critical reflection upon beliefs and meanings may be concerned (Appiah 1992a, chapter 6). Here he very clearly distances himself from those who have sought to characterize the indigenous African intellect as acritical, nonreflective, and therefore, in Western terms at least, nonrational. On a factual basis he argues that there is substantive evidence of critical thinking on the part of some members of "traditional" societies. On a moral basis he insists that "unless all of us understand each other, and understand each other as reasonable, we shall not treat each other with the proper respect. Concentrating on the noncognitive features of traditional religions not only misrepresents them but also leads to an underestimation of the role of reason in the life of traditional cultures" (Appiah 1992a, 134).

In an essay entitled "Akan and Euro-American Concepts of the Person" (2004b) his argument at a number of points indicates a continuing openness to the legitimacy of African departures from Western cultural (and, by implication, philosophical) norms. Indeed, his conclusion suggests that, at least as far as the essential components of the human being are concerned, Africans will be better off if they (and Westerners too, for that matter) continue to work at understanding, and achieving truth, from within their indigenous worldviews as opposed to abandoning them wholesale (presuming this was a realistic possibility) for those of another culture. This is the sensible way to proceed.

Finally, with an eye to the future, he discusses the seemingly inevitable problem of how Africa's cultures should come to terms with the antagonisms between the religious, or spiritual, and the scientific that seem to have become part and parcel of "development." This is a problem Africans will have to work through for themselves, but he sees no reason why the results should mirror what "has occurred among educated people in the industrialized world, in general, and in the United States, in particular" (Appiah 1992a, 135). These are cultures in which the so-called spiritual and the values it inspired have been severely curtailed by the influence of science and technology, cultures which are therefore sometimes said to have lost their soul.

> Scientific method may lead to progress in our understanding of the world, but you do not have to be a Thoreauvian to wonder if it has led only to progress in the pursuit of all our human purposes. In this area we [Africans] can learn together with other cultures—including, for example, the Japanese culture, which has apparently managed

a certain segregation of moral-political and cognitive spheres. In this respect, it seems to me obvious that the Ghanaian philosopher Kwasi Wiredu is right. We will only solve our problems if we see them as human problems arising out of a special situation, and we shall not solve them if we see them as African problems, generated by our being somehow unlike others. (Appiah 1992a, 135–36)

Here again one finds expressed that delicate dialectic between the universally human and the culturally relative, but never in a sense that should be taken as demeaning to either.

One obvious thing to notice about this synopsis of analytic philosophy in the African context is the level of technical sophistication displayed by these academic philosophers who have so obviously succeeded in adapting this complex methodology to a non-Western context. This statement is not in the least meant to appear patronizing. If anything, this introductory comment is meant to provide the basis for a complaint against the so-called mainstream Western philosophical establishment. Western philosophers' continuing preponderant attitude of benign indifference to the rich harvests produced by these analyses is unacceptable. To a lesser extent, the same can be said of colleagues who work in other disciplines within African Studies. African philosophy, as an autochthonous and important area of research in its own right, definitely has arrived, and it deserves far more attention from the international academy than it is presently receiving.

Another important achievement of African analytic philosophy is that it amply demonstrates that African scholars have regained the initiative with regard to the complex task of defining rationality as it relates to Africa's intellectual heritage. There is no question that this achievement was motivated in part by the unflattering portrayals of African cognition and the African intellect that made them somehow qualitatively distinct from those of cultures that were said to be somehow better endowed with regard to these fundamentally human attributes.

One outstanding issue that merits further discussion is the need to reflect again on the basis for the distinction between those who have been typed as universalists and those who have been typed as relativists. Is it really a difference in kind, or is it more one of emphasis—insofar as some African philosophers have preferred to focus primarily upon what they see as commonalities while others have preferred to concentrate upon what they see as differences?

This may be true to some extent—insofar as it is a consequence of their *methodological* assumptions. For example, it is apparent that some of these philosophers prefer to begin their analyses on the basis of a presumption that there is—indeed, that there must be—a shared rationality (otherwise one group would not even be able to understand the other). Others think that

this kind of commitment should be avoided, or at least delayed, until sufficient piecemeal, detailed, concrete, empirical analyses of specific elements
of the African intellectual heritage have been undertaken and the results
assessed. This is seen as a more cautious way to proceed and as a way that
contains the ever-pervasive influence of the paradigm of rationality that is
treated as a virtual sinecure of Western philosophy.

Last but not least, it is important to note that African analytic philosophers themselves are well aware of this split within their ranks. It is and will
doubtless continue to be a source of vigorous debate and criticism, but that,
after all, is an activity that can acceptably distinguish the discipline known
as philosophy in any culture.

5

Ethnophilosophy and Philosophical Sagacity

Paulin Hountondji is another major figure in contemporary African philosophy whose influence spans the Francophone-Anglophone divide. He is from the République du Benin (formerly Dahomey) and for years has been professor of philosophy at the University of Cotonu. Hountondji is best known for his critique, *African Philosophy: Myth and Reality* (1996a), of philosophers in and of Africa who propound what he calls "ethnophilosophy."

His intention is to condemn the intellectual injustice that he believes to be enshrined in publications purporting to be African philosophy when they display the following essential characteristics. Ethnophilosophy presents itself as a philosophy of peoples rather than of individuals. In African societies, therefore, one is given the impression that there can be no equivalent to a Socrates or a Kant. Ethnophilosophy speaks only of Bantu philosophy, Dogon philosophy, Yoruba philosophy; as such, its scope is collective, tribal, and of the worldview variety. Ethnophilosophy's sources are in the past, in what is described as authentic traditional African culture of the precolonial variety, of the Africa prior to modernity. These sources are to be found primarily in products of language: parables, proverbs, poetry, songs, myths—oral literature generally. From a methodological point of view, ethnophilosophy tends to portray African beliefs as things that do not change, that are somehow timeless. Disputes between ethnophilosophers arise primarily over how to arrive at a correct rendering of oral literature and traditions. African systems of thought are depicted as placing minimal emphasis upon the rigorous argumentation and criticism that are prerequisites to the sort of search for truth that involves discarding the old and creating the new. Tradition becomes suspect as a justification that something is "true" and is portrayed as antithetical to innovation (Hountondji 1996a).

If this material was presented as cultural anthropology or as ethnology, Hountondji would find it less objectionable. But when it is introduced as philosophy, as African philosophy, a demeaning and subversive double standard is introduced that excuses African thought and philosophy from having critical, reflective (it becomes, in effect, prereflective), rational, scientific, and progressive content produced by individual thinkers in any significantly cross-culturally comparative sense. Of the philosophers whose work has been discussed or mentioned in this text, Hountondji would certainly claim that the work of John Mbiti, Placide Tempels, Alexis Kagame,[1] and Marcel Griaule (Ogotemmeli) is of an ethnophilosophical character. And he would likely characterize the approach of analytic philosophers who use African languages as a basis for African philosophy[2] (since languages are shared and thereby also collective) as also guilty of the ethnophilosophical sin.[3]

Hountondji does not hold these creators of unphilosophical African philosophies criminally responsible for their crimes. In their own intellectual circles, they believe they are doing something genuinely professional and progressive in their attempts to link Africa and philosophy. Also, Hountondji appreciates the problematic sources of Africa's modern intellectual history that may be traced back to the colonial period, when academic philosophers—African or expatriate—were a rare species. The principal Western initiatives for serious scholarly studies of African cultures came from ethnography and anthropology. Given the holistic parameters of the social sciences, it is understandable—if still not ideologically or professionally acceptable—that something like ethnophilosophy came about. But that is not reason enough to encourage its continued development—as African philosophy.

1. "Scientific rigour should prevent us from arbitrarily projecting a philosophical discourse on to products of language which expressly offer themselves as something other than philosophy" (Hountondji 1996a, 43).

2. There is anticipation of Quine's indeterminacy in the following quote from Hountondji, in which he derides the usually unspecified methods these ethnophilosophers use to educe African philosophy from oral literature: "The discourse of ethnophilosophers, be they European or African, offers us the baffling spectacle of an imaginary interpretation with no textual support, of a genuinely 'free' interpretation, inebriated and entirely at the mercy of the interpreter, a dizzy and unconscious freedom which takes itself to be *translating* a text which does not actually exist and which is therefore unaware of its own *creativity*. By this action the interpreter disqualifies himself from reaching any *truth* whatsoever, since truth requires that freedom be limited, that it bow to an order that is not purely imaginary and that it be aware both of this order *and* of its own margin of creativity" (1996a, 189n16; his italics).

3. For a postmodernistic defense of ethnophilosophy, see Salemohamed 1983. For a comparatively strident condemnation of virtually the whole of "African philosophy" as non-philosophy, as too culturally specific and descriptive (in other words, as ethnophilosophy yet again), see Pearce 1992.

In 2002 Hountondji published *The Struggle for Meaning: Reflections on Philosophy, Culture, and Democracy in Africa*. Written as a form of intellectual autobiography, it both clarifies and refines his views on philosophy in the African context. He underlines the point that his underlying motive throughout has been political (2002, xx): to liberate Africa from external intellectual, economic, and political dominance and control, and to reorient and revitalize the cultures of Africa so that the continent regains control of its own destiny. This is why he has so severely chastised both foreign and African philosophical expositions of the African intellect that fit the definition of ethnophilosophy.[4] For this kind of pseudo-philosophy, as far as Hountondji is concerned, is another false and demeaning way of presenting Africa to the world that makes it appear not just different from, but inferior to, other cultures. I suspect he would not hesitate to suggest that such an approach to portraying Africa's intellectual potential was politically motivated as well.

What he now proposes is that there is a role for traditional beliefs and practices to play in the revitalized Africa he foresees, but only if they are subjected to substantive critical analysis and reflection in order to determine whether they are worth keeping:

> The important question is how to demarginalize "traditional" knowledges, to open them up, integrate them into the movement of living research; by which methodologies they could be tested, verified, and as the case may be, proved, or on the contrary disproved; how to separate wholly or partially "the wheat from the chaff," to distinguish the rational from the mythical. How can the valuable and true in these real or alleged knowledges be reactivated and updated? How can they be reappropriated in a critical way? How can the silent coexistence between an institutional and scientific discourse and a so-called traditional discourse be transcended by organizing between the two a peaceful confrontation, and by trying to recreate beyond the current divide, the unity of knowledge? (2002, 252)

Though this is phrased as a question, there is no question that Hountondji is advocating "the critical, methodological reappropriation of one's [Africa's] own knowledge" (2002, 255). Hountondji goes so far as to suggest that this process might result in "the construction of an expanded rationalism that would enable the incorporation of categories of fact that had hitherto been excluded from the spectrum of possible facts by the dominant discourse of science. That was only a suggestion, an extreme hypothesis, but I was ready after all, to go to that extent to think through the unity of human

4. See Hountondji 1997b for a fascinating account of Nkrumah's unfinished Ph.D. thesis manuscript (in which Nkrumah first coins the term "ethnophiloso-phy," even if with a meaning very different from that given it by Hountondji).

knowledge" (2002, 255). In other words, even if Africa was found to be the repository of genuine knowledge unknown to the rest of the world, it would be knowledge that could then be confirmed [his reference to "unity"] by the rest of the world.

But this is not the only point of his program to resuscitate Africa (and, of course, African philosophy). For real progress to be made in both a meaningful and a comprehensive manner, Africans must disengage from thinking of themselves primarily as oriented to the past. They must as aggressively set out to be future-oriented in that they actively seek to discover new knowledge that can then be reviewed for possible incorporation into the African context (2002, 256–57): "to recapture the initiative at all levels, to gain and regain, within the realities of the present-day world, the independence lost, to enable these margins [i.e., what he sees as Africa's current marginalization by much of the rest of the world] to become their own center, and to participate, actively and responsibly, in the construction of a common future" (2002, 257).

Another complementary theme in Hountondji's published work that should be seen as an essential component of this overall process is the importance he assigns to the development of science and technology in Africa as independent and vital research disciplines in their own right. From a practical point of view, this is the sort of enterprise (and knowledge) that African governments and universities must encourage if international intellectual independence is to be achieved and secured. From a philosophical point of view, the literacy, inventive critical thinking, analytic argumentation, and competitive testing of alternate hypotheses intrinsic to such disciplines which, appropriately, would address themselves to African research priorities are also sure to contribute to the kind of independent individualized theoretical thinking that Hountondji finds essential to philosophical discourse that is truly worthy of the name.

It would be unfair to discuss the work of the late Kenyan philosopher H. Odera Oruka only as a reaction or response to Hountondji's critique of ethnophilosophy. In Oruka's methodological writings and fieldwork focused on the approach to African philosophy that he christens "philosophical sagacity," he believes that he is creating a genuinely novel approach to the discipline that both suits the African context and rebuts the claims of those who insist that the philosophical enterprise in Africa must be a mirror image of philosophy in the West.

Oruka suggests that the activity of reflection upon certain themes of fundamental importance to human life—the existence of a supreme being (or God), the nature of time, the nature of freedom, the nature of death, the nature of education—has always been of concern to a select number of people in all human societies. This kind of thinking does not presuppose a modern education or even literacy, so it is false to presume that it can take place only in societies that are typed as "developed." Therefore one task of the academically trained philosopher becomes to identify the sages in a culture and then to record their potentially unique insights on these and related topics (unique because their beliefs may very well differ from conventional beliefs in their societies).[5] In a sense, Oruka remolds and rechristens Wiredu's "folk philosophy" as "culture philosophy," which he says includes the shared, fundamental, conventional beliefs of a society or culture on a variety of important human concerns, topics, and questions of philosophical prepossession. But for this "culture philosophy" to then metamorphose into "philosophical sagacity," individual thinkers (sages) in that society must also reflect upon and critically assess such conventional beliefs on the basis of their own experience and intellectual prowess, and on this basis possibly suggest either criticisms or novel alternatives. It is this that contributes that element of individuality that both Hountondji and Oruka insist is a sine qua non of philosophy in any culture.

> In the ultimate sense philosophy is not a language analysis, not the exercise enjoyed in a logical dialogue, and not a special insight of the world reserved for some race or gender. Philosophy is a perspective of the whole or part of the human predicament and insightful suggestions on how to get out or conform. This sort of perspective can be found in anybody (white, black, yellow, female or male). But in every community there are always persons who specialize in offering or studying such perspectives (in traditional Africa this role was left to the Sages). (Oruka 1990b, 35–36)[6]

Oruka first presented his position on sagacity in a seminal paper that probably should be considered the first serious attempt to introduce an Africanized system to differentiate the various approaches to African philosophy that could then be used as a basis for writing the history of contemporary African philosophy, "Four Trends in Current African Philosophy" (1981b). The four trends, schools, or approaches to African philosophy he identifies are ethnophilosophy (Tempels, Griaule, Mbiti, and, as this category was first delimited, Gyekye, Hallen, and Sodipo); philosophical sagacity (Oruka); nationalist-ideological philosophy, which included African social-political

5. Oruka does not regard Griaule's Ogotemmeli as a sage because basically all he does is summarize Dogon beliefs (no matter how esoteric) on a variety of topics. Oruka argues that there is minimal evidence of critical and independent reflection on the beliefs by Ogotemmeli himself (Oruka 1990d, 45–46).

6. Oruka refers to the mental ability responsible for such reflection on the part of sages as "intuition" (1990b). Compare with Léopold Senghor: "White reason is analytic through utilization: Negro is intuitive through participation" (1956, 59).

thinkers (Senghor, Nkrumah, Nyerere); and professional philosophy, which he associates with the orthodox Western academic tradition (Bodunrin, Hountondji, and, as this category was first delimited, Wiredu and, most interestingly, Oruka himself again[7]). There is not time to discuss Oruka's detailed critical assessments of each of these categories, but it is important to note that he later refined their terms of reference and added (Oruka 1990a, xx–xxi) an additional two: the hermeneutic, to more specifically accommodate those who choose a linguistic approach[8] (Wiredu, Gyekye, Hallen, and Sodipo) and the artistic or literary, to apply to African intellectual figures in the humanities who address themselves to themes basic to Africa's cultural identity (Okot p'Bitek, Ngugi wa Thiong'o, and 'Wole Soyinka).

The tragic death of Odera Oruka did not result in the demise of philosophical sagacity, or, as it is also known, sage philosophy. Several contemporary Kenyan philosophers, including F. Ochieng'-Odhiambo (2006), as well as the American philosopher Gail Presbey (2007) have continued to both clarify and elaborate Oruka's and their own visions of the future of sage philosophy. Philosophical sagacity also continues to attract its share of commentaries by African philosophers who do not identify themselves as committed to this methodology (Kalumba 2004, Masolo 2005).

One point of particular interest is that Oruka saw his approach as providing a way to reconcile the dispute over whether African philosophy was compelled to choose between universalism and relativism, in that African sages would prove to be critical and reflective (universal) in terms of their own cultural frameworks (relative) (Masolo 2005, 25; Ochieng'-Odhiambo 2006, 24–25). Another is that Oruka had mapped out much grander programs and objectives than simply demonstrating (contra Hountondji) that Kenyan sages were capable of both first- and second-order thinking. He had drawn up an agenda for collecting foundational philosophical material from the sages of all of the various ethnic groups within Kenya, with a view to identify the differences among those cultures that then might be revised and reconciled via further contributions from the relevant sages, and that would as well contribute to a more future-oriented thinking on the part of the populace (what traditions is it best we keep, what should we dispense with, where is new thinking required, etc.) (Ochieng'-Odhiambo 2006, 22, 26–27; Presbey 2007, 146–47). In other words, his was not a perfunctory "ivory tower" exercise. It was also to serve as a *practical* step toward nation

7. Oruka evidently views "philosophical sagacity" as a species of the genus "professional philosophy" specially designed for accommodating "traditional" African cultures.

8. Which he understands as involving "the philosophical analysis of concepts in a given African language to help clarify meaning and logical implications arising from the use of such concepts" (Oruka 1990d, xx).

building—something that would promote human welfare in the most genuine sense of the term.

Something also needs to be said about the strong reactions by both Hountondji and Oruka against a linguistic approach to African philosophy and their view of it as a further extension of a one-sidedly ethnophilosophical approach directed only at non-Western (more specifically, African) peoples and cultures. Twentieth-century Western analytic philosophy is perhaps best known for its own "linguistic turn."[9] Western analytic philosophers have spent much of their time analyzing language—either in an idealized or paradigmatic form, by exploring the nature of meaning, reference, and so forth in any language, or more concretely, by identifying and evaluating the criteria governing usage of certain concepts or fields of discourse in a specific natural language that is actually used by human beings (not surprisingly, usually the English language). For example, they attempt to determine the criteria that are involved in English-language discourse for a piece of information to be classified as "true" or for a particular action to be labeled "good" or "moral." This kind of approach to English-language discourse was instrumental to the fundamental distinctions incorporated by epistemology (or the theory of knowledge) between "knowledge by acquaintance," "knowledge how," and "knowledge that" (or "propositional knowledge").[10] But if both Hountondji and Oruka (at least at one point in time) would condemn the linguistic approach as misguided because it is based on a shared, collective, "tribal" enterprise such as a common language, then much of the contemporary orthodox Western philosophical canon itself qualifies as perhaps the most gross example of ethnophilosophy ever! Therefore, it would seem there must be a place for some sort of accommodation between Hountondji and Oruka and mainstream Western linguistic philosophy.[11]

It appears Hountondji and Oruka would have no objection to the individual philosopher observing and reflecting upon the world and human experience and on that basis propounding a speculative theory derived from those sources. Indeed, in a sense this is their paradigm for the philosophical (and sagacious). So if the linguistic philosopher proposes to substitute language, either in its idealized form or as a specific natural language (English, Akan [Twi]), for the world and human experience as an alternative basis for his or her observations, reflections, and speculations, are the parameters involved really so different? Only, it would seem, if linguistic philosophy is made out to be so parochial and prosaic an enterprise as to amount to nothing more

9. As expressed by Richard Rorty's well-known anthology *The Linguistic Turn* (1967).

10. See, for example, Feldman 2003, 8–12.

11. See Hallen 1996b.

than the simplistic representation of a language's grammar and vocabulary that can be found in an elementary-level foreign-language textbook. On the other hand, if the networks of concepts and fields of discourse of every natural language might be looked at as potentially original and unique creations of human genius setting out to comprehend the world, theoretical incentives much more exciting than mere grammar and vocabulary become involved. Furthermore, if the philosophical backgrounds, interpretations, and critiques of the different linguistic philosophers who reflect upon and critically analyze those conceptual networks and fields of discourse differ, as indeed they do, does this not highlight or underscore that essential element of individuality, of significant creative input by the individual thinker, that Hountondji and Oruka find vital to the philosophical enterprise?

6

Phenomenology and Hermeneutics

Contemporary African academic philosophy is as noteworthy for the variety of methodological approaches it evidences as it is for the diversity of views that are consequential to application of those methodologies to a variety of topics and problems. Up to this point, the only mainstream methodological approach to the discipline that has been explored in any detail is that conventionally referred to as analysis, or analytic philosophy. Another approach that deserves consideration is that derived from the phenomenological tradition and is conventionally, at least as far as its African manifestations are concerned, referred to as hermeneutics.

The technical terminology intrinsic to the phenomenological-existential-hermeneutical tradition[1] has frequently been criticized (by persons outside that tradition, of course) as excessively dense and difficult to interpolate. Without some sort of introductory primer or dictionary, the non-initiated often find themselves hopelessly befuddled when they try to take on a text that is based upon it. It is, some say, like landing on a different (albeit philosophical) planet. But the analytic tradition too has managed to generate its own technical vocabulary which, if abused rather than used in a sensible manner, is no less notorious for its befuddling effects upon the casual reader. The goal of this chapter on hermeneutics is to summarize this important approach to African philosophy with a narrative text that will do it justice and still communicate with the reader who has no firsthand experience of or prior exposure to it. Within African philosophy itself, it would be unfortunate if analytic and hermeneutic philosophers begin to congregate

1. Some major figures in Western (notably Continental European) philosophy linked to or identified with this tradition are Hegel, Kierkegaard, Nietzsche, Husserl, Heidegger, Jaspers, Gadamer, Sartre, Marcel, Merleau-Ponty, and Ricoeur.

in increasingly segregated intellectual circles (as has been the case in the Western academy [Hallen 2005b]).

The modern-day founder of the philosophical approach that has come to be known as phenomenology was the German philosopher Edmund Husserl (1859–1938). As did many of his analytic contemporaries who sought universalist philosophical principles, Husserl sought to formulate a methodological approach that would focus on a level of (human) experience that was common to all peoples, in all historical periods, in all cultures. To reach this most fundamental level of experience, Husserl insisted that phenomenologists would have to be trained in a rigorous manner to enable them to see through, to discard, and to discount all of the more superficial interpretative frameworks that they had inherited or invented in the particular historical and cultural contexts in which they happened to live and with which they were most familiar as supposedly representing the world the way it "really" is.[2] Such frameworks include a person's cultural identity, "common" sense, religious identity, professional identity, and, in the academy, philosophical identity. Husserl regarded analytic philosophy itself as, relatively speaking, just another one of those comparatively superficial but fashionable philosophical frameworks for interpreting human experience invented by scholars who were the products of a particular phase of human history—in this case, a period overwhelmingly influenced by the paradigms and propaganda of the empirical sciences.

Precisely what Husserl believed that most fundamental level of experience to contain has remained an issue of some controversy. The English-language adjective most frequently used to describe it is "structured." In other words, freeing ourselves of all preconceptions about what the world 'is' composed of or about what experience really consists of or means (such as 'people,' 'trees,' 'atoms,' and so forth) does not result in all forms of stability and order disintegrating so that we are left with the experience of disorder or chaos. In fact the 'structures' (which Husserl unfortunately christened *Ideen* in German, a term transliterated into English as "ideas") that remain constitute an ordered, if most fundamental (and universal), level of experience upon which all of those more superficial creations of the human intellect (national cultures, empirical sciences, religions, and endlessly so forth) are erected, superimposed, and therefore effectively obscure.

Both the possibility and the nature of Husserl's 'ideas' provoked controversy within the phenomenological movement itself. There were and are those who labeled him a (philosophical) idealist, implying that he had become the victim of or had fallen prey to that conventional philosophical superstition

---

2. An objective reminiscent of the philosophy of Zar'a Ya'aqob. See p. 17 above.

that entities entertained by the mind (hence 'ideas') somehow have a more primordial ontological or metaphysical status than, for example, those communicated to us by the five physical senses. However this debate internal to the phenomenological movement may ultimately be resolved, several of Husserl's intellectual descendants who challenge the primacy of a universal and necessary level to experience have become of particular importance to African philosophy. They prefer to concentrate explicitly upon the distinctive 'ideas,' worldviews, or priorities that are characteristic of particular historical and cultural contexts, and these are the philosophers who have become most prominently associated with the name "hermeneutics."

The best known of these maverick descendants is Martin Heidegger (1889–1976), who is frequently, and many would say misleadingly, identified with the post–World War II literary-philosophical movement known as existentialism. The Heideggerean corpus of writings (1962) is far too complex to do it justice here. What this chapter shall attempt is to extract several relevant themes from that corpus and then conjoin them with several others derived from the work of one of Heidegger's students and intellectual descendants, Hans-Georg Gadamer (1900–2002).

With regard to the relationship between language and philosophy, one of the reasons phenomenologists (and in this regard one thinks primarily of Heidegger) have deliberately created a unique vocabulary is to sunder the preconceptions generated by the words of ordinary discourse about the things that it persuades us to regard as "real." The avowed purpose of this vocabulary (and the methodology of which it is an indispensable element) is to facilitate a hermeneutical or "interpretative" (the more conventional term to which "hermeneutical" is most frequently equated) approach to historically and culturally relative periods and processes of understanding—of how human beings then and there happen to relate to and understand the world, themselves included. Perhaps Heidegger's most controversial claim is that most of these conventional interpretative efforts fabricated by human beings—including science, philosophy, religion, and even "common" sense— are granted a grossly exaggerated truth status. This error enables humankind to embrace a false or inauthentic conviction that it really does understand the nature of existence.

A primary aim of Heidegger's existential phenomenology is to identify the truly authentic nature of human being (or being human) that underlies and gives rise to all of these comparatively *in*authentic modes of understanding the world and ourselves that we have invented with the passage of time. Indeed "Time" with a capital "T" becomes the key to that authenticity— what characterizes human being most fundamentally—in the sense that every person is suddenly thrust ('born') into a world they did not choose, then they distract themselves from the possible meaningless of their existence ('life') with the invention and sustenance of all manner of projects and situations that keep them occupied. Yet they also must somehow come to terms with future possibilities (the most irrevocable and terrifying of these being death, of course). There is then still an element of theoretical and methodological transcendence[3] ('universality') to Heidegger's philosophy in that this phenomenological portrait of 'authentic' human being is meant to be fundamental to and formative of all social and historical contexts.[4]

Gadamer is important because of the frequent references made to his work by African philosophers who align themselves with his distinctive form of hermeneutics. Gadamer argues that the various frameworks that have been invented or created by human beings over the course of their history (including all the arts and sciences) should constitute the objects of obvious and important, if comparatively less fundamental (thinking of Husserl and Heidegger), hermeneutical or interpretative exercises. There is no clear sense of transcendence here, apart from his encouraging us to have a self-consciously explicit appreciation of the fact that we all find ourselves in the world as products of specific historical, cultural, and intellectual contexts. Hermeneutics as "interpretation" can certainly promote understanding of the nature of those contexts, and our own self-understanding, as well, of course, but always still as beings who have no choice but to continue to exist, to learn, to understand, and perhaps even to struggle against or to overcome within those contexts. In other words, human understanding is always affected by, a consequence of, the various contexts in which it is sited. In other words, human understanding is always and inevitably interpretation (keep in mind the significance of this word for Gadamer's hermeneutics), a rendering arising from the contexts of which it is a product and which it, in turn, may thereafter transform.

This is an appropriate point for a brief diversion before we move on to consideration of specific philosophers who choose to work with this kind of approach in the African context. If this synopsis is to practice what it preaches regarding the importance of intellectual intercourse between different philosophical traditions, it should be of interest to compare the approaches of the analytical and hermeneutical traditions to something—language—that is of common concern to them. Gadamer's work, in particular, demonstrates a special interest in the relationship between language and philosophy.[5]

As intellectual descendants of the Anglophone tradition of (British)

3. Perhaps "descendance" would more appropriately describe the stripping away of the relatively superficial, invented frameworks of human understanding.

4. For a more explicit discussion of Heidegger and African philosophy, see Hallen 2003.

5. "The key importance that the problem of language has acquired in philosophy" (Gadamer 1975, 350).

empiricism (manifested most notably by the sciences), analytic philosophers who concern themselves with language, concepts, or meanings appear to relate to these things as if they were stable and static 'objects' existing in a (culturally and historically) neutral environment that makes it possible to perform various definitive experiments and tests with and upon them that other philosophers may thereafter verify and confirm. This attitude is not manifested in an explicit manner, but it is frequently if tacitly implied by the manner in which the techniques of linguistic analysis are employed. Furthermore, the writings of analytic philosophers give the impression that the more important problems, topics, and questions of philosophy—on a purely rational basis—transcend any particular historical or cultural context. If time is assigned a role in the search for philosophical truth(s), it is that an essential cluster of those truths must be time*less*—universally applicable to all of humankind. There is, then, another form of transcendence here that is complementary to that sought by the more "radical" phenomenologists (Husserl and Heidegger). But while that of phenomenology places a priority on an accurate rendering of human existence and experience, analytic philosophy emphasizes the importance of reason(ing) as key for access to a level of 'truths' that will be undeniably transcendent or universal.

The idea of analyzing language in isolation from the particular social and historical contexts in which human beings use it is something Gadamer cannot accept and rejects as fundamentally flawed: "The instrumentalist *devaluation* of language that we find in modern times . . . makes it possible for 'language' as such, ie [*sic*] its form, [to be] separated from all content, to become an independent object of attention" (Gadamer 1975, 365; my italics). To Gadamer, language is like a living thing—in process and constantly adapting or being adapted to express new ideas, new understanding—rather than an object that can be regarded as if on display in a museum case (Gadamer 1975, 345). It cannot be isolated from human life because it is so fundamental to being human. "The language that lives in speech, which takes in all understanding, including that of the textual interpreter, is so much bound up with thinking and interpretation that we have too little left if we ignore the actual content of what languages hand down to us and seek to consider only language as form" (Gadamer 1975, 366).

As a shared vehicle of understanding and communication, language, as evidenced in conversation and dialogue, ensures that understanding is *inter*subjective rather than private. But since natural languages do differ from one another ("to see languages as views of the world" [Gadamer 1975, 364]), and since social and historical contexts also differ as well as change, Gadamer's orientation is most compatible overall with a relativistic appreciation of human understanding. In other words, he would regard it as culturally chauvinistic or ethnocentric for philosophy to anoint one particular natural language (English, Swahili) as some sort of paradigm or one particular approach to defining "rationality" (Western) at some point in time as a basis with which to assess the merits of others.

Obviously, this synopsis does not do Gadamer's extensive writings on this subject justice. Still, even on the basis of this brief diversion, one cannot help but wonder whether the genuine differences between the analytic and hermeneutic approaches to the study of languages are so fundamental as to make these two traditions irreconcilable. Certainly those analytic philosophers who themselves defend relativism, and who thereby provide a more flexible approach to human understanding, would seem to share some fundamental convictions in common with their hermeneutic colleagues (Hallen 2005b).

Theophilus Okere, a Nigerian philosopher, is one of the earlier advocates of a hermeneutical approach to African philosophy. A starting point he shares in common with most hermeneutical philosophers in and of Africa generally is the conviction that European imperialism and colonialism violently and profoundly disrupted Africa's social, cultural, and political continuity and integrity. One benefit of a hermeneutic approach, therefore, is that the fabric of African societies—which sometimes mix the indigenous and the European, the "traditional" and the "modern," in an unfortunate or unpromising manner—can be interpreted so as to single out what aspects or elements of the mélange are to be valued and reaffirmed as a sound basis for a progressive African social, political, and cultural heritage that will be a worthy tribute to that remarkable continent.

In his *African Philosophy: A Historico-Hermeneutical Investigation of the Conditions of Its Possibility* (1983),[6] Okere outlines a program for how such a hermeneutic approach might be implemented. The first major issue he addresses is what should be the proper relationship between such a hermeneutic philosophy and Africa's cultural heritage. He dismisses the work of the so-called ethnophilosophers[7] as not worthy of the label "philosophy." At the most, these collections of myths, proverbs, and worldviews qualify as ethnography, as compendiums of cultural beliefs and practices. Hermeneutic philosophers might work with such ethnographic materials to render them philosophical by *interpreting* them—distilling and assessing their meaning(s),

6. This is an edited version of the doctoral dissertation he presented in 1971.

7. He specifically mentions Tempels, Kagame, and Mbiti by name. Although suspicious of attempts to mine African languages for philosophical insights, he does not *absolutely* rule this out as a possibility: "Our scepticism does not, of course, refuse all validity to the thesis of linguists who have drawn attention to the close relationship between language and thought. According to the best researches, language seems to affect culture and thought at some level but there is not enough material yet to help determine precisely how" (Okere 1983, 9).

their true significance(s), and their value(s) to and for Africa's cultural present and future.

Okere is open-minded when it comes to the question of whether Africa
has always had or has its own indigenous philosophy and philosophers:

> Whether there is some black African philosophy or not, can be
> decided only after an exhaustive examination of every individual in
> the culture concerned. We have to allow for illiterate and unrecorded
> lovers of wisdom. More practically, we have, on examination of the
> current philosophy literature, objected not so much to the fact that
> they claimed the existence of philosophy in Africa as to what they
> claimed to be philosophy.[8] (Okere 1983, 114)

Adding a hermeneutical dimension to African philosophy would apparently
introduce something new—methodologically and intellectually—into the
African context. Certainly Africa has always had its culture(s), and herme-
neutically mining them for their progressive elements is something of which
he clearly approves:

> Here philosophy is really a manufacturing from raw materials. It is
> a forging out of thought from the materials of culture. It is an act of
> intellectual creation where the new creation is a meaning born from
> the melting of one's total experience. (Okere 1983, xiv)

Although he is appreciative of the Western philosophical tradition that
traces its roots to the Greeks, that tradition is most certainly not something
Okere would like to see transferred or transplanted into the African context.[9] He embraces Gadamer's notions of the relativity of cultural and social
contexts ("All philosophical discourse is first and foremost an answer to
problems and questions raised within a questioning horizon which means
always, a culture [Okere 1983, 64].""). In other words, to be genuinely
African, Africa's philosophers and philosophy must arise from and relate
directly to the particular culture(s) in which they are sited. These cultures are
sufficiently distinctive in their own right that it would be a reductive injustice
to claim or to conclude that they are somehow the "same" as their Western
counterpart(s). Clearly this again places Okere on the side of relativism when
it comes to the nature of philosophical "truths" and principles:

> The possibility of an African philosophy raises the question of the
> validity and universality of truth and of the communicability of cul-
> tures and their respective philosophies. Is truth relative? It seems this
> conclusion is inevitable. The historicity and relativity of truth—and

8. A further indictment of ethnophilosophy, no doubt.

9. Except insofar as it would be taught and studied as an alien philosophical
tradition, such as Chinese philosophy, Indian philosophy, and so forth.

this always means truth as we can and do attain it—is one of the
main insights of the hermeneutical revolution in philosophy and it
is on it that this thesis hangs. (Okere 1983, 124)

In the final chapter of his text, Okere identifies any number of "symbolic"
elements and practices in his native Igbo culture that he suggests could contribute to a positive basis for a philosophy arising from that culture as a
result of hermeneutical interpretation, such as the role of the *Chi* as guardian
spirit and symbol of destiny, the practice of polygamy, and the nature and
role of the extended family (Okere 1983, 115).

In 2005 Okere published a collection of his essays entitled *Philosophy,
Culture and Society in Africa*. The twenty-one essays included in this volume
cover as broad a range of topics as the title indicates. Okere also graciously
acknowledges the new generations of African philosophers to which his
teachings and writings have given rise (Oguejiofor and Onah 2005). One
passage from this text, which again addresses the issues of traditions and
modernity, is particularly relevant:

> At this stage let me enunciate what I consider the African cultural
> dilemma. We are in a position where we can no longer remain indif-
> ferent to our past. Therefore we must revive the past. But we cannot
> be expected to appropriate our past without any discrimination,
> after the slogan: My country, right or wrong! Further, we are in a
> position where we can no longer remain indifferent to the foreign
> culture that is now in contact with ours. Therefore we must borrow
> from that foreign culture. But we cannot swallow without discrimi-
> nation whatever the foreign culture has to offer. To revive or not to
> revive and if to revive, what to revive; to borrow or not to borrow
> and if to borrow, what to borrow: that is the question. That is the
> cultural dilemma of Africa. (2005, 32–33)

Congolese philosopher Okonda Okolo applauds the hermeneutical
approach to African philosophy outlined by Theophilus Okere (Okolo 1991,
201). To further its development he proposes to provide African-oriented
hermeneutical interpretations of two notions of fundamental importance to
Africa's indigenous cultures—Tradition and Destiny. His decision to concentrate on them is not accidental or haphazard. Apart from their genuine
importance to Africa's cultures, his decision also is motivated by his conviction that Western Africanists—as ethnocentric products of their own cultural
backgrounds—have managed to analyze and evaluate them in ways that are
both derogatory and false.

In Western anthropology, a culture based on Tradition is frequently portrayed as one devoid of change or development because it is also devoid of
critical or reflective thinking. Beliefs and practices inherited from the 'ancestors' are said to be preserved unchanged in the present and then handed on

to the next generation with the understanding they will be preserved and observed in a similar manner. Knowledge therefore does not progress, and those who dare to challenge established Traditions put their own welfare at risk. The belief in Destiny is portrayed as encouraging a rather severe manifestation of determinism, according to which it is believed that what will be, will be. This too is said to inhibit the development of independent or individual initiative.

Invoking the hermeneutic tradition arising from the work of Paul Ricoeur, Heidegger, and Gadamer, Okolo proposes to reinterpret and reappraise each of these notions and to do so as an African who can philosophize from within the African cultural and historical context. For example, he disagrees fundamentally with the stereotype that Tradition means unchanging beliefs and practices that are handed on from generation to generation. Tradition does involve a sense of transmission and of reception (Okolo 1991, 202), but in a context where the meanings of any particular tradition are constantly being interpreted and reinterpreted—and therefore always changing—by different individuals and in different historical contexts over the passage of time.

Tradition therefore does not inhibit invention or change, because new interpretations are made as a natural and normal part of making Tradition meaningful to the people who inherit it. Because of this, those societies will inevitably either eliminate or amend traditions as time passes and/or reinterpret them so that they again become newly relevant to the present generation. "The tradition, essentially defined as transmission, constitutes a hermeneutic concatenation of interpretations and reinterpretations. To read our tradition is nothing like climbing the whole chain of interpretations all the way back to its originative starting point; rather, it is to properly recreate the chain in actualizing it" (Okolo 1991, 204–205).

Destiny, from the vantage point of African hermeneutics, is not a symbol of determinism, where everything that happens is seen as inevitable. Destiny involves a people's "vision of the world" and as such represents the history of a people, of a culture, in the world. It represents that people's past, present, and future and whatever sense of identity they create and then recreate for themselves on the basis of reinterpreting and reinventing Tradition(s) over the passage of time. "We will have to, no doubt, explode the idea of destiny and recharge it anew starting from our hermeneutical situation. This hermeneutical situation is that of the formerly colonized, the oppressed, that of the underdeveloped, struggling for more justice and equality" (Okolo 1991, 208). Reinterpreting a sense of African Destiny must be linked to Africans' regaining the sense of being in control of their own societies, including the right to understand those societies in their own terms. These elements must constitute essential parts of the framework that will define African hermeneutics, that will reinterpret the nature of the African identity as expressed by and through African culture.

Eritrean philosopher Tsenay Serequeberhan,[10] along with the African American philosopher Richard Wright, deserve credit for having the foresight to produce the first two widely read anthologies of African philosophy. Serequeberhan's includes the essay by Okolo that has just been discussed (1991c). But here the principal interest will be his *The Hermeneutics of African Philosophy* (1994), which presents itself as a kind of manifesto about what the role of hermeneutical philosophy in Africa should be. Serequeberhan identifies Gadamer as "the father of contemporary philosophical hermeneutics" (Serequeberhan 1994, 16), which, he says, unlike "orthodox" phenomenology, is always explicitly and self-consciously sited in a specific historico-cultural context (1994, 3). Indeed, as far as Serequeberhan is concerned, *all* philosophy—not just the hermeneutical—must be so situated and, no matter how meticulously neutral and universal it pretends to be, must also have a political dimension (1994, 4). He castigates the Western philosophical establishment for playing along with the intellectual and political issues involved in the portrayal of Africa as irrational and primitive, especially when viewed against the background of European colonialism. Western civilization (philosophy included) was indeed propagandized as the cultural paradigm, and most things African were viewed as negations of that ideal.

Serequeberhan is an African philosopher who explicitly confronts the potential problem posed by the fact that hermeneutics itself is a methodology of European origin (Serequeberhan 1994, 10–11). In other words, how can it avoid being certified as just one more example of a European mentality that therefore cannot authentically apply to the African cultural context? His response to this potentially serious challenge is twofold. First, the hermeneutical approach to philosophy already has been adapted, filtered, and amended by the work within and about it by non-Western thinkers such as Frantz Fanon and Amilcar Cabral. Other non-Western intellectuals whose work is relevant to its political renovation (remember that for Serequeberhan *all* philosophizing has political ramifications) are Aimé Césaire and Cornelius Castoriadis (who was, in fact, Greek). At the same time, Serequeberhan does not hesitate to condemn Western icons such as Heidegger, Marx, Hegel, Hume, and Kant for the racist content of their writings (Serequeberhan 1994, 60–61).

Second, it would be hypocrisy for contemporary African intellectuals, philosophers included, to pretend that they remain unaffected by the colonial experience and the Western elements introduced thereby into Africa's

---

10. Which can be phonetically rendered as "Sen [as in the English-language 'den']-eye Sera-kway-burr-an."

own intellectual heritage. It makes more sense for Africans to come to terms with all of this in a deliberate and forthright manner. If that also involves the adaptation of an approach such as hermeneutics to the African context, then that may be all well and good, provided it is done in a positive, progressive manner—a manner that will benefit Africa rather than demean it:

> Thus, in terms of contemporary concerns—political, economic, scientific, cultural, etc.—the hermeneutics of African philosophy must engage in situated reflections aimed at the pragmatic and practical aim of enhancing the lived actuality of post-colonial Africa. It is only in this way that African philosophy, as the reflexive hermeneutics of its own historicalness, can grow and cultivate itself as a concrete contemporary philosophic discourse. (Serequeberhan 1994, 114)

Serequeberhan appears to have a fairly low tolerance for other methodological approaches to African philosophy. He rebukes the so-called ethnophilosophers for introducing themselves to the international community (and Africa) as a kind of new wave. Ethnophilosophers may argue that Africa's cultures have always contained a philosophical dimension, but it still took *them* to identify, codify, and somehow, in the end, take the professional credit for developing it. As for what I have been referring to as the "rationalist" approach, he criticizes Bodunrin, Hountondji, and Wiredu for too easily advocating, adopting, and imposing an essentially Western tradition of philosophy upon the African context (Serequeberhan 1994, 5).[11]

An African hermeneutics, if developed and applied in a sensitive manner, can make a positive contribution to Africa's social, cultural, and political restoration. The priorities he assigns to this hermeneutics are at least two. First, it must contribute to the true liberation of a continent that is still not truly independent, that still suffers the humiliating and destructive consequences of colonialism—neocolonialism (and all of the profound but negative factors that involves) and economic, political, and intellectual insecurity, instability, and underdevelopment. Second, it must promote a rediscovery and reevaluation of the authentic African past in every sense of the phrase—intellectual, social, political, and so forth. This does not mean that everything—every belief, practice, or social institution certified as (once upon a time) authentic will be resuscitated. But it does mean that Africans will be able to get on with the business of determining what really was and is their history, their culture(s); what they really want their rights and privileges to be; and how best to position themselves for the future. "From this point on, ancient/

11. Serequeberhan also mounts severe critiques of Kwame Nkrumah's "consciencism" (for its neo-Marxist "scientific" pretensions) and Léopold Senghor's theory of Negritude (for its racism arising from the special "traits" associated with being African).

ossified customs and traditions are not merely discarded out of hand . . . nor are they desperately held on to. . . . Rather, their preservation loses its inertia and becomes a process by which society is historically reinstituted out of the needs of the present mediated by the struggle" (Serequeberhan 1994, 100).

In this regard he has some nice things to say about Gyekye's suggested program for identifying and reexamining Africa's indigenous "traditions" to determine which deserve to be preserved and promoted (Serequeberhan 1994, 6). This obviously will also be a priority of African hermeneutics. With regard to the issue of whether there was philosophy in so-called traditional, or precolonial, Africa, because Serequeberhan is so insistent upon every people's and culture's right to define itself, clearly he is open to the idea that Africa's cultures are entitled to claim their own philosophical heritage, even if it is manifested in a substantially different form from that taken as conventional by other societies: "The foundational wondering and musing of traditional African sages have—in their continuous critical and safeguarding relation to the traditions (i.e., the ethnic world-views) they inhabit—a hermeneutic and philosophic function. To this extent, it has to be conceded in principle that their reflections and intellectual productions are products of philosophic effort" (Serequeberhan 1994, 126n11).

In *Our Heritage: The Past in the Present of African-American and African Existence* (2000), Serequeberhan makes a deliberate effort to enunciate the concerns, from both historical and hermeneutical viewpoints, that Africans and African Americans today share. They are linked, first and foremost, by their common struggles against oppression and for liberation. This is also manifested by a body of literature which, it appears, he means to introduce as the basis for a kind of canon—a body of essential, foundational writings that may serve to define Africana philosophy. His chapters are devoted to critical evaluations of the heritage left by a variety of Africana philosophers and intellectuals from both sides of the Atlantic—Frantz Fanon, W. E. B. Du Bois, Frederick Douglass, Kwame Anthony Appiah, and our old friend, Zar'a Ya'aqob.

Serequeberhan again affirms, even more explicitly, the right of peoples of African descent to define their own priorities:

> We are, at the close of the twentieth century, at a point in time when the dominance of the *uni*verse of European singularity is being encompassed or engulfed by the *multi*verse of our shared humanity. The colonizer, selfdeified imperial Europe, is dead! (Serequeberhan 2000, 52–53)

The philosophical orientation that can best contribute to this ongoing process of liberation, again on both sides of the Atlantic, cannot derive from any universal tradition of philosophical thought, which is why he continues to insist on an *African(a)* hermeneutics (he regards "universalist" claims to be a covert strategy for the reassertion of Western paradigms):

> African philosophic practice has to engage in the systematic and critical exploration of indigenous forms of knowledge: practical and theoretic. . . . It must be done by sifting through our legacies: retaining that which is alive, casting off that which is lethargic, and critically fusing the heritage of the past with modern scientific conceptions. (Serequeberhan 2000, 55)

Political independence (as the Fourteenth Amendment to the U.S. Constitution, U.S. civil rights legislation, and the end of European colonialism have demonstrated) is one thing. But achieving and securing intellectual independence is something else entirely. It is this second dimension of the liberation struggle to which a philosophical hermeneutics can make an indispensable contribution.

As a further step toward securing this intellectual independence, Serequeberhan has published *Contested Memory: The Icons of the Occidental Tradition* (2007), which contains severe critiques of three of the Western canon's most influential figures: Immanuel Kant (1724–1804), Georg Wilhelm Friedrich Hegel (1770–1831), and Karl Marx (1818–1883). The inspiration for this text was a question formulated by the American philosopher Robert Bernasconi (see below, pp. 92–93): "[W]hat would it mean to do Continental [in philosophical vernacular "Continental" refers to the European continent] philosophy in the light of African philosophy" (Bernasconi 1997, 183, as quoted in Serequeberhan 2007, xiii). In harmony with his previous insistence on Africa's right to formulate its own philosophical approaches, Serequeberhan interprets this question as an invitation to do a critical review of these three Western philosophical 'icons' from a thoroughly critical, non-Western point of view.

What he finds, in each case, is that the philosopher involved somehow embraced the inevitability of the domination of other cultures by the West as a progressive dimension to human history. Kant is found to promote European Enlightenment culture as a paradigm that should be embraced by all of humanity (an implicit justification of European imperialism) while at the same time he "bemoans and finds outrageous . . . [the] conquest of the non-European world" (2007, 56). Hegel provides a metaphysical justification for European imperialism and African slavery as inevitable milestones of world evolution, ironically as humankind progresses to "Freedom" (2007, 93). Marx, the controversial champion of universal human liberation, characterizes what he refers to as "ancient" societies as follows:

> Those ancient social organizations of production are, as compared with [European] bourgeois society, extremely simple and transpar-

ent. But they are founded either on the *immaturity of man* as an individual, *who has not yet severed the umbilical cord that unites him with his fellowmen in a primitive tribal community,* or upon direct relations of subjection. They can arise and exist only when the development of the productive power of labor has not risen beyond a low stage, and when, therefore, the social relations within the sphere of material life, between man and man, and between man and Nature, are correspondingly narrow. (*Capital,* 1:79 as quoted in Serequeberhan 2007, 127; italics Serequeberhan)

As far as Serequeberhan is concerned, this too amounts to a justification of European imperialism insofar as: "The explicit presupposition of the passage quoted above is that the development of the forces of production [via colonialism] will transform this limited and inferior mode of life" (2007, 127). In all three thinkers, therefore, enslavement and exploitation of the non-Western world by the Western world become the keys to 'freedom' and human welfare.

Finally, in answer to his original question, what does Serequeberhan see as the appropriate role for Western philosophy vis-à-vis the non-Western world? His response, as evidenced by the above, is that it should be very realistically evaluated, as much for its limitations and ethnocentrism as for its positive contributions to human understanding:

> Rather, the arrogant Eurocentrism in which these values are incased is purged and Occidental values and technics are accepted for what they are; the achievements of *a particular* culture. In this recognition the universalized particularism of the West is discarded and elements—technics and values—of European culture are appropriated and become indigenous aspects of reemerging African cultures. (Serequeberhan 2007, 152)

Once this is achieved the people of Africa will be in a position to *reposition* themselves, their cultures, and their philosophies in a manner that suits their prioritized aims and objectives rather than those that the Western world, even today, seeks to persuade humanity generally to accept as appropriately universal.[12]

There is one final dimension of African hermeneutics that must be included if this summary is to be arguably comprehensive. In a sense, it represents its most radical, even revolutionary, posture with reference to the

---

12. Though at times Serequeberhan is less sanguine: "But, thus far, having achieved political independence, Africa has opened itself up to being nothing more than the distorted mirror image of the Occident, obsessively seeking 'the modern' glitter of that which still controls it, and like Achilles chasing the tortoise, destined never to catch up" (2007, 154).

status and role of African philosophy. Although this position is explicitly present in Serequeberhan's writings, to do its frequency justice we must also refer to the work of three other Africana philosophers—Lewis Gordon (1997b),[13] Lucius Outlaw (1996), and Robert Bernasconi (1997).

This unifying theme is introduced by Serequeberhan's claim that any people have the right to define their own cultural heritage with regard to philosophy. This also may and should imply that African philosophy will go so far as to turn the tables on the (Western) philosophical establishment and treat it as just one other tradition of cultural philosophizing or, even more radically, as nothing more than a subspecies of a major discipline whose redefined limits, given the postcolonial political realities of the international academic and cultural marketplace, will be defined as much or more by non-Western (more specifically, African) philosophy.[14]

The truly revolutionary status[15] of such a possibility is more clearly highlighted when one recalls that it was the West that labeled the African intellect as primitive and irrational, as virtually a-philosophical and ahistorical. If African philosophers do proceed, as many seem to be doing, to construct their own paradigms of the rational and the philosophical—paradigms that are in part reactions to those that have been iconized by the West—then they may also supersede as well as encompass those of the West, as Gordon points out:

> The artificial situating of the African outside of the universal leads to a particular conception of the "scope" of reality. . . . African philosophy is treated by many theorists as a type of suppressed prime.[16] . . . The white/Western philosophical reality becomes the "governing fiction." . . . Now although this governing fiction suggests at first that "real philosophy" is Western, there is a logic that can show that African philosophy is broader in scope than Western philosophy because it *includes* the Western in its self-articulation. In *practice*

13. Specifically, "African Philosophy's Search for Identity: Existential Considerations of a Recent Effort" in Gordon 1997b.

14. It should be noted that many of these philosophers have serious reservations about the term "African philosophy" itself. For one thing, the terms "Africa" and "African" were originally products of Western application and definition more than they were products of the peoples of the subcontinent (Gordon 1997b, 143). For another, should it be taken for granted that there is a single, static set of principles or beliefs that are, by definition, common to that Africa?

15. "The thought of revolutionary thinking in philosophy has become such a thing of the past that those of us who expect no less are often greeted by raised eyebrows or condescending laughter" (Gordon 1997b, 140).

16. "*Suppressed* prime" in the sense, perhaps, that it is portrayed as never realizing a potential.

Western philosophy may be a subset of African philosophy. (Gordon 1997b, 145; my italics in part)

In *Existentia Africana: Understanding Africana Existential Thought* (2000), Gordon continues to identify himself as a representative of "black *radical* existential thought" (21; my italics) who would certainly agree with Serequeberhan that the struggle of all Africana peoples against racism is something that must continue unabated. Gordon goes into considerable detail in order to map what he sees as the various schools of thought that constitute Africana philosophy (African-American, Afro-Caribbean, African) (2000, 10). This is a taxonomy Gordon develops in detail in *An Introduction to Africana Philosophy* (2008), which will be discussed in chapter 9. This also involves outlining a kind of canon or set of foundational thinkers and their works (2000, 39–40). In doing so, he explicitly acknowledges that Africana *existential* philosophy is just one approach to an Africana philosophy that is methodologically diverse:

> Africana philosophy's history of traditional Africana Christian, Marxist, feminist, pragmatic, analytical, and phenomenological thought, then, has been a matter of what specific dimensions each of these approaches had to offer the existential realities of theorizing blackness. (Gordon 2000, 11)

But he remains minimally hermeneutical in this more diverse overview insofar as he still maintains that for all examples of human thought, existence precedes essence—individual thinkers must always begin from whatever particular social and historical contexts in which they find themselves. For contemporary purposes, undeniable aspects of existence that must define Africana philosophers and philosophy are race and racism—oppression and therefore a continuing, multidimensional struggle for liberation.

Lucius Outlaw employs a deconstructive critique to demonstrate how Western "philosophy" is used as an ideological weapon to denigrate the intellectual significance of non-Western, in particular African, cultures. His strategy for combating this coalesces with that of Serequeberhan and Gordon when he re-views African philosophy as a movement to dis-place the West from its paradigmatic role (Outlaw 1996a, 65):

> [Western canonical] Philosophy has been . . . one of the most privileged of disciplines, especially in its self-appointed role as guardian of the self-image of the brokers of Western history and culture. Were this not the case, there would have been no debate about "African philosophy." Thus, any discussion of *African* philosophy involves, *necessarily*, confronting this privileged self-image. It is this confrontation that problematizes "African" and forces its deconstruction/reconstruction in its relations of difference with "European." But

this confrontation leaves the complex fields and histories of philosophizing in the West—past, present, and future—forever altered, in ways similar to (because part and parcel of) the alterations of sociopolitical landscapes involving the West, Africa, and the African diaspora. The fraudulent Greco-European monarchy *philosophia* is no more.

Does this mean that [Western canonical] Philosophy is left without universality and unity? Yes. Does this mean that philosophy [as a transcultural enterprise] is without universality and unity? "Yes" again. (Outlaw 1996, 72)

Early on (1992–1993) Outlaw also recognized that a fundamental step to achieving this aim was to constitute a canon of historical and contemporary writings that could serve as an explicit foundation and reference point for African(a) philosophy. As a philosophical tradition "born of struggle," to borrow Leonard Harris's (1983) phrase, African philosophy as the "unknown," the "irrational," the "unknowable," has no choice but to contest the formidable monopoly established over the philosophical domain by Western civilization and culture: "Why is Western philosophy hegemonic when it *excludes* other philosophies, yet African philosophy, which *includes* Western philosophy, lacks such influence?" (Gordon 1997b, 145; my italics).

If this situation overall is just one more manifestation of Eurocentrism (to borrow a term from Samir Amin [1989]), of the West's systematic program for imposing its culture on the rest of the world, then non-Western philosophy has every right to challenge the gross presumptions (as well as arrogance) that program involves. Especially since in the views of many Western and non-Western philosophers and intellectuals, the Western philosophical tradition has *failed* because it has not achieved its most radical and well-publicized goal—to achieve a level of "rational" truth that transcends (and thereby applies to) all of humanity's diverse cultures.

Finally, Robert Bernasconi, writing explicitly as a Westerner versed in the phenomenological-hermeneutical tradition, finds favor with the idea of an African philosophy that can critically engage the Western tradition about its philosophical ethnocentrism and attendant ideological pretensions. He indicts the European-Continental philosophical tradition (the birthplace of modern phenomenology-hermeneutics) for being as much in need of ethnocentric cleansing as its Anglophone analytic counterpart (Bernasconi 1997, 190; 2001). But what is most pertinent about his critique is that he too sees the real possibility and value to Western philosophy and to philosophy as a transcultural enterprise of an African philosophical tradition, independent of the West, engaging in dialogues *with* and deconstructive critiques *of* that West:

The powerful critiques of Western philosophy by African and African-American philosophers exceed Western philosophy and cannot simply be re-inscribed within it, even when they rely on the idiom of Western philosophy for their presentation. This is because these critiques spring from the pre-philosophical experience of racism and colonialism to which neutral reason is inevitably deaf, just as it is deaf to the role of tradition within philosophy. If Continental philosophers would open themselves to a critique from African philosophy and thereby learn more about their own tradition seen from "the outside," they would find that the hegemonic concept of reason had been displaced, and they would be better placed to learn to respect other traditions, including those that are not African. (Bernasconi 1997, 192)

One important concern analytic and hermeneutic philosophers share is the determination to come to terms with the damage done to Africa by the era of colonialism and Western intellectual imperialism. African hermeneutic philosophers appear to be more outspoken in this regard, but there is no question that it is also an underlying and formative influence to the development of African analytic philosophy.

Another important interest the two traditions share is the degree to which African languages may serve as a basis for African philosophy. The hermeneutic tradition appears to place far more emphasis upon recognizing and accepting the historical and cultural contingencies of a language at any given point in time. Indeed, it would not be surprising to find hermeneutic African philosophers accusing their analytic colleagues of the intellectual sin of reifying language and treating it, comparatively, as a cultural artifact to which change is not fundamentally important.

But here again the difference is perhaps more one of degree or of emphasis than it is of substance. Analytic philosophers are interested primarily in a/any language's deeper substructure—in those elements that might be found constitutive of it in any historical period. The relativist African analytic philosophers would appear to share a bit more in common with their hermeneutic colleagues insofar as they explicitly and implicitly allow for both greater and more fundamental variety of expression.

Both varieties of African analytic philosophy could probably come to terms with that seemingly most radical claim of African hermeneutical philosophy—that it may someday, or in fact already does, subsume the whole of the Western tradition as just one other cultural anomaly thanks to a broader, revisionist view of "philosophy." Universalists such as Wiredu could even now be said to be working toward a definition of the "rational" or "rationality" that does transcend all cultures and therefore can subsume the West as just one other subspecies. Individual relativists, in some cases, already have intimated this in their published work: "Reigning paradigms of rationality and morality that were once labeled explicitly 'Western' can then be re-assessed as just other alternatives which human beings have devised to explain and to order their experience" (Hallen 1998a, 204).

The important thing, as far as Africa's overall philosophical future is concerned, is that analytic and hermeneutic philosophers interact and communicate with one another on the professional or intellectual level. In the Western academy this is not the case, and the split between them is sometimes viewed as irreparable. But with reference to Africa, the two share some concerns and interests that should be explored, hopefully to the mutual benefit of both approaches.

7

Socialism and Marxism

African philosophers, intellectuals, and political figures who identify them-selves as socialists or Marxists constitute yet another category of philo-sophical thinking. The non-Western socialist and Marxist philosophical tradition with specific reference to Africa has a distinguished Caribbean and South American, as well as African, ancestry and may be associated with some of the most brilliant and radical thinkers who address the issues of (European) colonialism, neocolonialism, Africa as a victim of the so-called Cold War—the ideological and political struggle between "West" and "East"—and where Africa's best interests lie when it comes to contemporary social, political, and economic development. Here one has in mind intellec-tual figures such as Claude Ake (1939–1996), Samir Amin (1931–), Amilcar Cabral (1921–1973), Aimé Césaire (1913–), Frantz Fanon (1925–1961), Paulo Freire (1921–1997), Samora Machel (1933–1986), Albert Memmi (1920–), Eduardo Mondlane (1920–1969), Walter Rodney (1942–1980), and Léopold Sédar Senghor (1906–2001).

There is no way this comparatively brief text can do justice to all of these important and seminal thinkers. At the same time, it would be inexcusable not to say at least something about two of the founding fathers of what has come to be known as African socialism—Kwame Nkrumah (of Ghana) and Julius Nyerere (of Tanzania). Nkrumah (1909–1972) actually completed an M.A. in philosophy at the University of Pennsylvania, but he could not afford the time to complete his doctorate as he became increasingly involved in various African liberation movements (always with a special interest in his native Ghana, of course) and then became the first president of an inde-pendent Ghana in 1960.

Nkrumah continued to retain an interest in philosophy throughout his life. Despite a hectic political career, he continued to produce texts of remarkable originality in that they are deliberately crafted to express an African point of view. Their titles speak for themselves: *Towards Colonial Freedom* (1962), *I Speak of Freedom: A Statement of African Ideology* (1961), *Consciencism* (intended principally as an philosophical explication of the African mind or consciousness, rather than the more conventional 'moral' conscience; first published in 1954, reprinted in 1964 as *Consciencism: Philosophy and Ideology for Decolonization* [1970c]), *Neo-Colonialism: The Last Stage of Imperialism* (1965), *Handbook of Revolutionary Warfare* (1969), *Class Struggle in Africa* (1970a), *Africa Must Unite* (1970b).

Nkrumah was no overt enemy of the so-called West but, obviously, he was no champion of it either, since he had successfully negotiated the liberation of his country from European (British) rule. The Cold War between East and West unquestionably had an effect on his international policies and status. In certain respects he was forced to play both ends (East and West) against the middle (himself and his country's interests), eventually at some cost. But, above all, he was an African patriot who appreciated full well how much independence could mean to his nation and continent.

It is essential to begin by appreciating Nkrumah's view of African socialism as an original social, political, and philosophical theory of African origin and orientation. He recognized that Africa's indigenous cultures were more communally than individually oriented. He therefore argued that capitalism, with its pronounced emphasis upon individual self-interest (if necessary at the expense of the community), was a sinister force that, if further encouraged, would result in the further deterioration of Africa's indigenous moral values and quality of life overall. For example, in Africa traditionally land ownership was not personalized. Land *usage* was (at the present time this parcel of land is being farmed by so-and-so), but overall the land itself was regarded as a communal resource. If capitalism was to be contained, the obvious alternative was to promote the importance of centralized state control (though lest we be misled by terminology, "state control" was to be viewed as a further expression of African communality and its underlying spirit of humanism). After independence, capitalist institutions, influences, and practices that were leftovers of colonialism (now labeled "neocolonialism") were to be contained or eliminated.

In *Consciencism,* in particular, Nkrumah develops an ideological view of philosophy that sees it as the effect, the expression, the articulation (rather than some kind of spontaneous and independent creation of a gifted thinker) of a people's cultural predispositions at a particular point in time. Once articulated (by someone like him), it can then be refined and explicitly instituted by deliberate social and political programs. Hence socialism in the African context was to be a formalized, (economically and politically) institutionalized expression of indigenous humanitarian social and moral values.

Julius Nyerere (1922–1999), known in Africa popularly as "Mwalimu" (Swahili for "The Teacher") during his lifetime, was the leader of the party and movement that led Tanzania to independence (from Britain, again); he became his country's first president in 1961. Although he is also recognized as the founder of a form of African socialism associated with the Swahili term *ujamaa* (which is awkwardly rendered into English as "familyhood" and is the title of his best-known collection of published essays [1968c]), Nyerere's approach to socialism as a cultural phenomenon was more pragmatic and less overtly theoretical/philosophical than Nkrumah's.

Nyerere argued that there was a form of life and system of values indigenous to the culture of precolonial Africa, Tanzania in particular, that was distinctive if not unique and that had survived the onslaughts of colonialism sufficiently intact to be regenerated as the basis for an African polity. While it might take an intellectual such as Nkrumah to identify and articulate, as well as reconcile and systematize, the implicit tenets of philosophical ideology that were latent in Ghanaian culture, Nyerere maintained that this precolonial worldview was still a conventional and self-conscious element of Tanzanian society and culture. He argued that what was needed was to arrive at a happy reconciliation of it with the apparatus of the so-called nation-state.

For Nyerere, the "traditional" values of greatest significance to that culture were: that every member of society was expected to do work of some form as a contribution to their own well-being and thereby that of the community, and for that reason everyone deserved to be rewarded sufficiently to satisfy their needs; that land was owned communally and used individually, as and if needed; that the sense of being a community (*ujamaa*) on the part of the people was conscious and was significant in terms of determining their relationships with and regard for one another.

Capitalism, with its virtues of self-interest and exploitation, could not be happily reconciled with such an essentially humanitarian worldview. In fact, it would destroy it. Theoretical Marxism or communism, which emphasizes class conflict (between capitalists and workers, for example) as a motivating force for social and political change, also did not seem obviously relevant to a population that consisted largely of subsistence farmers. What was needed was a social and political ideology more realistically tailored for the African context.

For Nyerere, this ideal was encapsulated by a one-party democratic state in which everyone (from the president to the smallest farmer) would continue to be "just" a worker (an ideal Nyerere certainly tried to live up to during his presidency). Policies would be formulated and differences would be discussed and reconciled on the basis of discussion and compromise in a national population that self-consciously identified itself as a more expansive version of the extended family.

In Africa today, African socialism, as outlined by Nkrumah and Nyerere, is no longer a dominant (some would say "significant") factor on the political landscape. Various explanations are given for this change (Friedland and Rosberg 1964; Sigmund 1963), but that does not diminish its importance as an original contribution to African intellectual history. Both socialism and Marxism in the African context were forced to contend with the cloud of ideological suspicion cast over them by European-inspired adherents of colonialism and neocolonialism—for example, that their popular association with atheism was enough to qualify them as "un"-African. Perhaps it is because of this that African Marxists, in particular, expend considerable effort in their published writings to clarify the basic tenets of theoretical Marxism—hoping thereby to defuse or to neuter such negative and largely Western-inspired anti-Marxist propaganda.

African philosophy's heritage from Frantz Fanon (1925–1961) is monumental. Fanon was originally from the Caribbean island of Martinique, where Aimé Césaire was his teacher and thereafter confidante. Although he was professionally trained in France as a psychiatrist, his interests and influence extend to philosophy, literature, and the social sciences. It is sometimes suggested that, as Fanon's most important and well-known works, *Black Skin, White Masks* (1952) and *The Wretched of the Earth* (1961), were written against a background where organized, violent, armed resistance to European colonialism was taken to be appropriate, it is important to appreciate that particular historical context as formative of his excessively radical (e.g., outright advocacy of violent revolution as the only solution, etc.) thought. But today there continue to be any number of diverse efforts to mine his writings for provocative stimuli in this era that has christened itself "postcolonial."

One of those efforts which I am going to concentrate upon, because it serves to highlight the thought of yet another African academic, is the Ghanaian Ato Sekyi-Otu's *Fanon's Dialectic of Experience* (1996). Sekyi-Otu[1] is forthright about this attempt to reconstitute the body and message of Fanon's writings as a composite (rather than disparate) whole. "The result is a critical and visionary narrative that provides a vantage point from which we may measure the promise and performance of postcolonial life" (1996, 5).

In contemporary African studies the movement that has come to be associated with the term "postcolonialism" has diverse meanings. It incorporates

1. Phonetic pronunciation: Se-she Owe-two.

the element of postmodernism that rejects Western cultural imperialism—of the right or status of the Western world to set the standards, or serve as any form of paradigm, for the rest of humanity. As far as Africa is concerned, postcolonialism rejects what is disparagingly referred to as "nativism" as an appropriate goal or objective—insofar as that term is associated with Africans making it a priority to try to resurrect some pristine, precolonial form of their indigenous cultures as a realistic solution to the problems of the present. It also rejects invoking any form of "historicism" insofar as that involves a vision of specific historical developments as inevitable, as things with which Africans must or will have to come to terms, regardless.

Fanon's premature death did not allow him to participate directly in this movement. And Sekyi-Otu objects to those who claim that Fanon's writings endorse a form of either nativism or historicism. But, he argues, Fanon did have a great deal to say about the *postcolony* (Sekyi-Otu 2003)—about the possibilities of the Africa that would come into being after regaining its political freedom.

The projections Fanon is commonly said to have made for the African postcolony do involve a period of neocolonialism, a transitional period following independence when the apparatus of the state and economy would be controlled by an unscrupulous African middle class and elite who would continue to emulate and serve their Western 'masters'—since it was clear the European powers were determined to continue to exploit their former colonial possessions via these paid African agents. And Fanon is said to have advocated that the road to true liberation could be achieved by a violent uprising of the African peasantry or masses, that would finally cleanse the continent of this alien infrastructure designed to do nothing more than secure and promote the interests of foreign powers.

Sekyi-Otu wants to argue, however, that the above simplistic synopsis does not do Fanon justice. Indeed that it reduces the richness of the contents of his thought to the outdated and radicalized stereotype[2] often used as an excuse to dismiss the significance of criticism emanating from the 'third world.' For what Sekyi-Otu finds in Fanon is a vision of a new and universal humanitarianism, based upon reason, that champions a notion of normative freedom, of liberation, in a world that has been deracialized (1996, 25), that is meant to be meaningful to every human being on the face of the planet (1996, 17). That this vision of liberty and freedom was so brutally subverted by the colonial world is what motivated Fanon, most fundamentally, to strategize against it (1996, 18). Given such a revisionist interpretation, the point

---

2. "I will take issue with the presumption that pictures of the world and rhetorics of the human situation evoked at determinate moments of Fanon's texts always commit him to a conclusive and unambiguous endorsement of such pictures and rhetorics" (Sekyi-Otu 1996, 5).

of Fanon's writings becomes to explore the various problems that human consciousness may have to go through,[3] may have to endure, may have to overcome, in order to attain what Sekyi-Otu believes Fanon had in mind as a "new humanism" (1996, 26).

Amilcar Cabral (1924–1973), the leader of the struggle against Portuguese colonialism in Guinea-Bissau on the coast of West Africa, is frequently identified as one of Africa's most important early Marxist thinkers (see Cabral 1969). But, as will prove to be the case with all of the African philosophers to be considered under the heading of Marxism, it is the originality of his approach to adapting elements of Marxism to the African context that makes him of particular interest from a philosophical point of view: "Experience of the struggle shows how utopian and absurd it is to seek to apply schemes developed by other peoples in the course of the liberation struggle and solutions which they found to the questions with which they were or are confronted, without considering local reality (and especially cultural reality)" (Cabral 1979, 151).

The above passage is taken from what seems to be Cabral's most often quoted theoretical statement with a humanities bent—a lecture entitled "National Liberation and Culture," given at Syracuse University, United States, in 1970. Though in characteristic Marxist fashion he briefly remarks upon the primacy of the means or forces of production in a society, the balance of the address is devoted to the importance of recognizing and resurrecting the popular (indigenous) culture of African peoples whose histories have been stopped (not just "changed") by the advent of colonialism. National liberation, therefore, is also essentially an *act of culture* (1979, 143), effectively a conscious renunciation by the mass of the population of the colonizers' attempts to alienate them from their history. When speaking in cultural terms, Cabral is no more specific about what is distinctive of Africa's indigenous values than the following:

> From Carthage or Giza to Zimbabwe, from Meroe to Benin and Ife, from the Sahara or Timbuctoo to Kilwa, across the immensity and the diversity of the continent's natural conditions, the culture of African peoples is an undeniable fact: in works of art as in oral and written traditions, in cosmogony as in music and dances, in religions and creeds as in dynamic equilibrium of economic, political and social structures that African man has been able to create. (1979, 148)

3. Sekyi-Out seems convinced that the "dramatical" (in the literal sense of "drama") tone of Fanon's exegesis is a technique used to enable readers to see beyond immediate realities to the more profound nature (and possibilities) of human experience.

Both Nkrumah and Nyerere have been criticized for allowing themselves to paint too idealized and romanticized portraits of "traditional" African society and culture. Perhaps this realization was responsible for Cabral's greater appreciation of the continent's cultural diversity:

> The fact of recognizing the existence of common and special traits in the cultures of African peoples, independently of the colour of their skin, does not necessarily imply that one and only one culture exists on the continent. In the same way that from the economic and political point of view one can note the existence of various Africas, so there are also various African cultures. (1979, 149)

Many conventional (and non-Marxist) expositions of Karl Marx's and Friedrich Engels's thoughts and theories divide them up into two major but supposedly irreconcilable phases: (1) an earlier "humanistic" period in which Marx, in particular, was outraged by the exploitation of some groups or classes in certain societies and sought to outline an alternative form of community in which such injustices might be corrected and human beings would be truly free ("Marx I"); (2) a later, comparatively "social scientific" period in which Marx (and Engels) sought to formulate a rigorous economic theory that would allow Marxist thinkers to demonstrate that the manner in which the means or modes of production in a society were controlled or administered exercised substantial influence upon its social, political, and cultural life ("Marx II").[4]

Oladipo Fashina and Olufemi Taiwo (both of Nigeria) reject this artificially imposed bifurcation of Marxist thought. In their writings they argue that Marx's economic theory can be understood correctly only as and if conjoined with fundamental commitments to moral or legal principles and ideals.

Nigerian philosopher Oladipo (better known as 'Dipo) Fashina addresses this point in an article (1988) in which he comments on the bifurcation between what have been labeled Marx I and Marx II: "According to some philosophers, all talk about human nature or human essence [Marx I] become irrelevant in Marx's outlooks as soon as he became a Marxist [Marx II]" (1988, 291). Fashina argues that Marx did reject certain forms of society on moral grounds but that, because his moral theory or viewpoint itself is atypical, this aspect of his overall thought has frequently gone unrecognized or unappreciated.

Fashina argues that portraying Marx as only a defender of human freedom (Marx I) places undue emphasis on one precondition of what he believes is required for human fulfillment. What is more fundamental to

4. See, for example, Venable 1946.

Marx's thinking is his view of human nature and the plurality of conditions he believes are required for its maximum fulfillment. Marx I and Marx II may therefore be better understood as reunited, in fact as never bifurcated, by his theory about the kind of society in which this can be achieved:

> In Marx's view, socialism is superior to capitalism by being more conducive to the realization of *human nature*: it enhances freedom (self-mastery), community, rationality, reciprocity, the development of talents, and other essentials of human nature." (Fashina 1988, 303; my italics)

That Marx may link his moral views regarding the fulfillment of human nature to more socially scientific notions of history and economics may indeed make them atypical. But this is as much because conventional Western moral philosophy continues to treat moral values as somehow independent of empirical realities and should not make Marx's more detailed views about the empirical preconditions for the fulfillment of that human nature any less moral in intent or content.

In a later article (1989), Fashina argues that so-called humanism involves acceptance of the following five basic tenets:

1. Assumption of a common humanity.
2. Assumption of the intrinsic moral worth of all human beings.
3. Inference to the appropriate treatment of human beings.
4. Human dignity and intrinsic worth as the standard for the assessment of social practices and institutions.
5. Assumption of the motivational force of humanity. (Fashina 1989, 181)

According to Fashina, points (4) and (5) prove especially relevant to Marx's moral views of social justice. Point (4) may be more explicitly summarized as follows: "Roughly, this amounts to the claim that the only justified institutions and practices are those which promote concern and respect for *all,* tend to minimize pain and suffering, and recognize the moral claim of *everyone,* irrespective of social class, status, or race" (Fashina 1989, 182; my italics).

The essence of point (5) is as follows: "Moral agents are, typically, moved to action by appeal to humanity; once we have shown a person that a certain desirable state of affairs will reduce or eliminate alienation, moral degradation and other forms of dehumanization, we have given her a necessary ground for endorsing or acting to bring about that state of affairs" (Fashina 1989, 183). Fashina insists that while Marx could agree with (4), he would never accept (5). This is because his theory (in this case of alienation) also depends upon and arises out of correcting unsatisfactory economic conditions. It is precisely this much-abused and so-called materialist dimension to his thought that effectively "makes him a nonhumanist, because for him the ultimate criteria of social progress are not [merely] justice, equality, and rights" (Fashina 1989, 184). In other words, the classic "liberal" social and political freedoms as defined by philosophers in capitalistic Western societies are insufficient unless conjoined with the economic freedoms best provided by a communist society: "Marx believed that the realization of *human nature* is possible only where each individual's labor-power is used by society for the purpose of satisfying the needs and developing the talents of *everyone*; not, as in capitalist society, for the sake of profit or mere survival" (Fashina 1988, 297; my italics).

With more direct reference to the African context, in an earlier essay (1981) devoted to the nature of mythical thought—something Western scholarship has frequently associated with indigenous Africa—he argues that philosophers such as Ernst Cassirer, who claimed to be a specialist on the mythical consciousness, fail to provide a reasonable or even sensible explanation for the origins of this kind of understanding. For example, they claim that "reality" is reduced to an "imaginary world produced by the mind [that is] nothing but an illusion" (Fashina 1981, 39). They also claim that, if this is the case, the basis for any kind of serious cause-and-effect relationships internal to the mythical world disappears.

Fashina argues that this kind of paradigm makes the so-called transition from the mythical consciousness to the scientific consciousness very difficult to imagine, much less to explain. Preferring to begin from a (ontologically) realist view of the world which, in philosophical terms, means that there are "real" mind-independent things and causal mechanisms in the world, Fashina argues that imputing this (realist) presumption to the mythical consciousness as well makes more sense of it as a form of cognition. Then it too recognizes the existence of causal (rather than purely palliative "emotional" or "affective") relationships in the world but intellectually, analogously, even if mistakenly, identifies their nature with the same kinds of powers that human beings discover within themselves (emotions, feelings, morals). The mistake of the mythical consciousness is to generalize in too hasty a manner and believe that similar kinds of things (emotions, feelings, morals) must exist in the other kinds of objects in the world and that they can be employed, causally, to make something happen.

In effect, then, the explanatory basis for scientific thought—that there are cause-and-effect relationships in the real world—is already an essential component of the mythical consciousness. What is missing is a more objective and less (humanly) subjective presumption about the nature of the "powers" inherent in non-human being that can be used to cause desired effects. This is something mankind learns about, gradually but most importantly, through laboring in that external world: "It follows that human labour is not merely a means of physical survival. It is a way of *knowing* the external world. And, over and beyond that, it is a way in which human beings know (in a rather loose sense) their own powers, i.e. labour is a source of self-knowledge" (Fashina 1981, 43; my italics).

Nigerian philosopher Olufemi Taiwo has done interesting work in the area of African philosophy (see bibliography) as well as Marxism. But this narrative will concentrate on the latter, particularly as represented by his book *Legal Naturalism: A Marxist Theory of Law* (1996a). His overall strategy is encapsulated by the title's initial phrase, "legal naturalism." What Taiwo sets out to do is to establish a Marxist theory of natural law. He does this principally by arguing that there are legal priorities or principles that constitute an essential intrinsic part of any economic system:

> I argue that there is a subset of social relations that are *legal* and necessary to or constitutive of the *mode of production*. These conjointly form the *natural law* of the relevant mode. The natural law of a mode of production is that regime of law which is essential to its constitution, is discoverable in its operation, and provides the outer limits of possible *positive laws* within it. . . . If [for example] there is some species of law that is part of the nature of *capitalism,* then, we can say that a capitalist society which lacks this law is not really a capitalist society. In such a case the law is a *necessary* part of the capitalist mode of production. (Taiwo 1996a, 59)

Perhaps the most important initial point to establish about Taiwo's text is his explicit acknowledgment that the end result will be a novel synthesis of Marxist theory with natural law theory:

> I do not claim that what follows is the theory of law Marx would have written, had he had the time or turned his mind to it. I insist only that this foundation yields a theory of law substantially different from those which have hitherto dominated Marxist discourse about law. Whether it is a better or worse theory will be judged by how well it enables us to make sense of legal phenomena. (Taiwo 1996a, 33)

As does Fashina, Taiwo begins by arguing that the so-called bifurcation (Marx I and Marx II) attributed by some commentators to the Marxist canon between the economic "substructure" of a society and its more explicitly humanitarian, moral, cultural "superstructure" is an error: "What we may not do is behave as if the early writings [Marx I] were merely the confused, exuberant outpourings of a youthful spirit which in the soberness of age were found embarrassing and therefore jettisoned" (Taiwo 1996a, 8).

Taiwo distinguishes his analysis of law from that of most Marxist theoreticians because:

> ["Orthodox"] Marxist theories of law are dominated by a positivist orientation that sees law as the will of the ruling class in its efforts to make the subaltern classes cooperate with or accede to its dominance. . . . In the main they treat law within a general discussion of politics or philosophy of history. They all, in their different ways, accept the base/superstructure dichotomy of society. Thus law is usually discussed as a component of politics or economics and banished to the superstructure. (Taiwo 1996a, 2, 45)

Yet according to Taiwo and to Marxism generally, the moral value of any legal system (and the economic order of which it is part and parcel) can be rated by the degree to which it facilitates freedom. "Freedom is the essence of human beings" (Taiwo 1996a, 23).

At this point some readers may well be wondering what exactly is meant by the theory of natural law or the natural law tradition:

> Natural law is identified with the ideal legal system which is striving for realization and, being ideal, is desirable and ought to be. (Taiwo 1996a, 37)

Whether its ultimate source is said to be the divine, human reason, or the material or economic basis of society (the option Taiwo favors), this is the system of legal values that humankind should strive to institute/instantiate in order to fully realize the ideals that define that particular form of society (and its particular notions of what are considered to be "happiness," "freedom," "justice," etc.).

Though he also acknowledges the diversity of the natural law tradition (as evidenced, for example, by the various origins attributed to natural law in the preceding paragraph), Taiwo suggests that the core of the theory may be summarized by three basic principles:

(1) that it is necessary to make a *distinction* between so-called 'positive law' (the laws that are *in fact* enacted or legislated by a particular society at a particular point in time) and the 'natural law' (the ideal law(s) that serve as guiding principles for positive law, and that *ought* to be enacted by a society to maximize its notions of 'happiness,' etc.);

(2) that, in terms of both values and rationality, natural law *rates higher* than positive law, and so may be used as a *standard* on the basis of which to evaluate whatever positive law is in place at a given point in time;

(3) that, in some instances, natural law may be invoked as a justification for *rejecting* or *disobeying* positive law because the latter is said to violate the principles of natural law and therefore, in fact, is not entitled to be regarded as 'law' (Taiwo 1996a, 37–38).

Taiwo notes that any number of Marxist theoreticians have rejected natural law theory as nothing more than one more ideological invention of a burgeoning middle class out to challenge the European feudal aristocracy

(Taiwo 1996a, 34–35). But, and this perhaps is where the originality of his approach is most evident, Taiwo argues that the natural law framework may be used to make explicit the legal content inherent in any economic system. He does this first by arguing that it is not necessary for natural law to be immutable (1996a, 40)—that there in fact can be different systems of natural law that emerge as human societies undergo economic and legal change over the course of time. His point is that if this theoretical innovation is incorporated into Marxism, it would mean that "the concept of law is not exhausted by" (1996a, 56) a society's positive law system, its legislated law(s).

Next, he argues that because it enunciates certain basic, if very generalized, values, natural law can be used as an independent but practical standard for the evaluation of the positive law(s) in place in a society at a given point in time:

> Natural law . . . is a system of norms. This characteristic distinguishes it from the natural laws of physical science. . . . It prescribes the norms of acceptable conduct, obligations, duties, and mutual forbearances in respect of the issues that fall within the structure of rights etc. concerned. However, natural law shares one significant attribute with the natural laws of physical science: *it is objective;* that is, *it is independent of human will.* Natural law exacts obedience in the same way that physical laws do. (Taiwo 1996a, 67–68; my italics)

To make the implications of the above more clear, it is helpful to apply the recommended perspective to a more specific social situation. For example, with regard to capitalist society:

> Capitalist natural law must be observed in a capitalist polity if its laws are to remain capitalist and the society itself wishes to realize as much of its capitalist potential as is possible or desirable for it. If people living in, say, a capitalist society believe that their social formation has a lot to recommend it and very little to be disapproved of in it, and if they want it to survive or be improved, they must pay heed to capitalist natural law when they work out their positive laws. The objective, independent character of natural law becomes quite significant when one considers the situation of a ruling class under, to continue with our example, capitalism.
>
> In the objective, independent character of capitalist natural law is contained the real limit on the actions of the ruling class. In this sense, natural law performs a regulative role. If the ruling class understand that theirs is an example of the capitalist mode of production and they hold beliefs approbative of their society, they may not make positive laws that contradict the norms of the natural law of capitalism. If they lack adequate understanding of what capitalism entails or if they are interested in committing class suicide, they

can make positive laws that are violative of the norms of capitalist natural law. (Taiwo 1996a, 68)

In other words, every variety of economic system or social formation, whether feudal, capitalist, socialist, or communist, has inherent in it a distinctive, defining set of natural law(s) which constitute part of its essence. These natural laws also set certain limits to the positive law(s) that society may choose to enact. If those limits are exceeded, on the basis of either ignorance or revolution, the nature and future of that society may be undermined or overturned: "We will, for example, deny that a mode of production is capitalist if it forbids the ownership of private property, makes profitmaking illegal, and decrees that commodities shall be produced only for use, not for exchange" (Taiwo 1996a, 66).

This allows Taiwo to offer a more comprehensive interpretation of "natural" law that he suggests is compatible with a Marxist perspective:

> The natural law of the mode of production provides the foundation for the positive law of each society. It is the law that positive law seeks officially to express. It is the law that legislators seek to formulate in conscious positive law.
> [But the so-called] "law*makers*" formulate . . . [the laws they do] because they have to operate within specific or specifiable limits imposed by the natural law of the given mode of production in which they are located. For example, if a social formation is feudal, no matter how determined the legislators are they cannot make or implement laws that will guarantee capitalist commodity production and exchange, or liberty, equality, etc. (Taiwo 1996a, 67; my italics)

The theoretical and the empirical addition of this natural law framework provide a substantive basis that individuals or groups may invoke to justify demands they make of their society. It also provides a more clear framework for individuals or groups whose aim is to reform or overthrow a society:

> People in this last group can be expected to make demands for a positive law regime that they know, or have reason to think, will generate consequences that are potentially or actually destructive of the existing social structure, including its natural law. (Taiwo 1996a, 69)

Does the fact that such individuals or groups reject the established system of positive (and natural) law mean that there are also some transhistorical criteria on the basis of which the various systems of natural law may themselves be evaluated or rated? According to Taiwo, the answer is yes: "One can say that Marx does affirm such a normative standard of human and social evolution" (1996a, 73). Namely: "to strive to bring about better and better social orderings, where the best possible social ordering is one in which human beings are enabled to realize their human potential as fully as possible, limited only by the constraints of physical nature, human and material" (Taiwo 1996a, 73).

The final major topic that Taiwo addresses in his text is Marx's controversial notion of the "withering away" of the state and, by obvious implication, the law. In a truly communist society—in which human freedom and potential could be maximized, where the means of production were not used by some to profit at the expense of others, and where everyone's material needs could be satisfied—there would be no place for one group or class to administer or to govern the rest; hence the so-called classless society.

Perhaps no other element of Marx's overall theory has been subjected to as much ridicule as these notions of the state's "withering away" and a "classless" society—both have been regularly characterized as hopelessly utopian. But Taiwo asks us to reconsider one more time. He begins his argument by asking us to be completely forthright with ourselves about our feelings and attitudes toward the "law" in our society. The "us" that seem most directly involved are those who live in the various contemporary societies that constitute our increasingly capitalistic world order. Taiwo believes that if we reflect objectively upon the natural law framework of capitalism and the positive law(s) to which it gives rise, we will conclude that it "is too limited for purposes of making the world better and improving the human condition" (Taiwo 1996a, 73). In other words, we can do better!

The conventional justification for having (positive) law(s) is that it provides "the best means for ensuring peaceable living in society" (Taiwo 1996a, 165). But this does not mean that most people regard law as an unqualified good. In most cases, it is in fact considered the lesser of evils, or perhaps even a necessary evil (1996a, 75). Certainly in everyday life it is not something which people invoke or to which they feel they must have recourse. Taiwo's argument here is that the status law has attained in contemporary society and the way it is regarded by the ordinary person have important negative elements as well as positive ones. For example, the character law has assumed is primarily one of coercion—do what the law says or else (1996a, 176). Another negative consequence is the ever-increasing recourse to litigation to settle even the most minor dispute (1996a, 180). "It is arguable that at no other time in human history has law enjoyed so much acceptance or attracted so much enthusiasm as it does now in all parts of the world" (1996a, 181). But this is still not enough to mitigate its negative attributes. If anything, this too is a negative, rather than positive, development.

Law does not coerce or litigate where the most important and distinctive of human values are concerned:

Law does not require us to love our neighbors; it does not ask us to befriend lonely hearts; it generally does not require us to rescue people in distress; rather, it quibbles over whether we should be Good or Bad Samaritans; it does not ask us to be exemplary husbands, wives or parents, or siblings; it does not ask us not to cheat on our spouses; it does not ask us to strike friendships; nor does it facilitate the operation of friendships once they are struck; it does not ask us to be good employees or employers. The list goes on. (Taiwo 1996a, 181)

In effect, law becomes involved only when and if such relationships become destructive rather than constructive:

Law intervenes when amity breaks down between friends; when consensus is lost among associates—the law has no role where a handshake will do; when spouses have become each other's scourge; when families are no longer united in love; when employer and employee are no longer talking to or with each other; when neighbors are snarling at each other. *Law is inseverably linked to the breakdown of accord.* (Taiwo 1996a, 181; my italics)

The conclusion Taiwo reaches is that in most instances, human beings choose to relate to one another on a basis of "good faith, on the assumption that the other party will not seek any undue advantage so long as we do not. Only when there is a failure or noncompliance do we invoke law" (Taiwo 1996a, 182).

I conclude that in all those activities which define what we value most in our humanity—social harmony, good-neighborliness, loving and being loved—the law is completely excluded or, at best, plays a negative role. The argument that without law we would be at one another's throats assumes that without law we cannot trust ourselves to be human, that law is essential to our humanity. But if what I have been saying is true, then this assumption and the argument founded on it are implausible. For even in its best manifestation, in its most positive form, we try to hide the play of law, we strive to banish it from our most treasured relationships. Law is an acknowledgment of failure; it is what we resort to when we are unable otherwise to achieve our ends. *Law is always a second-best option.* (Taiwo 1996a, 182–83)

Taiwo, in accord with Marx, attributes the "problem" of law, including the emphasis upon coercion and the ever-increasing frequency of recourse to litigation—in short, all of positive law's negative attributes—to the breakdown of the sense of community in modern society (Taiwo 1996a, 186). Contemporary modern society prides itself on the unparalleled freedom and independence that are now accorded the individual. But the increasingly ato-mistic society to which this notion of individual rights is giving birth results in dramatically lessened importance being assigned to the human commu-nity—and consequently relations between individuals and between the indi-vidual and his or her society, which have increasingly come to be defined and constituted by "law." "The victory of individuality has been achieved at a very great price: the loss of genuine community" (Taiwo 1996a, 187).

If humanity, if the quality of life, is to advance further, the natural law basis for human society must change once again—to a social order where "instead of proceeding from a presupposition of the sovereignty of the individual, we proceed from one concerning *the value of social solidarity*" (Taiwo 1996a, 189; my italics). In effect, such solidarity will constitute the essence of this kind of society's natural law. And just such a society, Taiwo suggests, would be provided by "that mode of life which Marx called 'com-munism'" (1996a, 190).

This postcapitalist, postlegal society, in which the need for (positive) law would diminish radically, must be based upon those two Marxist fundamentals:

(1) "the transformation of private property in the means of production to public ownership," and the conscious rational regulation of those means of production for the benefit of all;

(2) the deepening of the meaning and sense of democracy and the impor-tance of society as a human community as the fundamental directing and controlling forces (Taiwo 1996a, 190).

One is tempted to wonder whether there would be reason for Taiwo to regard the humanitarian values of "traditional" African society, as outlined by Nkrumah and Nyerere, for example, with approval, because they do in many respects seem compatible with the changes he has in mind. Overall Taiwo is optimistic about the possibilities for overcoming the practical obstacles to such a postcapitalist, postlegal society. He argues that once such a sense of community is achieved, there will be virtually no need for (posi-tive) law. Human beings in most cases will simply relate to one another on the basis of their common and positive humanity. In effect, then, the natural law of this postcapitalist or communist society would make conventional or positive law superfluous.

Congelese historian and philosopher Ernest Wamba-dia-Wamba was for many years professor of history at the University of Dar es Salaam, Tanzania. Later he attracted the attention of the international community as the leader of one of the contending forces in the post-Mobutu Democratic Republic of Congo. In much of his writing, Wamba-dia-Wamba is more concerned with social praxis in Africa than he is with Marxist theory per se. But it is cer-tainly true that his interest also extends to a variety of ways in which Marxist theory has been abused rather than used, internationally as well as in Africa. This synopsis shall consider select points derived from two articles published in 1984 and 1994. The first, entitled "History of Neo-Colonialism or Neo-Colonialist History? Self-Determination and History in Africa," is principally of interest here for what Wamba-dia-Wamba has to say about the progress being made by the bulk of the African subcontinent's population (what used to be called the masses) toward "self-determination and social emancipation" (Wamba-dia-Wamba 1984, 2). As the first interrogatory sentence of his title implies, he is concerned by the fact that, economically, Africa continues to be so subservient to the West (in particular) that most of the political and economic priorities imposed upon Africa during the era of colonization remain in place. In effect, many African countries continue to be run much as they were during the age of Western imperialism.

This article is also of interest for what Wamba-dia-Wamba has to say about the state of contemporary African Studies and about African intellectuals and the African university systems in which they are principally based. He laments the fact that the priorities and parameters of African Studies still are principally determined by Western political, cultural, and economic interests (Wamba-dia-Wamba 1984, 5). Although he appreciates the efforts of African academics who challenge this dimension of Western imperialism, he also is concerned that this crusade must occupy so much of their time and effort. What then happens is that the field of African Studies itself becomes a political and ideological battleground rather than a source of new ideas and initiatives that would be of direct benefit to the bulk of the African population that exists without, rather than within, the university system. Yet surely this must and should be, above all, the *raison d'être* for the existence of African Studies in the first and final place.

> Imperialist "African Studies," their socio-democratic marxist/radical critique and to some extent, the nationalist African critique—the one putting emphasis on struggles against eurocentrism—have failed to provide any knowledge capable of educating African masses of people's initiative to make their history, i.e. capable of controlling the movement of their social processes. Needless to say that this would have exposed the mechanisms of the reproduction of dominant colonial social relations of production, of power and of cultural hegemony. (Wamba-dia-Wamba 1984, 6)

The second article, "Africa in Search of a New Mode of Politics," is a forthright and devastating critique of the evils of both capitalism and Marxism as practiced (this is clearly a very important concept in Wamba-dia-Wamba's vocabulary) virtually everywhere in the world. This is not to say that he forsakes Marxism, but he is relentless in his criticisms of social, political, and economic policies of supposedly mainstream Marxist states (the old Soviet Union and China, for example) that violate basic tenets of Marx's theory. "The basic needs and aspirations of the large masses of people ceased to be the objective basis of the modes of politics" (Wamba-dia-Wamba 1994, 250).

However, this synopsis shall concentrate on what Wamba-dia-Wamba has to say about the state of Marxism in Africa and several suggestions he makes that seem aimed at adapting and instituting a Marxist framework in Africa's indigenous cultures. His principal goal remains the same as in the first article—to create conditions that will further the self-determination and social self-emancipation of the entire African population. He begins by roundly condemning the institution of the so-called modern nation-state in Africa. Essentially the creation of foreign interests, it remains an element that is foreign to the continent's indigenous heritage:

> From a political point of view, even to those who militated for eman-cipatory politics—complete abolition of colonial conditions of life—the occupation of the colonial state rather than the destruction of the colonial state itself was seen as the condition for the realization of [independence]. That is, the occupation of the machinery of the enemy rather than its destruction and the deployment of a different machinery, was seen as the content of politics. . . . Ultimately, national independence was won on the basis of the abandonment of eman-cipatory politics rooted in the large masses of the people and their needs and aspirations. The constitutional frameworks taken from the colonialists, to be part of the machinery of government, were almost universally never submitted, through referendum, for approval by the large masses of people. (Wamba-dia-Wamba 1994, 251)

In addition, the nation-state has been a source of violence, corruption, class societies, and economic underdevelopment:

> Having a revolutionary *sounding* ideology was seen to be enough to make the state serve and be accountable to the people. . . . One party or one-party state, a bureaucratic and patrimonial management of the economy, the seizure and control of the state and its foreign policy by a gang of people *speaking* in the name of the common interest ('national unity,' 'national development'), the scope of the repressive apparatuses (leading to cases of political assassinations, persecution of opponents, etc.), legal arbitrariness, censorship of mass media and cultural, intellectual and spiritual productions, etc. are elements which became common to almost all African post-colo-nial regimes. Society increasingly became *statized*: society is forced to service the state which is controlled by an authoritarian gang of people. (Wamba-dia-Wamba 1994, 252; my italics in part)

In those instances where the terms "socialism" or "Marxism" have been linked to particular regimes or policies of an African nation-state, they have often meant nothing more than a government-run or government-sponsored industrial or agricultural initiative. "Even Marxism ('Marxism,' 'Scientific Socialism,' etc.) has become, in our countries, a form of ideology for capitalist development carried out by the State" (Wamba-dia-Wamba 1984, 4).

As a result, the status of politics or of the political in much of Africa has become abysmal. The mass of the population, whatever hopes they may have had reduced to cynicism and despair, no longer look to the nation-state or its agents as sources of positive developments. For Wamba-dia-Wamba, therefore, the only and best hope for rectifying this deplorable situation is a revolutionary restructuring of the political arena to make it do what it is supposed to—meaningfully involve the mass of the population and improve their standards of material, social, and cultural existence.

He suggests that any number of steps must be taken in order to achieve this. Some of the most important are: (1) deliberate deemphasis of the entire notion of territorial nationalism (or the "nation-state") as an important and independent component of a person's identity (Wamba-dia-Wamba 1994, 257); (2) abandonment of "development" policies which are defined by and oriented toward external agencies or foreign powers (1994, 257); (3) deconstruction of the "colonial legacy," in particular as it involves the vision of an Africa defined by stagnant traditions and, in fact, all foreign notions of what supposedly is involved in being a "traditional" society or culture (1994, 257–58); (4) gaining indigenous control of the economy and of the basis upon which it is to be related to the "world economy" (1994, 258); (5) democratization of "the knowledge process" so that what constitutes "knowledge" is not defined by other cultures and so that the bulk of the population is involved in both its dissemination and creation (1994, 258).

> Without a new historical mode of politics, a new vision of politics, which would demarginalize the large masses of people (women, youth, workers, poor peasants, people-without identity, the invisible majority), de-freezing their creativity and allowing them to move themselves to the centre stage of history-making in our countries, we cannot succeed. (Wamba-dia-Wamba 1994, 258)

In order to meaningfully involve the bulk of the African population in this enterprise, Wamba-dia-Wamba turns, again, to Marxism:

> Politics (political capacity, political consciousness), the active prescriptive relationship to reality, exists under the condition of people who believe that politics must exist. Marx and Engels assigned to proletarians the modern revolutionary capacity of realizing communism. . . . Proletarians may have this capacity under the conditions that they satisfy the requirements and conditions of that politics. They must take a position on politics, i.e. take a position on the factory, on the question of the state and power, on the question

of war and national liberation. That is, they must have political consciousness. . . . Generally, in Africa, the tendency has been to assign [political consciousness] to the state (including the party and liberation movements functioning really as state structures) *per se*. Unfortunately, the state cannot transform or redress itself: it kills this prescriptive relationship to reality by imposing consensual unanimity. Internalization, by people, of the state, and state orientation in handling, for example, differences among the people, provokes self-censorship in people and arrests political consciousness. (Wamba-dia-Wamba 1994, 258)

Wamba-dia-Wamba is, in fact, disenchanted with the role political parties have played in the African state (Presbey 1998). In a one-party state they prove to be oppressive. In a multi-party state they prove to be divisive, often along ethnic lines. He therefore is in favor of the abolition of political *parties,* but this does not mean he is against the idea of all political *organizations.* As examples of such organizations that might be derived from Africa's indigenous cultures and synthesized with Marxism, he mentions the "Palaver (where public, collective, open, mutual self-questioning and self-criticism takes place as a way of treating differences among the people)" (Wamba-dia-Wamba 1994, 258), and the "*Mbongi* (lineage assembly), and perhaps now the national conference (when it is independent of the state)" (1994, 258), as a suitable forum or venue for Palaver.

Our starting point must be: in Africa too *people think* and this is the sole material basis of politics. We must investigate the internal content of what they actually think. . . . It is through a scheme like the one suggested above, that peoples' viewpoints on matters of politics, as opposed to that of the state and parties, will be kept alive, and that the state can be contained, made accountable and democratized. Regulations aimed at silencing people's political viewpoints must be made the first target for a politics of democracy and social emancipation to develop. (Wamba-dia-Wamba 1994, 259)

It is remarkable how fresh and intriguing, even exciting, many of these ideas are and how regrettable it is that this school of thought is often implicitly stigmatized because it is underrepresented in more generalized discussions of African philosophy. In some measure, this is no doubt a hangover from past propaganda contests between the East and the West. Anything linked with the words "socialism," "Marxism," or "communism" still is suspect to a substantial portion of the world's population today. But it is time people learned to look beyond these labels to the new ideas and insights being produced by socialist and Marxist philosophers in and of Africa today. There appears to be much here that is of value and should be of common concern.

8

Philosophy and Culture

As was first indicated by Wiredu's discussion on pp. 33–34, an issue that at one point or another concerns virtually every contemporary contributor to African philosophy is how to do African philosophy justice when doing it using a methodology that originated in, or at least was formalized by, a *non-African* culture. In other words, can cognitive frameworks that have been crafted and elaborated by one culture really and truly be used to achieve an accurate understanding of another? One could also challenge the legitimacy of making prescriptive recommendations about how Africa's cultures should be invigorated or its nations governed on the basis of non-African social and political ideological paradigms, or the relevance of not just translating but actually doing African philosophy in Western languages.

It is not by accident that two of the more prominent texts in the recent history of African philosophy (Wiredu 1980b and Appiah 1992a) have as their titles *Philosophy and an African Culture* and *Africa in the Philosophy of Culture*. The real bottom line is whether the way philosophy is conventionally defined in Western culture—its methodologies (analysis, hermeneutics, Marxism, etc.), subdisciplines (metaphysics, epistemology, logic, etc.), and priorities (what it means to be 'rational,' the relationship between 'mind' and 'body,' whether human thought and action are free or determined, the nature of the 'good,' etc.)—must be replicated by whatever is referred to as philosophy in non-Western cultures. To an extent, this is the same question that underlies many of the discussions and differences between analytic and hermeneutic philosophers in the African context. Yet after all is said and done, such philosophers could still be said to be working within methodological frameworks, however loosely defined and however carefully adapted to the African(a) cultural context, that somehow relate to or derive from Western philosophy and therefore culture.

The point of this chapter is to represent the views of scholars who argue that virtually all of the philosophers previously considered (Sogolo is an obvious exception; see pp. 57–58) may have misconstrued the nature of African Studies (hence philosophy) if they believe Africa can truly be given fair representation using methodologies that are in some sense of Western origin. Many of these scholars did not obtain their academic qualifications in philosophy, but in their view that is no shortcoming, because becoming "qualified" in that so-called discipline effectively amounts to being brainwashed by a Western cultural ideology. Many would also reject being identified, despite their comparatively radical stance, with contemporary intellectual movements such as postmodernism, deconstruction, feminism, or even postcolonialism, since each of these movements uses alternative methodologies devised within the context of, or still addresses itself to issues defined by, Western culture. These scholars argue that Africa should define itself in and on its own terms regarding methodologies, subject areas, and issues without reference or deference to any alien culture. For then, and only then, will Africa's cultures be in a position to speak for themselves about what philosophy should or should not mean to them.

There is anticipation of this point of view in Eritrean scholar Asmarom Legesse's postscript to his *Gada: Three Approaches to the Study of African Philosophy* (1973), entitled "An Essay in Protest Anthropology":

> Africans who wish to learn about their cultures find themselves in a peculiar position. They must fall back on sources written by Westerners on the basis of data largely gathered by European scholars for the benefit of their own societies. Not surprisingly, *the literature rarely addresses itself to African concerns.* Moreover, *the analytical procedures developed by the social scientist are all products of specific cultures [Western] and tend to be associated with particular cultural presuppositions.* (Legesse 1973, 272)

> *[Africans] study African cultures so that they may live and grow to become the enduring foundation of a distinctive African civilization.* (Legesse 1973, 291; my italics in part)

'Wole Soyinka in *Myth, Literature, and the African World* (1976) provided another harbinger of this point of view:

> We are at a definitive stage of African self-liberation [that] is particularly crucial. . . . On the continent [there] must come *a reinstatement of the values authentic to that society.* Could this be why of late *we Africans* have been encountering a concerted assault, decked in ideological respectability, on every attempt to *re-state the authentic world of the African peoples and ensure its contemporary apprehension through appropriate structures?* (Soyinka 1976, x; my italics)

Similar sentiments are expressed in Okot p'Bitek's *African Religions in Western Scholarship* (1970) and Ngugi wa Thiong'o's *Decolonizing the Mind: The Politics of Language in African Literature* (1986). But what also distinguishes many of these texts is their concern to refute, to rebut, the misguided accounts of Western scholars about Africa. Those who today defend the integrity of Africa's cultures in a more radical—indeed, one might sometimes say polemical—manner argue that the predominant emphasis should shift from *defenses* against, corrections of, or attacks on Western scholarship to authentic, autochthonous, straightforward "Africa speaks" accounts by scholars about whatever is the relevant subject or issue—period.

A recent book that is at least compatible with this point of view is Paget Henry's *Caliban's Reason: Introducing Afro-Caribbean Philosophy* (2000). "Compatible" in the sense that this text begins with the admission that there is no explicit formal "school" of Afro-Caribbean philosophers and philosophy that may be compared with Western philosophy in the formal (professionalized) academic (institutionalized) sense. But this does not mean that there is no Afro-Caribbean philosophy in the relevant culture(s). In other words, Henry's point is that, for various reasons, philosophy may be expressed and found in different forms and formats in different cultural contexts.

Many of these scholars who assess the basis for philosophy in non-Western cultures are not "professional" philosophers, and Henry, for one, introduces himself as a "trained . . . sociologist[1] [who has] undertaken to write a book addressed primarily to philosophers" (Henry 2000, xii).

> *From the Afro-Caribbean perspective,* philosophy is an intertextually embedded discursive practice, and not an isolated or absolutely autonomous one. . . . However, it is a distinct intellectual practice that raises certain kinds of questions and attempts to answer them by a variety of styles of argument that draw on formal logic, paradox, coherence, the meaningful logic of lived experiences, and the synthetic powers of totalizing systems. (Henry 2000, 2; my italics)

Nevertheless, the format, the content, the subject matter, the topics and issues that express or represent philosophy in a particular cultural context ("by no stretch of the imagination can this philosophy be considered an autonomous one" [Henry 2000, 7]) also may be relative ("philosophy is *neither* an absolute *nor* a pure discourse. It is an *internally* differentiated and discursively embedded practice" [2000, 3; my italics]).

---

1. Another reason so many of the scholars considered in this chapter come from a non-philosophical background (literature, sociology, anthropology) may be that these disciplines are more compatible with the idea of viewing "philosophy" generally as a culturally relative by-product.

In the Afro-Caribbean context, one of the earliest issues that had to be dealt with was that of European colonization and the consequent valorization of European (versus non-European) culture. This created an atmosphere which, Henry says, promoted such binary alternatives as "colonizer/ colonized, colony/nation, or black/white . . . [rather than more philosophically conventional issues such as] those of being/nonbeing, spirit/matter, good/ evil, and so forth" (Henry 2000, 4). Nevertheless, over the course of the development of what would become an indigenous syncretic Caribbean culture (composed of "Euro-Caribbeans, Amerindians, Indo-Caribbeans [Indians from India], and Afro-Caribbeans" [2000, 3]), Henry suggests it is possible to distinguish three historical periods. Each is distinguished by the emphasis placed upon the input of incoming and, eventually, outgoing cultural foci: (1) traditional African thought, primarily through the medium of imported African slaves (1630–1750); (2) Afro-Christianity, as expressed by the various syncretic religious movements that eventually emanated from the Caribbean (1750–1860); (3) a contemporary period marked by literary-poetic and political-historical figures who have become internationally as well as regionally significant. Consequently, the pool of cultural resources on which to draw for Afro-Caribbean philosophy is rich and ethnically diverse. It includes movements such as African religions and "traditional" thought— Voudou, Santeria, Obeah, and Rastafarianism—and intellectual figures such as Edward Blyden, Aimé Césaire, Frantz Fanon, Marcus Garvey, C. L. R. James, Jamaica Kincaid, George Padmore, Derek Walcott, and Sylvia Wynter (2000, 6–7).

According to Henry, it is the African contributions to Caribbean (or creole) philosophy that have been accorded the least significance. Not surprisingly, the reasons for this are the pervasive influence of the lowly status assigned to Africa's intellectual heritage by Western scholars as well as downright racism. European-oriented influences dictated that philosophy, as the proverbial queen of the sciences, be protected from the perceived vulgarities of Africa's cultures. In consequence, the growth of a truly indigenous *Afro*-Caribbean philosophy was seriously inhibited, and what philosophy there was tended to be of distinct and direct European pedigree (Henry 2000, 7–11).

Hence the movement to constitute a genuinely Afro-Caribbean philosophical tradition must, of necessity, incorporate a movement to oppose racism and encourage a philosophical tradition that is critical of the West in a region that, historically, has every reason to be so. This chapter will focus almost exclusively on Henry's treatment of what he himself refers to as "the African philosophical heritage" (chapter 1) inherent in Caribbean culture. But simply acknowledging and embracing this African heritage cannot be the final objective if a truly indigenous Afro-Caribbean philosophy is to emerge. For that, Henry insists, a further step is required:

Caribbean philosophy must creolize itself by breaking its misidentifi-
cations with European and African philosophies and allowing them
to remix within the framework of more organic relations with local
realities. (Henry 2000, 89)

The bulk of Henry's book is devoted to detailing the nuances of a Caribbean
creole culture and philosophy as expressed in a variety of formats (religious,
literary, artistic, political, etc.) that are the original products of disparate
cultures brought together by diverse historical circumstances. And, as Henry
himself has just made clear, Afro-Caribbean philosophy cannot be the same
as African philosophy precisely because of those circumstances.

Paget Henry might have mixed feelings about finding his text placed
in this chapter, for sometimes he writes as if his aim involves, in Appiah's
sense, building bridges between African and Afro-Caribbean philosophy and
Western philosophy.[2] But why should it necessarily be the case that, even
if Western and non-Western traditions do differ in the most fundamental
manner over the substance of "philosophy," they have no reason to discuss
their different points of view? Perhaps this is why Henry's exposition does
not always preface the noun "philosophy," when it is being used to refer to
the "established" tradition, with the words "European" or "Western." Yet,
in repeated instances, he also very deliberately and forcefully presents the
African dimension of the Caribbean philosophical heritage in a manner that
would be found unacceptable by mainstream academic (Western) philosophy. This becomes understandable once one appreciates that his philosophical approach of choice is a blending of the rational and the hermeneutic that
could be characterized as a "discursive phenomenology" (2000, 151–66)
with an explicitly Africana orientation. This enables him to include source
material that Western philosophy would conventionally exclude:

> Throughout the exposition I make the assumption that the charac-
> ter of traditional African philosophy has been profoundly shaped
> by its intertextual relations with the religious, mythic, genealogi-
> cal, and proverbial discourses that dominate African cultural sys-
> tems. Indeed, it is a central argument of this book that traditional
> African philosophy emerged in the philosophical positions that were
> implicitly taken by sages[3] in these and other important discourses.
> (Henry 2000, 21–22)

> The claim that authoritarian and dogmatic tendencies of myth
> and religion void them and their intertextual relations of all philo-
> sophical significance is a false one. Dogmatism is not unknown to
> philosophy. . . . Thus, in spite of their dogmatic tendencies, I will

2. "This critique and transcending of egoism establishes quite certainly the
place of traditional African philosophy at the table of cross-cultural philosophical discourse" (Henry 2000, 62).

3. See chapter 5 for the discussion of Odera Oruka's sage philosophy.

take the position that there is much in religious and mythic discourses that is of philosophical importance. (Henry 2000, 22)

We need to look at traditional African philosophy with eyes that have been freed from European constructions of the premodern/modern dichotomy. . . . We need to look anew at the problems that traditional African philosophy has attempted to address, and then define and evaluate it in terms of its contributions to the resolving of these problems. (Henry 2000, 62)

Henry then proceeds to document these claims by drawing directly on the myths, religions, and genealogies of a number of African cultures: Igbo, Yoruba, Baluba, Akan, and Tallensi, for example. In doing so, he sometimes draws upon the published works of Western anthropologists, and that might seem to violate the a-Western orientation of scholars featured in this chapter. But as long as such works are drawn upon selectively in a manner that targets straightforward ethnographic reporting and excludes accompanying value judgments and supposed interpretations of the significance of what is being reported, this would seem to be an acceptable methodological recourse.

In his 2002 essay, "Culture, Politics and Writing in Afro-Caribbean Philosophy: A Reply to Critics," Henry summarizes his position with regard to the transcultural character of philosophy:

From all that I have said earlier about philosophy and its capabilities for cultural transcendence, it should be clear that . . . I attribute [a transcultural dimension] to all philosophies, whether African, Indian, Chinese or Latin American. Each standing within its own cultural particularity can, via their logical and phenomenological capabilities, partially enter the sphere of the transcultural while always remaining embedded in cultural particularity. (2002, 183)

In "Between Hume and Cugoano: Race Ethnicity and Philosophical Entrapment" (2004) Henry reemphasizes that philosophy transculturally must be construed in a much broader sense than (Western) analytic philosophy and (Western) phenomenology. He also continues to reflect upon the denigration of philosophical thinking in non-Western cultures that amounts to "racialization or ethnicization" (2004, 130). But this deliberate downgrading of the non-Western by the Western has not succeeded in suppressing the fact that "philosophy is a fundamental discourse, that helps to articulate the visions of existence in cultures all over the world" (2004, 131). Western philosophy may continue its attempts to claim ultimate legitimacy and pride of place as the definitive manifestation of the discipline. But, as Henry points out, this is also the source that sought to provide a philosophical (rational) justification for racism and slavery (similarly to Tsenay Serequeberhan, he targets Hume, Kant, and Hegel).[4]

The issue for Africana[5] philosophy, as broadly as it may come to be construed, is how much of the Western philosophical approach to understanding, which has produced this obvious example of its own shortcomings, should be adopted/adapted as elements of an Africana methodology. There is no question that the priorities of the Africana approach to philosophy (which Henry aligns prominently with "spirituality") have been profoundly altered by its confrontations with Western imperialism. Hence the necessity to address issues such as "race, freedom, decolonization, and rehumanization" (2004, 146). Referring to the work of Sylvia Wynter, Henry therefore characterizes this ever-increasing self-awareness and independence of Africana philosophy as still problematic, but also healthily indicative of a progressive "post-Western" orientation (2004, 147–48).

Nigerian sociologist Oyeronke Oyewumi issues a strong indictment of Western culture's African Studies establishment and offers a detailed revisionist study of the significance of gender in her native Yoruba culture in *The Invention of Women: Making an African Sense of Western Gender Discourse* (1997). Her thesis (and conclusion), simply put, is that "despite voluminous scholarship to the contrary, *gender* was not an organizing principle in Yoruba society *prior to colonization* by the West" (Oyewumi 1997, 3; my italics). Oyewumi complains of

> the uncritical imposition on African cultures of *supposedly objective conceptual categories and theories that are in origin and constitution bound to Western culture.* (Oyewumi 1997, xiv; my italics)

> This book grew out of the realization of Western dominance in African studies. That realization made it necessary to undertake a re-examination of the concepts underlying discourse in African studies, *consciously taking into account African experiences.* Clearly, all concepts come with their own cultural and *philosophical* baggage,

---

4. "[R]acial discourses were integral parts of the work of these philosophers" (2004, 136). Africana philosophers have no reservations about highlighting the fact that such racist discourses were produced during a period that is termed the (European) "Enlightenment." Henry remarks on the manner in which such discourses are treated by the Western mainstream as minor "embarrassments" which are not relevant to the priorities of contemporary academic philosophy (2004, 137). To characterize this attitude, Henry uses the term "self-deflection" rather than "self-reflection" (2004, 147; also see Wynter 1984).

5. "Africana" as opposed to "African" is meant to be inclusive of philosophy both on the continent and in the diaspora.

much of which becomes alien distortion when applied to cultures other than those from which they derive. (Oyewumi 1997, x–xi; my italics)

The first thing is to be clear about what is meant by the term "gender." In English-language culture, most people probably first encounter it as a grammatical classification of masculine and feminine pronouns. Think of "he" and "she" or "his" and "hers," as said to reflect the masculine and feminine genders respectively. But in Western social history, the fact that both spoken English and publications in English favored the use of the male pronouns over female pronouns when referring to human beings generally is now taken as just one more sign of the secondary or second-rate status assigned to women in that culture. Hence when a sociologist like Oyewumi refers to "gendering," she is speaking of a sociological as well as a grammatical phenomenon, whereby women, simply because biologically they are women, are regarded as different, usually inferior, from men with respect to any number of other attributes (Oyewumi 1997, 39).

In sociological terms, then, "gendering" as a practice refers to a society in which a person's sex predetermines the positions they may occupy and the roles they may play. Oyewumi's use of the word "colonization" in the introductory quotation also applies to the ways in which Africa's cultures have been misrepresented and thereby transformed in print by Western scholarship. The social sciences, in particular, are supposed to operate on the basis of methodologies that are culturally universal, that can in principle apply to any society. But she argues that in fact they have been "infected" and biased by the Western cultural context into assuming that gendering must be a universal attribute of all human societies.

What Oyewumi is suggesting is that not just in Western *culture* but also in the (Western) *social sciences* it came to be assumed that the biological differences between men and women "naturally" result in their being assigned different social status and roles in every society that provided for preferential treatment of one sex with respect to the other. For example, one elementary indication of the importance of gendering in (Western) social science is the typing of virtually all societies as either (and usually) *patriarchal/patrilineal* (households/kinship headed and defined by the male line) or, occasionally, *matriarchal/matrilineal* (households/kinship headed and defined by the female line). But the fact that Western culture happened to elaborate the biological differences between the sexes into social distinctions that resulted in the preferential status of one sex (men) does not necessarily make this distinctive Western worldview, much less the entire process of gendering itself, into some universal "truth" to which every other culture in the world must then somehow be assumed to subscribe. But that is precisely what did happen[6] when a biological basis for generating stereotypes of the male and the female was adopted by [Western] sociology/anthropology as fundamental and universal and presumed to apply in an indiscriminate manner to non-Western societies. "In African studies, historically and currently, the creation, constitution, and production of knowledge have remained the privilege of the West. Therefore, body-reasoning and the bio-logic that derives from the biological determinism inherent in Western thought have been imposed on African societies" (Oyewumi 1997, x).

The second phase of Oyewumi's critique requires a concrete example of a society that does not gender human beings—that does not make "sexist" value judgments about people purely on the basis of biological/anatomical differences. To be more explicit, this would not be a society in which the social hierarchy of men over women (conventionally referred to as patriarchal) would be reversed (conventionally referred to as matriarchal). This would be a society which is neither patriarchal nor matriarchal because *biological sex is irrelevant to determining what positions or roles a human being can occupy or play.*

In choosing this example, Oyewumi is scrupulous about delimiting the empirical basis for her claims—her study is centered on the culture of the historic city of Oyo, in Yorubaland, in Nigeria.[7] In Oyo, she argues, the "social categories 'men' and 'women' were nonexistent, and hence no gender system was in place" (Oyewumi 1997, 31). Male and female were of course acknowledged as differing physically and as playing different physical roles in the reproductive process (1997, 36). But these facts of life were not then used as a basis for a socially gendered hierarchy in which human beings who, biologically, were men were privileged more than human beings who, biologically, were women (or the reverse). Therefore gender was not a factor in determining what *social* role an individual was fit or not fit to occupy. This applied to rulers as well as to all the professions.

In a systematic manner Oyewumi proceeds to document the absence of gendering in Oyo society and culture in a variety of ways:

(1) *Language:* The Oyo dialect tends to be the lingua franca of Yorubaland, and it is not gendered with respect to nouns or pronouns (the

6. Philosophers could regard this as an example of the "naturalistic fallacy," when what "is" the case in *one* culture is assumed to be what "ought" to be the case in *every* culture.

7. "There is no question that Africans have many things in common and that some generalizations are possible. But care must be taken in deciding how these claims are to be made and at what level they are to be applied given the paucity of detailed, historically grounded, and culturally informed studies of many African societies" (Oyewumi 1997, xiv).

same word may mean "he" or "she"—which specific person is being referred to becomes dependent on context, etc.) and, in most cases, with respect to "given," or first, names (Oyewumi 1997, 34–43);

(2) *Lineage:* Along with *seniority* (age), a person's ancestral household or "family" of origin become the principal determinants—rather than gender, or "sex"—of status and role in a household (for example, whether an individual was originally born into the household where they are living or whether they married into it from outside that household); in which case a female as well as a male can be the overall head of a household (47–48);

(3) *Marriage:* This is regarded most importantly as the conjunction or joining of lineages rather than of "man" and "woman" (even if, physically, that was the case). The social identity of a female who left the household of her birth to join that of the male who was to be her "husband" was never severed from that of her original lineage (51–64);[8]

(4) *Market* (including "professional" identities): As one of the most important economic institutions in the society, proprietary rights to the market were not favored with regard to a particular gender (despite misleading images of the proverbial "African market women"). Different lineages came to be identified with particular professional skills, and this, rather than gender, was the principal determinant of an individual's—male or female—right to practice a particular profession (trading, farming, hunting, alternative medicine, divination, etc.) (64–71).

In addition to lineage, seniority was the other principal determinant of an individual's social status:

> Seniority is the primary social categorization that is immediately apparent in Yoruba language. *Seniority is the social ranking of persons based on chronological ages.* The prevalence of age categorization in Yoruba language is the first indication that age relativity is the pivotal principle of social organization. (Oyewumi 1997, 40)
>
> *Seniority is highly relational and situational* in that no one is permanently in a senior or junior position; it all depends on who is present in any given situation. Seniority, unlike gender, is only comprehensible as part of relationships. Thus, it is neither rigidly fixated on the body nor dichotomized. (Oyewumi 1997, 42; my italics)

If this is in fact the way Oyo society "traditionally" functioned, how is it that the world has a completely different and mostly negative impression of the status of women in Africa generally? Is this not the continent where women are oppressed, exploited, and downtrodden, virtually degraded into

---

8. See especially pp. 58–64 for an interesting discussion of the role of polygamy in Oyo Yoruba society.

a form of commodity?[9] Oyewumi has already answered this question in part by suggesting that one reason for this misrepresentation of Yoruba (and, by extension, African) society by traders, missionaries, colonial administrators, and foreign scholars was that they could not really understand the language or customs of the society they were observing, added to the fact that they arrived in Africa already convinced that social sexual discrimination was a human universal. Other contributory causes that have in fact served to undermine indigenous Oyo social traditions and that have introduced Western elements of biological gendering into it were the policies of the British colonial government, which tended to assign African men and women the different roles and status assumed to be "natural" to each sex according to European standards (i.e., men were assumed to be "superior"). And last, but far from least, during and after colonialism the influence of internationalized Western culture, with its popular stereotypes (i.e., the "housewife") of the proper roles for men and for women, was ever pervasive.

One obvious question that begs to be addressed at this point is how a professional African sociologist like Oyewumi would view "Western" feminism. Since its announced aim is to liberate all women from male dominance and to achieve genuine social equality, especially when it asserts itself as a formidably organized internationalized force, should it not be viewed as a movement that could help to salvage gender neutrality in a society like that of the Oyo Yoruba? Interestingly, this does not seem—at least at present—a realistic possibility as far as Oyewumi is concerned. Her assessment of Western feminism seems to be that it is precisely that—*Western* feminism. It is a movement that was engendered in a particular cultural context that continues to associate biology with gender, that continues to approach the cultures in the non-Western world as if they are grounded on the same association (but the social status of non-Western women is assumed to be even lower than in Western society), and that therefore is incapable of appreciating the truly radical alternative of *genderlessness* that a culture such as that of the Oyo Yoruba has to offer:

> In effect, [every] society was assumed to have a sex/gender system. (Oyewumi 1997, 12)

> From a cross-cultural perspective, the more interesting point is the degree to which feminism, despite its radical local stance [in the Western social context], exhibits the same ethnocentric and imperialistic characteristics [the situation of women in their society must be similar to what it *was* in ours; we are in a better position to know

9. "The emphasis, erroneously, is on how tradition victimizes women" (Oyewumi 1997, xiv).

what should be done about this] of the Western discourses it sought to subvert. This has placed serious limitations on its applicability outside of the culture that produced it. (Oyewumi 1997, 13; my italics)

In *African Women and Feminism: Reflecting on the Politics of Sisterhood* (2003), Oyewumi continues her critique of Western feminism: "feminism's role in the projection of Western culture and culture forms in the contemporary period must not be underestimated" (2003, 3). She challenges (Western) feminism's adoption of the terms "sister"/"sisterhood" and their explicit identification with "women's activism" (2003, 3) as further evidence of the hypocritical "dishonesty of white feminists in advocating an unconditional love and solidarity amongst all women, even as they exercised their race and class privileges on the backs of non-white women" (2003, 4).[10]

Oyewumi suggests that a more transculturally meaningful choice would be "motherhood"/"co-mother," although she immediately acknowledges that Western feminists would likely protest against this because it reverts to an element of the gender inequity (the status of "wife" in a patriarchal family) that (Western) feminism designates as unacceptable:

> To an African reader . . . the model of motherhood is absolutely natural, because if anything binds women together in collective experience, it is childbearing and the mothering of children, and consequently *the nurturing of community*. . . . Simply put, since sisterhood is a kinship term that emerges from the logic of the nuclear family, which is a specifically Euro-American family form, one must ask why Africans and other peoples whose family systems may have a different logic and hence articulate and privilege a different set of kinship and non-kin relations should adopt the term. (2003, 5, 6; my italics)

In non-Western cultures, where the nuclear family is not a given, it is the extended family, the collectivity, the *community* that takes as much precedence as the individual. In this kind of environment motherhood becomes a much more prestigious and powerful form of identity, as it is foundational to the sense of unity without which such communities or cultures could not exist, and recognizes the manner in which women also contribute to their *communities'* economic, political, and religious institutions (2003, 11–13).

But what has all of this to do with philosophy? Philosophy in the African context does not have to replicate philosophy as defined and practiced in Western culture. Oyewumi certainly believes that there is a philosophical

---

10. Oyewumi also acknowledges the original importance (and different meaning) attached to "sisterhood" by the African American community during the Civil Rights struggle (2003, 9).

dimension to her arguments. Very early on she establishes a bridge between her study, as relating to "the *sociology* of knowledge" (Oyewumi 1997, xi), and philosophy with her claim that "since there is a clear epistemological foundation to cultural knowledge, the first task of the study is to understand the *epistemological* basis of both Yoruba and Western cultures" (ix).

A variety of epistemologies/methodologies would appear to be involved here. On a first-order (more fundamental or basic) level are, as matters of fact, the languages and forms of discourse actually used by the populations of the relevant cultures (Western and African) to define what the world is like for them (certainly a form of understanding). On another, comparatively second-order (more abstract and theoretical) level, are the cognitive frameworks of the more specialized technical disciplines—in this case, the (Western) social sciences—used to study non-Western societies. Finally, there is the alternative critical second-order approach Oyewumi herself, as an African professional sociologist, uses to identify, to understand, and to assess the cognitive frameworks used by the indigenous populations and by professional (Western) social scientists to study those cultures (which would certainly include "sisterhood" and Oyewumi's "co-mother").

She gives any number of indications of how her own second-order framework is constituted when she introduces such words and phrases as "hermeneutics" (Oyewumi 1997, x), "archaeological" (ix), "and "unpack the concept" (73). Hermeneutics is an old friend from chapter 6, where a key element of it as a methodological point of view was said to be accepting, as it seems Oyewumi clearly does, the difficult fact that any attempt to go beyond the conventional, even in scholarship, necessitates beginning from and with what is taken as conventional scholarship at that point in time. One may attempt (and succeed) to understand the presuppositions underlying ("archaeological") such conventional scholarship in a more profoundly critical and insightful manner than was achieved before ("unpacking"), and that certainly is Oyewumi's aspiration. But it would be unrealistic to expect results that would be theoretically comprehensive methodological miracles that suddenly and totally alter the course of human history and understanding. Such new understanding is achieved piecemeal at great cost, effort, and controversy. It seems quite clear that all of the scholars whose work is discussed in this chapter appreciate that.

Contemporary Nigerian anthropologist Ifi Amadiume undertakes a critical reassessment of various theories put forward by Senegalese anthropologist, Egyptologist, historian, physicist, and founder of Afrocentrism, Cheikh Anta Diop (1923–1986), in her *Reinventing Africa: Matriarchy, Religion and Culture* (1997). Amadiume too is concerned to shift the emphasis in Africa-based or Africa-oriented scholarship from attacks on Western scholarship to autonomous studies or statements ("Africa speaks") about African cultures that take their integrity (in cross-cultural terms) for granted. To christen or to type such studies, she suggests the Igbo term *nzagwalu* as a general name for such "Africa speaks" statements, or studies of Africa's cultures (2000a, 2000b, 2008).[11]

Cheikh Anta Diop waged war for decades against an international academic establishment that in his opinion had denied Africa a place in the ranks of "civilized" cultures, cultures that were entitled to articulate their own intellectual heritage and history. Along with his colleague Theophile Obenga (1992, 1995, 2004), Diop is primarily responsible for the reclamation of the Egyptian cultural heritage for all African peoples. Because Amadiume is concerned to place Africa's precolonial and contemporary indigenous cultures into a historical context, it makes good sense for her to reevaluate Diop's own claims about that subject as possibly complementary to her own.

The corpus of Diop's published writings is substantial, and it is difficult to do him justice in an abbreviated summary such as this; I will emphasize those elements of the corpus that serve to restore an African sense of historical and intellectual continuity. In this regard, during his lifetime Diop's most controversial claim was that ancient Egyptian culture was a "black" African culture. In physiological and linguistic, as well as cultural, terms, he argued, the ancient Egyptians were Africans (Diop 1974). But imperialism and colonialism, under Western auspices, engaged in a deliberate conspiracy to deprive peoples of African descent of this aspect of their heritage by portraying Egyptian civilization as somehow independent of (the legendary "fertile crescent") or not relevant to the rest of Africa.

Another thesis put forward by Diop that attracts Amadiume's interest is his claim that historical (indeed, also prehistorical) African society, Egypt included of course, was matriarchal rather than patriarchal in character (Diop 1987, 1989).[12] In an earlier work, *Male Daughters, Female Husbands* (1987), which will be discussed below, she undertakes an analysis of gendering in her native precolonial Igbo (Nnobi) society. In addition to providing some interesting points of comparison with Oyewumi's work on the Oyo Yoruba, it is indicative of Amadiume's interest, as a social anthropologist, in the basis for societies in precolonial Africa.

Diop argued that matriarchal cultures tended to privilege specific moral virtues. "Diop's point is clear, 'Great Civilizations' can be built on a pacifist

---

11. "*Nzagwalu* is an Igbo word meaning *answering back;* when you have suffered an insult, you have to *answer back*" (Amadiume 1997, 4; my italics).

12. "[Diop] argued that the African systems were matriarchal with inheritance and succession traced through the female line, either through the sister as in Pharaonic Egypt or the sister's son as in the African kingdoms and all the so-called matrilineal African societies" (Amadiume 1997, 7).

moral philosophy" (Amadiume 1997, 57). Amadiume finds a comparable set of "motherly" values in her Igbo hometown of Nnobi. She names some of them as compassion, love, and peace (1997, 18, 84). But gradually, over the course of history, as Africa suffered the consequences of repeated and violent invasions, dating from Egyptian times through European colonization, African societies shifted to patriarchy in self-defense because that form of social order is better suited to dealing with violence.

> As a result of the militarization and gradual masculinization of the African continent over the past two thousand years, the ideological structure of patriarchy has [gradually] been reproduced in all our current forms of social organization, along with associated exploitative modes of production such as family, lineage, feudalism, slavery, capitalism, and totalitarian centralized planning. (Amadiume 1997, 22–23)

What Amadiume disputes about Diop's historical portrait of Africa as shifting from matriarchal to patriarchal societies is that he focuses disproportionately upon the ostentatiously patriarchal roles and values of "supreme" heads of state (emperors, kings, emirs, chiefs) and ignores the "forms of life" represented by the common people living in the society at large. For here, she believes, matriarchal values survived and retained a prominent place in Africa's cultures that also, by the way, argues for further distinctive evidence of historical continuity: "Every conceivable African political system had communities at its base. What are the social organizations of these communities? What are their moral philosophies? This appears to be the subject given the least importance by African academics. Africans have not yet written their social history" (Amadiume 1997, 15). This is something Amadiume believes she is helping to establish by arguing for "a fundamental African *moral philosophy*. This was [Diop's] theory of matriarchy as a *unifying* African moral code and culture" (Amadiume 1997, 24; my italics).

This thesis is developed further in a chapter devoted specifically to Diop's historical analyses of moral philosophy in the African social context (Amadiume 1997, chapter 2). Here Amadiume explores the cultural consequences of the gradual "militarization and masculinization of the African continent" (1997, 60). This trend would be further reinforced by European colonization, since the colonial powers favored and imposed systems of values that were the expression of their own patriarchal morality, one that justified violence and conquest (of which the slave trade is the icon) as morally "right" and "just."

For Amadiume, one important lesson to be learned from all of this is Africa's need and right to recognize and revitalize the distinctively gendered, motherly/matriarchal, moral values that were and to a significant extent are still a part of the continent's contemporary cultural history:

Coupled with the removal of Africans from their own self-history is a problem with the continuous presentation of Africans as a people with no *philosophical* history. There is usually a marginalization of the question of *epistemology* as history of ideas [presenting it as a "story" rather than as cogent examples of critical thinking], and intellectual debate in all fields of learning are introduced with reference to European thought, without concern or respect for *Africans as a people who should be understood within their own self-constructed status and identity and as creators of their nations.* (Amadiume 1997, 64; my italics)

In *Male Daughters, Female Husbands* (1987), Amadiume undertakes a historical study of the moral values underlying some examples of gendering in precolonial Nnobi society. According to Amadiume, Nnobi culture was gendered, but not on a strictly sexual (biological) basis. This meant that in certain contexts, (biological) men could be addressed as women and (biological) women could be addressed as men. She characterizes the gendering system in Nnobi as "flexible" or as "neutered" because "women could play roles usually monopolized by men, or be classified as 'males' in terms of power and authority over others. As such, roles were not rigidly masculinized or feminized" (Amadiume 1987, 185).[13]

How is it that a woman could "be" a man? "The two examples of situations in which women played roles ideally or normally occupied by men—what I have called male roles—in indigenous Nnobi society were as '*male daughters*' and '*female husbands*'; *in either role women acted as family head*" (Amadiume 1987, 90; my italics).[14] Since Nnobi was in large measure a farming community, ownership of land was one of the most important sources of wealth (1987, 30–35). But in a situation where a man had no son to serve as inheritor of his land, it was possible for him to appoint a daughter as a 'son,' who would thereby be entitled to inherit that part of his estate: "women owned land as 'male daughters' when they had been accorded *full*

13. Oyewumi (1997, 184n45) wonders whether it is conceptually possible to revamp the male-female (Western) gender dichotomy in this fashion, since it is based upon comparatively rigid (biological, sexual) distinctions between the sexes.

14. Although these examples of "flexible gendering" were clearly socially institutionalized, they should not be allowed to mislead readers into thinking there was not also a place in the society for family units in which (biological) males were recognized as the family "head": "The term for family, *ndi be*, which means people of one's home, is normally used in relation to the head of the family who is, ideally, a man" (Amadiume 1987, 90). Nkiru Nzegwu suggests that the contrary evidence and arguments Amadiume introduces in this regard have the (presumably unintended) consequence of making Igbo society appear to be patriarchal (Nzegwu 1998a).

male status in the absence of a son in order to safeguard their father's *obi* [ancestral home or compound]" (1987, 34; my italics).

"Female husbands" were (biological) women who demonstrated the potential to be exceptionally successful in business (traders), farming (Amadiume 1987, 31), or some other profession. Such talented individuals had need of others to work for them, since a one-woman (or one-man, for that matter) enterprise must of necessity be limited in scope. These additional personnel were obtained in one of two ways: (1) straightforward employment; or (2) "what was called *igba ohu,* woman-to-woman marriage. Such wives, it seems, came from other towns. The 'female-husband' might [thereafter] give the wife a (male) husband somewhere else and [then] adopt the role of mother to her but *claim her services.* The wives might also stay with her, bearing children in her name" (1987, 42).[15] What is striking about this arrangement is the social avenue it provided for the development of women who demonstrated a talent for professional careers that some stereotypes of Africa typically view as open only to male enterprise. There was a cultural as well as a social dimension to such achievements, because these women were then entitled to take a special title known as Ekwe, which was closely associated with a powerful female deity worshiped by all members of Nnobi society (1987, 42–44).

How is it that a man could "be" a woman? "In indigenous Nnobi society and culture, there was one head or master [who could be male or female] of a family at a time, and 'male daughters' and 'female husbands' were called by the same term, which translated into English would be "master." Some women were therefore masters to other people, both men and women. It was . . . [therefore] possible for some men to be addressed by the term 'wife,' as they were in service or domestic relationship to a [female] master" (Amadiume 1987, 90).

Once again, some may be tempted to ask what all of this has to do with philosophy. As far as *epistemology* is concerned, Amadiume's revisionist restatement of history from an African point of view demonstrates that the framework of "world" history constructed by Western scholarship is an "understanding" of world history weighted and consequently skewed

---

15. In another context, Amadiume describes this practice as follows: "As men increased their labour force, wealth and prestige through the accumulation of wives, so also did women through the institution of 'female husbands.' When a man paid money to acquire a woman, she was called his wife. When a woman paid money to acquire another woman, this was referred to as buying a slave, *igba ohu,* but the woman who was bought had the status and customary rights of a wife, with respect to the woman who bought her, who was referred to as her husband, and the 'female husband' had the same rights as a man over his wife" (Amadiume 1987, 46–47).

by Western ethnocentrism. The fact that it is possible to present a credible African-oriented alternative rendering of that history—which serves to highlight the integrity and uniqueness of Africa's cultures—demonstrates that such "understanding" is, to say the least, controversial. As far as *moral philosophy* is concerned, Amadiume defends a thesis that Africa had, and to some extent has retained, a unique, motherly/matriarchal system of social values that, in certain situations, also had the effect of neutralizing or relativizing (biological) gendering.

Nkiru Nzegwu is a Nigerian philosopher, artist, art historian, and scholar of Africana studies. She has formulated a number of explicit critiques of both Western and African scholars who, in her opinion, fail to have sufficient appreciation of African viewpoints in their subject areas. The range of Nzegwu's writings is considerable, and readers are referred to the bibliography for more specific references to relevant essays.

What is of particular interest in the context of the present discussion is her critique (Nzegwu 1998a) of Ife Amadiume's work. Although she appreciates Amadiume's motives in wanting to establish a distinct African social identity based upon Cheikh Anta Diop's thesis of an African matriarchal social tradition dating back to prehistoric times, Nzegwu suggests that Amadiume does not document the factual existence of matriarchy in Africa sufficiently on an empirical basis. Hence Amadiume's claim shifts from being anthropological to being ideological—to an "image" of Africa (as caring, etc.) that she appears to be promoting on other than socially scientific grounds.[16] Nzegwu is also concerned that this form of insufficiently documented "hasty generalization" about all of the continent's cultures may not do justice to the cultural diversity that is a part of Africa's heritage (Nzegwu 1998a, 4).

> In underplaying Africa as a complex terrain with complex histories, and whose societies and cultures cannot be collapsed into a grand explanatory master narrative, Amadiume theoretically recast Africa to reproduce the very same historical and epistemological distortions of the historians [for example, the numerous controversial generalizations about Africa produced by "Western" scholarship] she was critiquing. (Nzegwu 1998a, 5)

A second point that Nzegwu queries is Amadiume's use of the "male-female" gendering dichotomy as in any sense relevant to understanding the basis for individual identity in Igbo society. "If, indeed, a corpus of social roles and status transcend the politics and logic of gender ascription, so that 'monolithic masculinization of power was eliminated' (Amadiume 1997, 129), then it must be that the category of gender is not really foundational"

16. "Amadiume's matriarchal thesis is, at best, an emotional heartfelt ejaculation of the importance of mothers in Igbo society" (Nzegwu 1998a, 9).

(Nzegwu 1998a, 6).[17] If it is indeed the case that there are conventional practices whereby a (biological) female may become a "male" (and the reverse), does this not suggest the existence of deeper, more subtle criteria in the society for determining an individual's social status and role? Nzegwu suggests that jettisoning the male-female dualism altogether, rather than complicating it with females who have been "de-femaled" and males who have been "de-maled," would be of considerable help in bringing those deeper criteria to light.

Nzegwu then proceeds, on the basis of her own research among the Igbo, to develop an alternative, non-matriarchal, and non-gendered portrait of social status and roles in Igbo society. Resuming her critique of Amadiume's use of male-female (biological) gendering as a basis for understanding Igbo society, she argues that viewing the male-daughter phenomenon *essentially* as a process by which a female must *change her gender* to inherit her father's estate implies, more importantly, that *women really do have a second-rate status in the society at large,* rather than that, less importantly, in some situations their status may be enhanced (Nzegwu 1998a, 10). But Nzegwu argues that this too would give the wrong impression:

> It is precisely because of the importance attached to daughters, that when family survival is at stake, family obligations override marital relations. Under such conditions, a daughter has no qualms in either dissolving, or acquiescing to the dissolution of her marriage to ward off the obliteration of her *obi* (patricentric unit), and to become its *ide ji uno* (pillar that supports the house). (Nzegwu 1998a, 10)

Nzegwu proceeds to outline a system (which, she notes, is in decline given the onslaught of "modern" ways) of family and marital relations and obligations that, as was the case with Oyewumi's portrait of the Oyo Yoruba, would seem to make seniority and lineage more fundamental determinants of social status and role than any form of gendering:

> At the very least, Amadiume's anthropologized notion of *obi* [which Amadiume described as "ancestral home or compound"], as simply implying male and fatherhood must be urgently revised. What we have is *obi*-lineality, a *non-gendered* term that refers to the residence or house of fathers (socially not biologically understood) that encapsulates all the children of the family and lineage without implying that only males are the children in that house or compound. Because the *obi* is the term that references lines of descent, and daughters are

17. "Because Amadiume is committed to a gender frame of analysis, she fails to see the incompatibility of the two frames [a gendered versus a non-gendered model] and that the so-called neuter roles and status cannot evolve in a social practice in which gender is an ontological category" (Nzegwu 1998a, 7).

members of *obi,* they are automatically included. . . . Having eliminated daughters from the *obi,* the only way Amadiume can bring
them into that house is by turning them into males. This accounts
for why she represented such daughters as males and values them as
sons. (Nzegwu 1998a, 12; my italics)

In her 2006 book, *Family Matters: Feminist Concepts in African
Philosophy of Culture,* Nzegwu notes the current concern with human rights
in the African context as defined by an agenda that, in principle, privileges
the rights of the individual over his or her culture (2006, 1). She cannot
help but note the inconsistency between this initiative and the propensity
in contemporary African societies, including the courts, to legitimate the
inferior rights of women. This inferior status of women (their roles limited
to being "daughters and wives") is justified by appeals to the *community* (a
priority taken to be appropriately traditionally African, embracing Mbiti's "I
am because we are" maxim (see p. 26), but it is now a *community* in which
women's rights are judged to be inferior to those of men.

Her narrative in this book is based upon case studies in her native
Igboland, in which the three primary functions of women are now said to
have been reduced to: "the provision of labor, the production of children,
and the provision of sexual favors for men" (2006, 6). Nzegwu argues that
it is impossible to do justice to the indigenous social values and rights of
individuals in Igbo culture if tradition is now being *re*formulated to present
a gendered framework as foundational, for example, that because men are
men they are entitled to a privileged status, and that because women are
women they are relegated to an inferior status that makes them subservient
to both men and the community at large (2006, 8–9).

> Working within a gendered framework robs a researcher or theorist
> of the requisite flexibility to respond effectively to relations that
> are not products of patriarchy. The epistemological challenge for
> this study is to avoid the irresistible undertow of the assumptions
> and concepts of Western epistemology. Thus, in this study, the gen-
> der category will not dictate the terms and trajectory of research.
> (2006, 10)

The fundamental irony arising from the contemporary African situation,
at least in relation to the geographical area that concerns Nzegwu, is that
indigenous traditions that were the basis for a *genderless* culture have been
displaced and supplanted, thanks to Western colonialism and Western cultural imperialism, by gendered and discriminatory 'traditions' deriving from
the Western view of the family as patriarchal and the female as therefore
inferior and subservient.[18]

18. "[T]he dubious use of *tradition* to confer legitimacy on a family model
that is rooted in European family ideology and that is especially discriminatory
towards women" (2006, 7; my italics).

What were in fact the original traditions that governed relations between men and women in this culture? Nzegwu introduces alternative nomenclature into her analysis when she refers to the "African philosophy of culture" as involving "the sum total of a people's ways of living, histories, conventions, and practices that have been passed on from generation to generation and that endow them with a distinctive character" (2006, 14). Key to the (northwestern) Igbo culture was what she characterizes as "communities [that] possessed *dual-sex systems* in which there were separate lines of governance for men and women" (2006, 15; my italics). Political, economic, and social relations were thereby made separate but equal and, most importantly, *interdependent* (2006, 15). This meant that one group (rather than one 'sex')[19] had to seek the collaboration and cooperation of the other before any decision of communal consequence could be made.

The question then becomes, what is to be done? Elements of that precolonial, genderless culture persist, even if now in "attenuated form" (2006, 18). Therefore the first objective should be to outline in detail what role women did play in the culture. Here Nzegwu also places primary importance on the notion of *motherhood*:

> By understanding the constituent parts of the Igbo family and centering the ideology of motherhood, we are able to see the understated sources of power and channels of influence of Igbo women. In the past, the convergence of these channels on the mother had checked the development of patriarchal force by significantly curtailing the rights of fathers and husbands over daughters and wives. (2006, 19)

Nzegwu anticipates the objections and criticisms of those who might argue that by reverting to terminology that enunciates a dual-*sex* system, she is implicitly reintroducing gender as a foundational element. Her response is that gendering has become a controversial issue because of its own explicit association with the superiority and inferiority of the sexes. But the dual-sex system does not even entertain this as an issue because "it rejects the paradigm of female subordination and inferiorization," thereby making the notion of gender irrelevant as a basis for favoring the rights of one group over the other (2006, 20).

Contemporary consequences of the diminished role of the female are the increasing incidence of violence in Igboland and the increase of immorality in both the family and society in general (2006, 240–43). Self-interest, greed, and the accumulation of material wealth are supplanting traditional values, and Nzegwu links these unwelcome developments, at least in part, to the increased role of "male privilege" (2006, 243). The positive moral values of the past are now ridiculed as "primitive and backward" (2006, 244).

19. "[T]he dual-sex system in which the biological sex is recognized but does not affect the social valuation of human worth" (2006, 20).

> The crucial question we now face is, how do we rethink present Igboland, given the moral decay that is spreading over the entire landscape? We could start by reintegrating women back into society as equal partners with men and channeling their creative energies into rebuilding the society. In order to build a balanced society in which men and women function at their optimal level, gender equity and the rule of law must become the central pivots of society. (2006, 247)

Readers who find themselves distracted by such detailed discussions of gendering and its consequences must again bear in mind the epistemological and ethical basis all of these scholars invoke as of supreme importance to their concern about arriving at an understanding of Africa from an African point of view. The conceptual frameworks we use to "understand" a society are just about as fundamental as one can get with reference to that aspect of the theory of knowledge. If a conceptual framework that assumes gendering to be the fundamental social distinction, as evidently is the case in Western society, is used to "understand" a society in which gendering is not of such fundamental importance, obviously misrepresentation and misunderstanding will result.

A word of caution is also perhaps in order: one should resist the tendency to label Oyewumi, Amadiume, and Nzegwu as "feminists" just because they all happen to be women who concern themselves with the issue of gendering. It is best to think of them in the present context purely and simply as scholars. All three at various points and in the strongest terms reject "feminism" as a Western-based and Western-oriented movement that has yet to demonstrate that it is prepared to reject the misrepresentations of African societies generated by Western scholarship and is prepared to learn from rather than dictate to the non-Western world.

> The dilemma and anger for us African women is the contradiction implied in the actions of these Western women, whose cultural and historical legacies we know. Yet they leave their problems at home, and cross vast seas to go and dictate strategies of struggle and paths of development to Africans, as highly paid consultants and well-funded researchers. At the same time, their own imposed systems are eroding all the positive aspects of our historical gains, leaving us impoverished, naked to abuse, and objects of pity to Western aid rescue missions. (Amadiume 1997, 197)

The universality of gendering may be one particular topic of concern, but the broader issue at stake is that entirely original lines of inquiry may be required in order to appreciate what a *culture* or *community* or human relationship "is" from the African point of view. That this is an ongoing enterprise that still has vast territories to explore and map is indicated by the ongoing dialogue between Oyewumi, Amadiume, and Nzegwu. If Africa is finally to speak for itself, in self-critical philosophical terms as well, there must be very careful consideration of what that can and should involve.

As should now be apparent, in African cultures and African philosophy the status and role of community is distinctive. The arguments of Oyewumi, Amadiume, and Nzegwu, which promote lineage, seniority, co-mothering, and motherhood, would be pointless unless grounded in a social context that gives them both meaning and power. These discussions therefore provide a meaningful transition to the works of other contemporary African philosophers who are concerned to address themselves explicitly to the importance that should be given to *community* in the African context, whether from an empirical or a theoretical point of view.

As was indicated earlier on, the status of communalism, or communitarianism as it is also known, was important in the writings of the immediate post-independence leaders of Africa. Following independence in the early 1960s, it was those early political leaders—such as Kwame Nkrumah (see pp. 95–96), Léopold Senghor (see pp. 48–49), and Julius Nyerere (see pp. 97–98)—who invoked a heritage of what Nkrumah referred to as "communalism" (see 1970c), what Senghor described as "a community-based society" (see 1963), and what Nyerere christened *ujamaa* (1968c), which he translated into English as "familyhood."

With reference to John Mbiti (see p. 26) and his now popularized maxim: "I am because we are," Kwame Gyekye suggests that if one takes into account the remainder of the compound sentence of which this is only a portion—"and since we are, therefore I am" (Mbiti 1970a, 141), the statement as a whole places an exaggerated emphasis on the importance of *community* and therefore amounts to an implicit denial of any significant role for *individual* rights (Gyekye 1997a, 38). In *African Religions and Philosophy* (1970a) Mbiti also says:

> What then is the *individual* and where is his place in the *community?* In traditional life, the individual does not and cannot exist alone except corporately. . . . He is simply part of the whole (141). . . . [T]he highest authority is the community of which . . . [the individual] is a corporate member (268). . . . [A] person cannot be individualistic, but only corporate. (272; my italics)

The relative balance between individual rights and communal obligations establishes the framework for discussion of an issue that currently has become a topic of interest for a number of African philosophers: what precisely is meant by *communalism* or *communitarianism* in the African context? Furthermore, what is or should be the status of individual rights in a social context that evidently places a higher priority on communal rights than is conventional in Western culture or philosophy?

With regard to the discussion of communalism or communitarianism by contemporary African philosophers, and their thoughts about what it was, is, and should be, discussion will focus on three figures: Mogobe Ramose of South Africa and Kwasi Wiredu and Kwame Gyekye of Ghana. To begin with, there are a number of themes or theses about African communalism on which they seem to agree:

(1) That, on the basis of present-day beliefs and practices in Africa and numerous anthropological studies, on empirical grounds it is a safe generalization to say that Africa's cultures evidenced, and to a significant degree still evidence, a communitarian or communal character (Ramose 2003a, 230; Wiredu 1992b, 199; Gyekye 1997a, 36).

(2) "Community" in the African sense means much more than the Western notion of a "body of people living in the same locality" (a definition borrowed from the *Concise Oxford Dictionary*). In fact Ramose's view of the African community involves both natural and supernatural dimensions. It is human be-ing, taken as epistemologically foundational, that recognizes and articulates the multiple dimensions of the community. First there is the dimension of the living, based essentially on the family and extended family. Secondly, there is the dimension "of those beings who have passed away from the world of the living" (Ramose 2003a, 236). Ramose prefers referring to them as the "living dead," adapting a term from Mbiti, rather than the more conventional "ancestors" (2003a, 236). Finally there is the dimension of the "yet-to-be-born." "It is the task of the living to see to it that the yet-to-be-born are in fact born" (2003a, 236).

These dimensions interact, which gives rise to a potentially much more expansive notion of community, in that the living dead and the others are believed to have "a direct influence on the life of the living" (2003a, 236) and, hence, to form essential parts of the overall community.

> *Umuntu* [human be-ing] cannot attain *ubuntu* [be-ing] without the intervention of the living-dead. The living-dead are important to the upkeep and protection of the family of the living. This is also true with regard to the *community* at large. For this reason it is imperative that the leader of the *community,* together with the elders of the community, must have good relations with their living-dead. This speaks to the *ubuntu* understanding of *cosmic harmony.* (Ramose 2003a, 237; my italics in part)

For Wiredu, "a person is social not only because he or she lives in a community, . . . but also because, by his original constitution, a human being is part of a social whole" (Wiredu 1992b, 196).

> Thus conceived [here he is speaking specifically of Akan society], a human person is essentially the center of a thick set of concentric circles of obligations and responsibilities matched by rights and privileges. [These, he says, revolve] round levels of relationships irra-

diating from . . . household kith and kin, through the "blood" ties of lineage and clan, to the wider circumference of human familihood. (Wiredu 1992b, 199)

Gyekye's portrayal of the African community resonates with Wiredu's:

The notion of shared life—shared purposes, interests, and understandings of the good—is crucial to an adequate conception of community. What distinguishes a community from a mere association of individuals is the sharing of an overall way of life. In the social context of the community, each member acknowledges the existence of common values, obligations, and understandings and feels a commitment to the community that is expressed through the desire and willingness to advance its interests. Members of a community society are expected to show concern for the well-being of one another, to do what they can to advance the common good, and generally to participate in the community life. They have intellectual and ideological as well as emotional attachments to their shared goals and values and, as long as they cherish them, they are ever ready to pursue and defend them. (Gyekye 1997a, 42)

(3) That the underlying or foundational notion of community may be linked to a particular view of *morality*. In Ramose's case this view is expressed as:

be-ing human is not enough. One is enjoined, yes commanded as it were, to actually become a human being. . . . the maxim . . . that to be a human be-ing [*umuntu*] is to affirm one's humanity by recognizing the humanity of others and, on that basis, establish humane relations with them. (Ramose 2003a, 231)

Ramose's injunction that one must become a *human being* rather than merely a *human* replicates distinctions that are made by both Wiredu and Gyekye between being merely *human* and being a *person*. For all three of these philosophers, being moral in a communitarian or communal setting is what transforms the merely human into authentic personhood. Personhood therefore becomes a morally weighted ascription.

The communalistic orientation . . . means that an individual's image will depend rather crucially upon the extent to which his or her actions benefit others than himself . . . by design. . . . an individual who remained content with self-regarding successes would be viewed as so circumscribed in outlook as *not to merit the title of a real person*. (Wiredu 1992b, 200; my italics)

The moral significance of *denying personhood* to a human being on the grounds that his actions are known to be dissonant with certain fundamental norms or that he fails to exhibit certain virtues in his behavior is extremely interesting for communitarians.

> *Personhood*, in this model of humanity, is not innate but is earned in
> the ethical arena: it is an individual's *moral* achievement that earns
> him the status of a *person*. (Gyekye 1997a, 50–51; my italics)

(4) African humanism, as was previously the case with Senghor (see
pp. 48–49), finds the Western dichotomy between the rational and the emotional unacceptable when formulating an acceptable basis for moral values
and moral acts. This is because "duty" in the deontologically pure Kantian
sense, or as expressed by a purely rational sense of responsibility, is found
to be neither a sufficient nor a satisfactory basis for African humanism in
the communal or communitarian context. As Ramose puts it: "African philosophy would not subscribe to the radical opposition between reason and
emotion . . . but . . . [rather to] the mutual dependence of the 'rational'
and the 'emotional'" (2003a, 234). A similar repositioning of the emotional
appears to arise from Wiredu's point that it is his "injection of a dose of compassion into Kant's categorical imperative"[20] that converts it into a notion
of "*sympathetic* impartiality" (1996b, 29; my italics). Or Gyekye's emphatic
endorsement of "love, mercy, and compassion . . . as intrinsic to satisfactory
moral practice in the communitarian society" (1997a, 72).

It is the differences or, in some cases, differences in emphasis, among
these three philosophers that provide the material of greatest philosophical
interest. Because Ramose endorses a Bantu ontology or metaphysics of beings as foundational, his vision of the created universe is value-laden from
the outset. Moral values are therefore things that human be-ing inherits,
or even inhabits, though he also clearly indicates that individuals have to
struggle to implement them:

> In *ubuntu* philosophy a human being in the world of the living must
> be *umuntu* [morally astute] in order to give a response to the chal-
> lenge of the fundamental instability of be-ing. . . . Religion, politics,
> and law must be anchored upon the understanding of the cosmos
> as the continual strife for harmony. It is such anchorage which gives
> them authenticity and legitimacy. And this is the basis for consensus
> as the distinctive feature of *ubuntu* philo-praxis. (Ramose 2003a,
> 237)

Note that this is different from Akan thought in that the basis of the quest
for consensus, according to Wiredu (see p. 143) and Gyekye (see p. 143), is
social and secular rather than metaphysical.

Wiredu's approach to morality is that it is best understood first as a universal phenomenon manifesting certain principles or rules that every society
or community must strive to implement if it is to survive. His argumentation

---

20. A moral principle that is supposedly grounded upon "practical reason."

here is reminiscent of his discussion of rationality as culturally universal, in that, to paraphrase my earlier remarks, he is concerned to knock down the fences that have been created to morally segregate the African approach to ethics as somehow idiosyncratic, inadequate, and derogatory. Wiredu is committed to the notion that all of humanity share certain basic moral principles and that appreciation of how those principles are instituted in a particular culture should be assigned the highest priority for those committed (as Wiredu certainly is) to a vision of philosophy that truly crosses cultures.

How does he reconcile this universality with his claim that African societies are distinctively communal by comparison with, for example, their Western counterparts? There appear to be two fundamental steps in his argumentation here:

(1) That there are strictly ethical or moral universals. He justifies this claim via reasoning such as the following: "What we need to do is to specify a principle of conduct such that without its recognition—which does not necessarily mean its invariable observance—the survival of human society *in a tolerable condition* would be inconceivable" (1996b, 29). As an example of such a rule Wiredu introduces what he labels *"the principle of sympathetic impartiality"* (1996b, 29), which may be expressed by the imperative "Let your conduct at all times manifest a due concern for others" (1996b, 29), and acknowledges that it is reminiscent of the Golden Rule. But the reasoning he uses to justify its foundational character is as follows: "I suggest that it takes little imagination to foresee that life in any society in which everyone openly avowed the contrary of this principle and acted accordingly would inevitably be 'solitary, poor, nasty, *brutish*' and probably short" (1996b, 29).

(2) If Wiredu affirms the principle of sympathetic impartiality as *"a human universal transcending cultures"* (1996b, 29; my italics), then how does he reconcile this universalistic position with the apparent moral relativity evidenced by societies that embrace a communal as opposed to an individualistic orientation? He does this by means of two further arguments. One is the introduction of a form of sliding scale:

> [T]he distinction between communalism and individualism is one of degree only; for a considerable value may be attached to communality in individualistic societies, just as individuality is not necessarily trivialized within communalism. (1996b, 29)

In other words, according to Wiredu's model, even a society that is radically communal in nature would still have a place for a degree of individuality, or a society that is radically individualistic in character would have to make allowance for a degree of communality.

Secondly, he suggests that we cannot make sense of morality in any society unless we introduce, in addition to universal moral rules or principles, the supplementary categories of "customs" and "lifestyles," insofar as they are of instrumental and empirical value for highlighting the diversity of ways in which the universal moral principles are implemented in different cultures. "The real difference between communalism and individualism has to do with *custom* and *lifestyle* rather than anything else. . . . [B]oth are conceptually, of a kind and are distinct from morality in the strict sense" (Wiredu 1996b, 72; my italics).

Wiredu's point is that people who emphasize the relativity of moral values in different cultures are in fact themselves exaggerating the relatively contingent anomalies generated by differences in customs and lifestyles rather than foundational moral principles. He describes customs as "contingent norms of life" (1996b, 30) and argues that this could include "usages, traditions, manners, conventions, grammars, vocabularies, etiquette, fashions, aesthetic standards, observances, taboos, rituals, folkways, [and] mores" (1996b, 28). All of these, then, become the kinds of things that make cultures *differ* from one another. It therefore seems that every implicit or explicit value-laden belief or practice in any society, apart from sympathetic impartiality, would have to be regarded as pertaining to the category of *custom*.

Kwame Gyekye provides a number of interesting arguments for the status of individual rights in even a communitarian setting. He does this, in part, because he thinks it possible that some may still be mistakenly prone to exaggerating the 'power' the African community has over the individual, and because he thinks the individual must retain certain rights as privileges if he or she is not to become inhuman—a virtual automaton or robot.

Gyekye begins his argument by acknowledging that "the individual is not self-sufficient" (1997a, 38) and that the "community . . . alone constitutes the context, the social or cultural space, in which the actualization of the potentials of the individual can take place" (1997a, 39). But he then goes on to say:

> Besides being a social being by nature, the human individual is also by nature, other things as well. By "other things" I have in mind such essential attributes of the person as rationality, having a moral sense and capacity for virtue and, hence, for evaluating and making moral judgments: all this means that the *individual* is capable of choice. (1997a, 53; my italics)

Even in such a communal setting a relatively extreme form of individuality might be manifested by someone who decides to reject the values of his or her society:

> The capacity for self assertion that the individual can exercise presupposes, and in fact derives from, the autonomous nature of the person (Gyekye 1997a, 54). . . . The upshot is that personhood can

only be partly, never completely, defined by one's membership of the community. (1992, 113)

It may be the case that ordinary discourse in the communal setting does not make a fetish of individual rights in the sense of proclaiming them in a very public manner. But this is understandable, given the more fundamental commitment to a system of values meant to promote the good of the wider society as such. Gyekye therefore embraces a form of communitarianism that he describes as *"moderate"* in character (1997a, 65).[21]

Because Ramose's metaphysics extends to—in fact comprises—all be-ing, including "the greatest of the great, the ineffable [supremely supernatu-ral]" (2003a, 236) as well as more mundanely human be-ing, it would seem contrary to his vision of an *ubuntu* philosophy to analytically 'separate off' the realm of the ethical from that of the spiritual. Yet that, in a sense, is precisely what both Wiredu and Gyekye do when they argue that morality in the African communal setting is primarily *humanistic* in character.

> One important implication of the founding of value on human inter-ests is the independence of morality from religion in the Akan out-look: What is good in general is what promotes human interests. . . . Thus, the will of God, not to talk of any other extra-human being, is logically incapable of defining the good. (Wiredu 1992b, 194)

> In Akan moral thought the sole criterion of goodness is the wel-fare or well-being of the community. . . . The good is identical with the welfare of the society, which is expected to include the welfare of the individual. . . . It is clear that this definition does not at all refer to the will or commands of God. That which is good is decreed not by a supernatural being as such, but by human beings within the framework of their experiences in living in society. (Gyekye 1995, 132)

The discussions in this chapter serve to highlight at least two issues that are receiving increasing attention in the writings of contemporary African philosophers. One concerns the importance of the appropriate status and role(s) of women (and men) in contemporary (and historical) African cultures.

---

21. Most recently Wiredu has suggested that "communitarianism and indi-vidualism are both just different ways of arranging the pursuit of the interests of *individuals*. The difference is that there are many more issues of human well being regarding which an individual has obligations and rights in a communitar-ian society than in an individualistic one. I call the interests and concerns gener-ated by such issues *special* interests because they go beyond the province of pure morality (as defined by the principle of sympathetic impartiality or the Golden Rule). An individual's strictly ethical rights and obligations are shared by her with the entirety of mankind" (2007).

The second concerns the apparent increasing agreement about the positive consequences, at least in the African context, of a society that places as much emphasis on the welfare of the community as it does on the welfare of the individual.

With the benefit of hindsight, it would appear that these two issues are not unrelated. Though an interrelation is suggested at points in the arguments of Oyewumi, Amadiume, and Nzegwu, the incorporation of the gendering controversy into African communalism generally would seem to be a subject that warrants further attention and discussion by those who endorse the positive virtues of a communal agenda. It will therefore be of interest to see how philosophers in and of Africa set about more specifically addressing the relationships between these topics in days to come.

9

Histories, Anthologies, Introductions to African Philosophy, Journals, and Websites

In addition to the individual philosophers whose views we have explored, there are a substantial number of publications on and of African philosophy that are of a more diverse nature—usually because they incorporate the writings of a variety of African philosophers and intellectuals within a single text. At least some reference should be made to them here, for several reasons: (1) they too are important philosophical statements in their own right; (2) they further demonstrate the vitality and diversity of contemporary African philosophy; (3) they may be of use to newcomers to the field who wish to pursue their interest in the subject further.

In 2004 the publication of the Blackwell *Companion to African Philosophy,* edited by Kwasi Wiredu, represented a veritable milestone in the scholarship arising from philosophy in the African context. No previous text compares in either breadth or depth with the wide range of topics covered in a firsthand manner by many of Africa's prominent and promising philosophers. Its forty-seven chapters, grouped under seven different subject-headings (History; Methodological Issues; Logic, Epistemology, and Metaphysics; Philosophy of Religion; Ethics and Aesthetics; Politics; Special Topics), contributed by forty different authors, should make this volume a first-rate source for many years to come.

The first truly comprehensive and detailed history of African philosophy was written by Kenyan philosopher D. A. Masolo. Appropriately entitled *African Philosophy in Search of Identity* (1994), this important text devotes entire chapters to all of the topics touched upon here. Unfortunately, it is impossible to do justice to Masolo's much more sophisticated and detailed history in this brief historical synopsis. But it is important to point out that his text is also a philosophical statement in its own right. Masolo does more than merely chronicle ideas. He analyzes and provides critical assessments of the various philosophers and the traditions they represent. He does this, ultimately, from the standpoint of his own philosophical position, and it is therefore appropriate to at least say something about that here.

For example, Masolo is skeptical about the philosophical merit of an exclusively linguistic approach to African philosophy (1994, 95–102). Ordinary language exists primarily as a practical means of communication rather than as a philosophical statement of a people's worldview or metaphysics (their most fundamental beliefs about the nature of reality). Analytic philosophers may choose to explore the meanings and grammatical structure of language, but for Masolo this provides an insufficient basis for drawing systematic conclusions about the most fundamental or important theoretical precepts of a given African culture.

> When through some rigorous analysis we are able to trace word formation to the word's conceptual significances, we are actually doing an exercise that is essentially out of the context of the original function of the word. In other words, at this level we would be doing our own private abstractions and ploughing into fields completely unintended and possibly even unknown to the common native speaker of that language. . . . The philosopher's interests in meaning go beyond the limits of the linguist. His "meaning" searches for or denotes "essential" properties by which we identify things as belonging to a specific class. But this is beyond the communicative meaning that words denote in common language. . . . From the ordinary common language they build another language, a language of experts. The meaning of a specific word in ordinary language, on the other hand, must be sought in "what it stands for" for the majority of its speakers, who never have to qualify first as metaphysicians before they qualify as speakers of their own language, whether it is their native language or a new one. (Masolo 1994, 102)

One obvious problem with this "other language building" of the linguistic philosopher, and one apparently implied by Masolo's observations, is that the end result might be an African worldview or philosophy, attributed to an African people via their language, that was the product of the philosopher's own imagination and speculation. This would help to explain why Masolo insists that African philosophy must be grounded upon something more than mere linguistic analysis.

What Masolo does see as one of the most important and positive developments within contemporary African philosophy is the determination of African philosophers to explore the universal elements of rationality in

African thought (Masolo 1994, 44). For one thing, this kind of approach—for example, as evidenced by Wiredu—constitutes one of the benchmarks of the mainstream discipline known as "philosophy." For another, it will hopefully serve to counterbalance the claims of those extreme relativists who go too far in their efforts to prove that African cognition is qualitatively different from that of other cultures and who produce essentially ethnographic treatises (Tempels, etc.) of an "African traditional thought" that is both excessively exotic and bizarre in character.

Masolo suggests that even today, the most basic issue that continues to divide African philosophers and philosophy is precisely the degree to which cognition may be said to be distinctive in African thought (Masolo 1994, 247–48):

> The question of how to define the criteria of rationality has become a central theme in Anglophone philosophy. . . . On one side are the foundationalists [universalists], who argue that formal rational procedures are the defining features of science, which supersedes common sense and is universal. On the other side are the pluralists [relativists], who argue in favor of the diversity of human experience and systems of representation. These include the criteria for the definition of knowledge and for making judgments. (Masolo 1994, 247)

His own position is to try to strike a balance between the two:

> The position which states that our sense of the world and of personhood varies according to the varieties of experience takes a middle ground between the foundationalists and the pluralists by arguing that what are called products of the rational mind are not really conflictual with what are oppositionally referred to as the disorderly life of the body and the emotions. Rather, this third position argues, such products carry equal weight as they [both] are modes of thinking which illustrate the variant modalities of experience. This position avoids the Cartesian dichotomy which posits the cogito ["pure" reason] as separate from, opposed to, and more reliable than bodily experiences [sensory perception]. This position argues for *a historical and contextual approach* to the definition of knowledge and rationality. (Masolo 1994, 248; my italics)

He argues that this kind of "historical and contextual" approach will prove more beneficial because it will prevent African philosophy from being dominated by any absolute commitment to a single methodological or ideological paradigm. It will leave the future of the discipline open to the development of new insights and approaches that may prove of value or interest to philosophers working within the African context. In addition, it takes more explicit account of the fact that philosophy—philosophizing—is the product of the mind of the *individual* philosopher and his or her own creative interests, insights, and genius (Masolo 1994, 251).

Two texts that specifically discuss the possible relevance and/or irrelevance of "Western" approaches to philosophy in the African context are Tsenay Serequeberhan's *The Hermeneutics of African Philosophy* (1994), and Barry Hallen's *African Philosophy: The Analytic Approach* (2006).

John Pittman's anthology *African-American Perspectives and Philosophical Traditions* (1997) is a prime example of a collection that relates to African philosophy. It contains contributions by both African and African American philosophers (the two traditions increasingly grouped under the common heading "Africana Philosophy") and is of interest for the suggestions they make about how the two do and should interrelate. A similarly oriented anthology that has more of a textbook format is *African Intellectual Heritage: A Book of Sources* (1996), edited by Molefi Kete Asante and Abu S. Abarry.

Emmanuel Eze's *Postcolonial African Philosophy* (1997) is another anthology composed mostly of original essays. It is particularly noteworthy for the substantial number of contributions made by philosophers who come from a Continental, phenomenological, or hermeneutical background, traditions that, like Marxism, too often go underrepresented in the Anglophone philosophical context. *African Philosophy as Cultural Inquiry* (2000), edited by Ivan Karp and D. A. Masolo is an anthology of original contributions by philosophers, historians, anthropologists, linguists, and scholars concerned with the arts. It reaffirms the interdisciplinary and academically syncretic character of African philosophy by arguing, for example, that it is high time philosophers and anthropologists of Africa stopped attacking one another and begin to collaborate, because their fields really can serve to complement one another. More recent is the volume edited by Lee Brown entitled *African Philosophy: New and Traditional Perspectives* (2004), which is meant to address "traditional African conceptions of mind, person, personal identity, truth, knowledge, understanding, objectivity, destiny, free will, causation, and reality" (vii).

There is now a fairly wide variety of introductions to African philosophy, mostly in textbook format. Some are straightforward anthologies of canonical pieces. Prime examples are the collection edited by Richard Wright entitled *African Philosophy: An Introduction* (3rd ed., 1984), Tsenay Serequeberhan's *African Philosophy: The Essential Readings* (1991c), and Emmanuel Eze's *African Philosophy: An Anthology* (1998). Some are anthologies of canonical pieces supplemented by substantive, expository, editorial commentaries. Representative examples are the collection edited by Parker English and K. M. Kalumba entitled *African Philosophy: The Classical Approach* (1996), Albert Mosley's *African Philosophy: Selected Readings*

(1995), and P. H. Coetzee and A. P. J. Roux's *The African Philosophy Reader* (1998; 2nd ed., 2003). Finally, there are now at least two entirely original introductory texts that are meant to situate African philosophy in its historical context and then discuss major figures and traditions within it. These are *An Introduction to African Philosophy* (1998) by Samuel Oluoch Imbo, and *An Introduction to Africana Philosophy* by Lewis Gordon (2008).

Journals, unfortunately, go into and out of print, and it is sometimes difficult to keep up with their current state of health.[1] There never have been that many journals of African philosophy in print, but the *Journal on African Philosophy* (online via the African Resource Center website listed below), the *Journal of African Religion and Philosophy* (Uganda), *Quest* (Leiden, the Netherlands, and Zambia), and *Philosophia Africana* (USA) are some that might be found in university libraries.

Finally, there are a number of useful websites that are devoted to African philosophy. As with printed texts, they too tend to go in and out of fashion (and existence!). But several of the more enduring and useful are Africa Resource Center at www.africaresource.com, African Philosophy Resources at http://pegasus.cc.ucf.edu/~janzb/afphil, and the website of the International Society for African Philosophy and Studies (ISAPS) at www.isapsonline.com. These three sites also cross-reference a number of other websites that feature African philosophy.

---

1. Journals which appear erratically or of which publication has been suspended (temporarily or permanently) are: *African Philosophy* (UK); *African Philosophical Inquiry* (Nigeria); *Journal of African Philosophy* (Nigeria); *Second Order* (Nigeria); *SAPINA (The Society for African Philosophy in North America) Bulletin* (U.S.); and *Thought and Practice* (Kenya).

Conclusion

If anything, this narrative—incomplete and fragmentary as it may be—serves to demonstrate how dynamic, eloquent, and original a field African philosophy has become. Whether African philosophy involves restoring Africa's links with its precolonial intellectual heritage, exploring continuities between that past and the present, evaluating philosophical approaches best suited for understanding, appreciating, and developing Africa's cultures, or enunciating new priorities for philosophy in the African context, one thing is clear. African philosophers are fully aware of the role they rightfully must play, and fully engaged in addressing these concerns.

Though foreign scholars may have insisted that no value judgments were implied by their peculiar characterizations of the African intellect, it is difficult to deny that those characterizations led to a double standard that defined Africa's civilizations and cultures as somehow intellectually second-rate. The responses to this from philosophers in the African context vary—from new studies of Africa's cultures to prove that this was and is false, to charges of ethnocentrism, of racism, or simply to recasting such "scholarship" as a body of base rationalizations that justified the exploitation of the continent's resources (including, of course, its peoples). But there is also a sense of distress, of offense, of outrage that sometimes, even on academic and professional levels, such notions could be taken seriously.

It is this train of thought that has persuaded some African philosophers to suggest that, in the end, it is philosophy in the African context that will be more open-minded about and tolerant of the predispositions and peculiarities of other cultures' philosophical traditions. For, on the basis of sometimes bitter experience and hard-won political and intellectual independence, it is Africa that will be in a more informed position to appreciate the importance of every culture's inalienable right to intellectual integrity. How ironic it would be if the continent that was once denied having philosophical substance proved to be the place that is most appreciative of and receptive to the importance of philosophy!

Bibliography

Abimbola, Kola. 2005. *Yoruba Culture: A Philosophical Account*. Birmingham, UK: Iroko Academic Publishers.

Abimbola,'Wande. 1975. *Sixteen Great Poems of Ifa*. Niamey, Niger: UNESCO.

———. 1976. *Ifa*. Oxford: Oxford University Press.

———. 1977. *Ifa Divination Poetry*. New York: NOK.

———. 1997. *Ifa Will Mend Our Broken World*. Roxbury, Mass.: Aim Books.

Abimbola, 'Wande, and Barry Hallen. 1993. "Secrecy ('Awo') and Objectivity in the Methodology and Literature of *Ifa* Divination." In *Secrecy: African Art That Conceals and Reveals*, ed. M. Nooter, 212–21. New York: Museum for African Art; Munich: Prestel.

Abraham, W. E. 1962. *The Mind of Africa*. Chicago: University of Chicago Press.

———. 1996. "The Life and Times of Anton Wilhelm Amo, the First African (Black) Philosopher in Europe." In *African Intellectual Heritage: A Book of Sources*, ed. Molefi K. Asante and Abu S. Abarry, 424–40. Philadelphia: Temple University Press. (First published in *Transactions of the Historical Society of Ghana* 2, no. 1 [1963].)

———. 2004. "Anton Wilhelm Amo." In *A Companion to African Philosophy*, ed. Kwasi Wiredu, 191–99. Malden, Mass.: Blackwell.

Adeofe, Leke. 2004. "Personal Identity in African Metaphysics." In *African Philosophy: New and Traditional Perspectives*, ed. Lee M. Brown, 69–83. Oxford: Oxford University Press.

Ake, Claude. 1981. *A Political Economy of Africa*. New York: Longman.

———. 1993. "The Unique Case of African Democracy." *International Affairs* 69, no. 2.

———. 1996. *Democracy and Development in Africa*. Washington, D.C.: Brookings Institution.

Amadiume, Ifi. 1987. *Male Daughters, Female Husbands: Gender and Sex in an African Society*. Atlantic Highlands, N.J.: Zed Books.

———. 1997. *Reinventing Africa: Matriarchy, Religion and Culture*. London: Zed Books.

———. 2000a. *Afrikan Matriarchal Foundations: The Igbo Case*. Trenton, N.J.: Red Sea.

———. 2000b. *Daughters of the Goddess, Daughters of Imperialism: African Women Struggle for Culture, Power and Democracy*. London: Zed Books.

———. 2008. "African Women's Body Images in Postcolonial Discourse and Resistance to Neo-Crusaders." In *Black Womanood: Images, Icons, and*

Ideologies of the African Body, ed. Barbara Thompson. Seattle: University of Washington Press.

Amin, Samir. 1989. *Eurocentrism.* New York: Monthly Review Press.

Appiah, Kwame Anthony. 1981. "Structuralist Criticism and African Fiction: An Analytic Critique." *Black American Literature Forum* 15, no. 4 (Winter): 165–74.

———. 1984a. "An Aesthetics for Adornment in Some African Cultures." In *Beauty by Design: The Aesthetics of African Adornment,* 15–19. New York: African-American Institute.

———. 1984b. "Strictures on Structures: On Structuralism and African Fiction." In *Black Literature and Literary Theory,* ed. Henry Louis Gates Jr., 127–50. London: Methuen.

———. 1986a. "Deconstruction and the Philosophy of Language." *Diacritics* (Spring): 49–64.

———. 1986b. "Are We Ethnic? The Theory and Practice of American Pluralism." *Black American Literature Forum* 20 (Spring–Summer): 209–24.

———. 1986c. "The Uncompleted Argument: Du Bois and the Illusion of Race." In *Race, Writing and Difference,* ed. Henry Louis Gates Jr., 21–37. Chicago: University of Chicago Press.

———. 1986–87. "Racism and Moral Pollution." *Philosophical Forum* 18, nos. 2–3 (Winter–Spring): 185–202. (Reprinted in *Collective Responsibility: Five Decades of Debate in Theoretical and Applied Ethics,* ed. Larry May and Stacey Hoffman, 219–38. New York: Rowman and Littlefield, 1991.)

———. 1987. "Old Gods, New Worlds: Some Recent Work in the Philosophy of African Traditional Religion." In *Contemporary Philosophy: A New Survey,* vol. 5, ed. Guttorm Floistad, 207–34. The Hague: Martinus Nijhoff.

———. 1988. "Out of Africa: Topologies of Nativism." *Yale Journal of Criticism* 2, no. 1: 153–78. (Revised and reprinted in *The Bounds of Race,* ed. Dominic LaCapra, 134–63. Ithaca, N.Y.: Cornell University Press, 1991.)

———. 1989a. "The Conservation of 'Race.'" *Black American Literature Forum* 23 (Spring): 37–60.

———. 1989b. "Race." In *Critical Terms for Literary Study,* ed. Frank Lentricchia and Tom McLaughlin, 274–87. Chicago: University of Chicago Press.

———. 1990a. "Racisms." In *Anatomy of Racism,* ed. David Goldberg, 3–17. (Reprinted in *Introduction to Philosophy: Classical and Contemporary Readings,* 3rd ed. New York: Oxford University Press, 1999.)

———. 1990b. "Alexander Crummell and the Invention of Africa." *Massachusetts Review* 31, no. 3 (Autumn): 385–406.

———. 1990c. "But would that still be me? Notes on Gender, 'Race,' Ethnicity as Sources of Identity." *Journal of Philosophy* 87, no. 10 (Oct.): 493–99. (Reprinted in *Race, Sex: Their Sameness, Difference and Interplay,* ed. Naomi Zack, 75–81. New York: Routledge, 1997.)

——. 1990d. "New Literatures, New Theory?" *Mtatu 7 Canonization and Teaching of African Literatures,* ed. Raoul Granquist, 57–90. Amsterdam: Rodopi.

——. 1991a. "Is the 'Post' in 'Postcolonial' the 'Post' in 'Postmodern'?" *Critical Inquiry* 17 (Winter): 336–57.

——. 1991b. "Soyinka's Myth of an African World." In *Crisscrossing Boundaries in African Literatures,* ed. Ken Harrow, Jonathan Ngate, and Clarisse Zimra, 11–24. Washington, D.C.: Three Continents Press and African Literature Association.

——. 1992a. *In My Father's House: Africa in the Philosophy of Culture.* Oxford: Oxford University Press.

——. 1992b. "Inventing an African Practice in Philosophy: Epistemological Issues." In *The Surreptitious Speech: Presence Africaine and the Politics of Otherness 1947–1987,* ed. V. Y. Mudimbe, 227–37. Chicago: University of Chicago Press.

——. 1992c. "Social Forces, 'Natural' Kinds." In *Exploitation and Exclusion: Race and Class in Contemporary US Society,* ed. Abebe Zegeye, Leonard Harris, and Julia Maxted, 1–13. Oxford: Hans Zell.

——. 1992d. "African Identities." In *Constructions identitaires: questionnements theoriques et etudes de cas. Actes du Celat* 6 (May). Universite Laval, Canada: CELAT.

——. 1992–93. "African-American Philosophy?" *Philosophical Forum* 24, nos. 1–3 (Fall–Spring): 1–24. (Reprinted in *African-American Philosophical Perspectives and Philosophical Traditions,* ed. John Pittman, 11–34. New York: Routledge, 1997.)

——. 1993. "Thick Translation." *Callaloo* 16, no. 4 (Fall): 808–19.

——. 1994a. "Myth, Literature and the African World." In *Wole Soyinka: An Appraisal,* ed. Adewale Maja-Pearce, 98–115. London: Heinemann.

——. 1994b. "Identity, Authenticity, Survival: Multicultural Societies and Social Reproduction." In *Multiculturalism: Examining "The Politics of Recognition,"* ed. Amy Gutman, 149–64. Princeton, N.J.: Princeton University Press.

——. 1994–95. "Ancestral Voices." In *Salmagundi* 104–105 (Fall–Winter): 88–100. (Reprinted in *The New Salmagundi Reader,* ed. Robert Boyers and Peggy Boyers, 122–34. Syracuse, N.Y.: Syracuse University Press, 1996.)

——. 1995a. "Philosophy and Necessary Questions." In *Readings in African Philosophy: An Akan Collection,* ed. Safro Kwame, 1–22. Washington, D.C.: University Press of America.

——. 1995b. "Why Africa? Why Art?" In *Africa: The Art of a Continent,* ed. Tom Phillips, 21–26. London: Royal Academy.

——. 1996a. "Culture, Subculture, Multiculturalism: Educational Consequences." In *Public Education in a Multicultural Society,* ed. Robert Fullenwider, 65–89. New York: Cambridge University Press.

——. 1996b. "Against National Culture." *English in Africa* 23, no. 1 (May):

11–27. (Reprinted in *Text and Nation,* ed. Peter Pfeiffer and Laura Garcia-Moreno, 175–90. Columbia, S.C.: Camden House, 1996.)

———. 1996c. "Race, Culture, Identity: Misunderstood Connections." *The Tanner Lectures on Human Values.* Vol. 17, 51–136. Salt Lake City: University of Utah Press.

———. 1996d. "Reconstructing Racial Identities." *Research in African Literatures* 27, no. 3 (Fall): 58–72.

———. 1997a. "Identity: Political not Cultural." In *Field Work: Sites in Literary and Cultural Studies,* ed. Marjorie Garber, Rebecca L. Walkowitz, and Paul B. Franklin, 34–40. New York: Routledge.

———. 1997b. "Liberalism and the Plurality of Identity." In *Knowledge, Identity and Curriculum Transformation in Africa,* ed. N. Cloete, M. W. Makgoba, and D. Ekong, 79–99. Johannesburg: Maskew Miller Longman.

———. 1998a. "The Arts of Africa." In *Ideas Matter: Essays in Honour of Conor Cruise O'Brien,* ed. Richard English and Joseph Morrison Skelly, 251–64. Dublin: Poolbeg.

———. 1998b. "The Limits of Pluralism." In *Multiculturalism and American Democracy,* ed. Arthur M. Melzer, Jerry Weinberger, and M. Richard Zinman, 37–54. Lawrence: University of Kansas Press.

———. 1998c. "Race, Pluralism and Afrocentricity." *Journal of Blacks in Higher Education* 19 (Spring): 116–18.

———. 1998d. "Ethnophilosophy and Its Critics." In *The African Philosophy Reader,* ed. P. H. Coetzee and A. J. P. Roux, 109–30. London: Routledge.

———. 1998e. "Afterword: How Shall We Live as Many?" In *Beyond Pluralism: The Conception of Groups and Group Identities in America,* ed. Wendy Katkin, Ned Landsman, and Andrew Tyree, 243–59. Urbana: University of Illinois Press.

———. 2000. "Liberty, Individuality and Identity." *Critical Inquiry* 27 (Winter): 305–32.

———. 2001a. "African Identities." In *Race and Racism,* ed. Bernard Boxill. New York: Oxford University Press.

———. 2001b. "Ethnic Identity as a Political Resource." In *Explorations in African Political Thought: Identity, Community, Ethics,* ed. Teodros Kiros, 45–54. New York: Routledge.

———. 2004a. "African Philosophy and African Literature." In *A Companion to African Philosophy,* ed. Kwasi Wiredu, 538–48. Malden, Mass.: Blackwell.

———. 2004b. "Akan and Euro-American Concepts of the Person." In *African Philosophy: New and Traditional Perspectives,* ed. Lee M. Brown, 21–34. Oxford: Oxford University Press.

———. 2004c. "Language, Race, and the Legacies of the British Empire." In *Black Experience and the Empire,* ed. Philip D. Morgan and Sean Hawkins. New York: Oxford University Press.

———. 2005. "African Studies and the Concept of Knowledge." In *Knowledge*

Cultures: Comparative Western and African Epistemology, ed. Bert Hamminga, 23–56. Amsterdam: Rodopi.

———. 2006a. "How to Decide if Races Exist." *Proceedings of the Aristotelian Society* 106 (May): 363–80.

———. 2006b. "The Politics of Identity." *Daedalus* 135, no. 4 (Fall): 15–22.

———. 2007. *Cosmopolitanism: Ethics in a World of Strangers*. New York: W.W. Norton & Co.

Appiah, K. Anthony, and V. Y. Mudimbe. 2003. "The Impact of African Studies on Philosophy." In *The Impact of African Studies on the Disciplines,* ed. Robert Bates, V. Y. Mudimbe, and Jean O'Barr, 113–38. Chicago: University of Chicago Press.

Appiah, K. Anthony, Peggy Appiah, and Ivor Agyeman-Duah. 2008. *Bu Me Be: Proverbs of the Akans*. Banbury, Oxon, UK: Ayebia Clarke.

Asante, Molefi K. 2000. *The Egyptian Philosophers: Ancient African Voices from Imhotep to Akhenaten*. Chicago: African American Images.

———. 2007. *An Afrocentric Manifesto*. Stafford BC, Australia: Polity.

Asante, Molefi Kete, and Abu S. Abarry, eds. 1996. *African Intellectual Heritage: A Book of Sources*. Philadelphia: Temple University Press.

Beattie, John. 1966. *Other Cultures: Aims, Methods and Achievements in Social Anthropology*. London: Routledge and Kegan Paul.

Bedu-Addo, J. T. 1979a. "On the Alleged Abandonment of the Good in the *Phaedo*." *Apeiron* 13: 104–14.

———. 1979b. "The Role of the Hypothetical Method in the *Phaedo*." *Phronesis* 24, no. 2: 111–32.

———. 1983. "Sense-Experience and Recollection in Plato's *Meno*." *American Journal of Philology* 104, no. 3: 228–48.

———. 1985. "Wiredu on Truth as Opinion and the Akan Language." In *Philosophy in Africa: Trends and Perspectives,* ed. P. Bodunrin, 68–90. Ife, Nigeria: University of Ife Press.

———. 1991. "Sense-Experience and the Argument for Recollection in Plato's Phaedo." *Phronesis* 36, no. 1: 27–60.

Bell, Richard H. 2002. *Understanding African Philosophy*. New York: Routledge.

Bello, A. G. A. "Review of *Knowledge, Belief and Witchcraft*." *Journal of African Philosophy and Studies* (Lagos, Nigeria) 1, nos. 1–2: 93–98.

———. 2003. "In Praise of the *Onisegun*." *Journal on African Philosophy*, no. 3. www.africanphilosophy.com/issue3/toc3.htm.

———. 2004. "Some Methodological Controversies in African Philosophy." In *A Companion to African Philosophy,* ed. Kwasi Wiredu, 263–73. Malden, Mass.: Blackwell.

Ben-Jochannan, Yosef. 1994. *Africa, Mother of Western Civilization*. Baltimore: Black Classic.

Bernal, Martin. 1987. *The Fabrication of Ancient Greece*. Vol. 1 of *Black Athena: The Afroasiatic Roots of Classical Civilization*. London: Free Association Books.

———. 1991. *The Archaeological and Documentary Evidence*. Vol. 2 of *Black Athena: The Afroasiatic Roots of Classical Civilization*. New Brunswick, N.J.: Rutgers University Press.

———. 2001. *Black Athena Writes Back: Martin Bernal Responds to His Critics*. Durham, N.C.: Duke University Press.

———. 2006. *The Linguistic Evidence*. Vol. 3 of *Black Athena: The Afroasiatic Roots of Classical Civilization*. New Brunswick, N.J.: Rutgers University Press.

Bernasconi, Robert. 1997. "African Philosophy's Challenge to Continental Philosophy." In *Postcolonial African Philosophy: A Critical Reader*, ed. Emmanuel Eze, 183–96. Oxford: Blackwell.

———, ed. 2001. *Race*. Malden, Mass.: Blackwell.

Bewaji, J. A. I. 2003. *Beauty and Culture: Perspectives in Black Aesthetics*. Ibadan, Nigeria: Spectrum Books.

Bidima, Jean-Godefroy. 2004. "Philosophy and Literature in Francophone Africa." In *A Companion to African Philosophy*, ed. Kwasi Wiredu, 549–59. Malden, Mass.: Blackwell.

Bodunrin, Peter. 1975a. "'Theoretical Entities' and Scientific Explanation." *Second Order* 4, no. 1: 56–65.

———. 1975b. "The Alogicality of Immortality." *Second Order* 4, no. 2: 36–44.

———. 1978. "Witchcraft, Magic and ESP: A Defense of Scientific and Philosophical Scepticism." *Second Order* 7, nos. 1–2: 36–50. (Reprinted in *African Philosophy: Selected Readings*, ed. Albert G. Mosley, 371–85. Englewood Cliffs, N.J.: Prentice Hall, 1995.)

———. 1979. "Belief, Truth and Knowledge." *Second Order* 8, nos. 1–2: 28–46.

———. 1981. "The Question of African Philosophy." *Philosophy* 56, no. 216: 161–79.

———, ed. 1985. *Philosophy in Africa: Trends and Perspectives*. Ife, Nigeria: University of Ife Press.

———. 1992. "Philosophy in Africa: The Challenge of Relevance and Commitment." In *Postcolonial African Philosophy*, ed. H. Nagl-Docekal and F. M. Wimmer, 15–35. Munich: Oldenbourg.

Boele van Hensbroek, Pieter. 1999. *Political Discourses in African Thought: 1860 to Present*. Westport, Conn.: Praeger.

Bongmba, Elias Kifon. 2001. *African Witchcraft and Otherness: A Philosophical and Theological Critique of Intersubjective Relations*. Albany: State University of New York Press.

———. *The Dialectics of Transformation in Africa*. New York: Palgrave Macmillan.

Brown, Lee M., ed. 2004. *African Philosophy: New and Traditional Perspectives*. Oxford: Oxford University Press.

Cabral, Amilcar. 1969. *Revolution in Guinea: An African People's Struggle.* London: Stage 1.

———. 1970. "National Liberation and Culture." The Program of East African Studies, Occasional Paper No. 57. Syracuse: Maxwell Graduate School of Citizenship and Public Affairs, Syracuse University. (Republished in Cabral 1979, 138–54.)

———. 1979. *Unity and Struggle.* New York: Monthly Review Press.

Castoriadis, Cornelius. 1991. "Intellectuals and History." In *Philosophy, Politics, Autonomy,* ed. David Ames Curtis. New York: Oxford University Press.

Césaire, Aimé. 1972. *Discourse on Colonialism.* Trans. Joan Pinkham. New York: Monthly Review Press.

Clark-Bekederemo, J. P. 1991. *The Ozidi Saga: Collected and Translated from the Ijo of Okabou Ojobolo.* Ibadan, Nigeria: Ibadan University Press.

Coetzee, P. H., and A. P. J. Roux, eds. 1998. *The African Philosophy Reader.* New York: Routledge. (2nd ed., 2003, New York: Routledge).

Concise Oxford Dictionary. 1964. Oxford: Clarendon.

DePaul, Michael R., and William Ramsey. 1999. *Rethinking Intuition.* New York: Rowman and Littlefield.

Diagne, Souleymane. 2004a. "Precolonial African Philosophy in Arabic." In *A Companion to African Philosophy,* ed. Kwasi Wiredu, 66–77. Malden, Mass.: Blackwell.

———. 2004b. "Islam in Africa: Examining the Notion of an African Identity within the Islamic World." In *A Companion to African Philosophy,* ed. Kwasi Wiredu, 374–83. Malden, Mass.: Blackwell.

Diagne, Souleymane, and Heinz Kimmerle, eds. 1998. *Time and Development in the Thought of Subsaharan Africa.* Amsterdam: Rodopi.

Diagne, Souleymane, and Henri Ossebi. 1996. *The Cultural Question in Africa.* Dakar, Senegal: CODESRIA.

Diop, Cheikh Anta. 1974. *The African Origin of Civilization: Myth or Reality.* Ed. and trans. Mercer Cook. Westport, Conn.: Lawrence Hill; Paris: Presence Africaine.

———. 1978. *Black Africa: The Economic and Cultural Basis for a Federated State.* Westport, Conn.: Lawrence Hill.

———. 1987. *Precolonial Black Africa: A Comparative Study of the Political and Social Systems of Europe and Black Africa, from Antiquity to the Formation of Modern States.* Westport, Conn.: Lawrence Hill.

———. 1989. *The Cultural Unity of Black Africa: The Domains of Matriarchy and Patriarchy in Classical Antiquity.* London: Karnak House.

———. 1991. *Civilization or Barbarism: An Authentic Anthropology.* New York: Lawrence Hill Books.

Emmet, Dorothy. 1972. "Haunted Universes." *Second Order* 1, no. 1: 34–42.

English, P., and K. M. Kalumba, eds. 1996. *African Philosophy: A Classical Approach*. Englewood Cliffs, N.J.: Prentice Hall.

Evans-Pritchard, E. E. 1937. *Witchcraft, Oracles and Magic among the Azande*. London: Oxford University Press.

Eze, Emmanuel. 1997a. "The Color of Reason: The Idea of 'Race' in Kant's Anthropology." In *Postcolonial African Philosophy: A Critical Reader,* ed. E. Eze, 103–40. Oxford: Blackwell.

———. 1997b. "Democracy or Consensus? A Response to Wiredu." In *Postcolonial African Philosophy: A Critical Reader,* ed. E. Eze, 313–23. Oxford: Blackwell.

———, ed. 1997c. *Postcolonial African Philosophy: A Critical Reader.* Cambridge, Mass.: Blackwell.

———, ed. 1997d. *Race and the Enlightenment: A Reader.* New York: Wiley-Blackwell.

———, ed. 1998. *African Philosophy: An Anthology.* Malden, Mass.: Blackwell.

———. 2001. *Achieving Our Humanity: The Idea of the Postracial Future.* New York: Routledge.

———. 2008a. *Of Reason: Rationality for a World of Cultural Conflict and Racism.* Durham, N.C.: Duke University Press.

———. 2008b. *Postcolonial Social Theory, Religion, and Philosophy.* New York: Palgrave Macmillan.

Fanon, Frantz. 1967a. *Black Skin, White Masks.* New York: Grove.

———. 1967b. *The Wretched of the Earth.* Harmondsworth, UK: Penguin.

———. 1988. *Toward the African Revolution.* New York: Grove.

———. 1989. *Studies in a Dying Colonialism.* London: Earthscan.

Fashina, Oladipo. 1981. "Mythical Consciousness: Neo-Kantian or Quasi-Realist?" *Second Order* 10, nos. 1–2: 31–45.

———. 1988. "Marx, Moral Criticism, and Political Choice." *Philosophical Forum* 19, no. 4: 291–308.

———. 1989. "Frantz Fanon and the Ethical Justification of Anti-Colonial Violence." *Social Theory and Practice* 15, no. 2: 179–212.

Fasiku, Gbenga. 2008. "African Philosophy and the Method of Ordinary Language." *Journal of Pan African Studies* 2, no. 3 (Mar.): 100–116.

Feldman, Richard. 2003. *Epistemology.* Upper Saddle River, N.J.: Prentice Hall.

Forde, Daryll, ed. 1954. *African Worlds: Studies in the Cosmological Ideas and Social Values of African Peoples.* London: International African Institute and Oxford University Press.

Freire, Paulo. 1983. *Pedagogy of the Oppressed.* New York: Continuum.

Friedland, W. H., and C. G. Rosberg. 1964. *African Socialism.* Stanford, Calif.: Stanford University Press.

Gadamer, Hans-Georg. 1975. *Truth and Method.* Trans. W. Glen-Doepel. London: Sheed and Ward.

Garvey, Marcus. 1986. *Message to the People: The Course of African Philosophy.* Dover, Mass.: Majority.

Gbadegesin,'Segun. 1981. "Ethnicity and Citizenship." *Second Order* 10, nos. 1– 2: 3–12.

———. 1984. "Destiny, Personality and the Ultimate Reality of Human Existence: A Yoruba Perspective." *Ultimate Reality and Meaning* 7, no. 3: 173–88.

———. 1987. "God, Destiny and Social Injustice: A Critique of Yoruba Ifa Belief." *The Search for Faith and Justice in the Twentieth Century,* ed. Gene James, 52–68. New York: Paragon.

———. 1991a. *African Philosophy: Traditional Yoruba Philosophy and Contemporary African Realities.* New York: Peter Lang.

———. 1991b. "Negritude and Its Contribution to the Civilization of the Universal: Leopold Senghor and the Question of Ultimate Reality and Meaning." *Ultimate Reality and Meaning* 14, no. 1: 30–45.

———. 2004. "Toward a Theory of Destiny." In *A Companion to African Philosophy,* ed. Kwasi Wiredu, 313–23. Malden, Mass.: Blackwell.

———. 2005. "Origins of African Ethics." In *A Companion to Religious Ethics,* ed. W. Schweiker, 413–422. Malden, Mass.: Blackwell.

Gettier, Edmund L. 1963. "Is Justified True Belief Knowledge?" *Analysis* 23: 121–23.

Goody, Jack, comp. 1972. *The Myth of the Bagre.* Oxford: Clarendon.

Gordon, Lewis. 1997a. "Tragic Dimensions of Our Neocolonial 'Postcolonial' World." In *Postcolonial African Philosophy: A Critical Reader,* ed. Emmanuel Eze, 241–51. Oxford: Blackwell.

———. 1997b. *Her Majesty's Other Children: Sketches of Racism from a Neocolonial Age.* New York: Rowman and Littlefield.

———, ed. 1997c. *Existence in Black: An Anthology of Black Existential Philosophy.* New York: Routledge.

———. 2000. *Existentia Africana: Understanding Africana Existential Thought.* New York: Routledge.

———. 2008. *An Introduction to Africana Philosophy.* Cambridge: Cambridge University Press.

Griaule, Marcel. 1965. *Conversations with Ogotemmeli.* Oxford: Oxford University Press.

Graness, Anke, and Kai Kresse, eds. 1997. *Sagacious Reasoning: Henry Odera Oruka in Memoriam.* Frankfurt am Main: Peter Lang.

Gunn, Battiscombe. 1909. *The Instruction of Ptah-hotep and the Instruction of Ke'gemni: The Oldest Books in the World.* New York: Dutton. (Reprint, Kila, Mont.: Kessinger, 1999.)

Gyekye, Kwame. 1974. "Substance in Aristotle's *Categories* and *Metaphysics.*" *Second Order* 3, no. 1: 61–65.

——. 1975a. "Review of John Mbiti's *African Religions and Philosophy.*" *Second Order* 4, no. 1: 86–94.

——. 1975b. "Philosophical Relevance of Akan Proverbs." *Second Order* 4, no. 2: 45–53.

——. 1977. "Akan Language and the Materialist Thesis: A Short Essay on the Relation between Philosophy and Language." *Studies in Language* 1, no. 2: 227–34.

——. 1978. "The Akan Concept of a Person." *International Philosophical Quarterly* 18, no. 3: 277–87. (Reprinted in *African Philosophy: An Introduction,* 3rd ed., ed. Richard Wright. Lanham, Md.: University Press of America, 1984.)

——. 1981. "Philosophical Ideas of the Akans." *Second Order* 10, nos. 1–2: 61–79.

——. 1988. *The Unexamined Life: Philosophy and the African Experience.* Accra: Ghana Universities Press.

——. 1992. "Person and Community in Akan Thought." In *Person and Community,* ed. Kwasi Wiredu and Kwame Gyekye, 101–22. Washington, D.C.: Council for Research in Values and Philosophy.

——. 1995. *An Essay on African Philosophical Thought: The Akan Conceptual Scheme.* Rev. ed. Cambridge: Cambridge University Press.

——. 1996. *African Cultural Values: An Introduction.* Philadelphia and Accra, Ghana: Sankofa.

——. 1997a. *Tradition and Modernity: Philosophical Reflections on the African Experience.* New York: Oxford University Press.

——. 1997b. "Philosophy, Culture, and Technology in the Postcolonial." In *Postcolonial African Philosophy: A Critical Reader,* ed. Emmanuel Eze, 25–44. Oxford: Blackwell.

——. 2003. *Beyond Cultures: Perceiving a Common Humanity.* Accra, Ghana: Ghana Academy of Arts and Sciences.

Hallen, Barry. 1975. "A Philosopher's Approach to Traditional Culture." *Theoria to Theory* 9, no. 4: 259–72.

——. 1977. "Robin Horton on Critical Philosophy and Traditional Thought." *Second Order* 6, no. 1: 81–92. (Revised and republished as Hallen 1996a.)

——. 1979. "The [African] Art Historian as Conceptual Analyst." *Journal of Aesthetics and Art Criticism* 37, no. 3: 303–13.

——. 1981. "The Open Texture of Oral Tradition." *Theoria to Theory* 9, no. 4: 259–72.

——. 1988. "Afro-Brazilian Mosques in West Africa." *Mimar* 29: 16–23.

——. 1995a. "Some Observations about Philosophy, Postmodernism, and Art in African Studies." *African Studies Review* 38, no. 1: 69–80.

——. 1995b. "Indeterminacy, Ethnophilosophy, Linguistic Philosophy, African Philosophy." *Philosophy* 70, no. 273: 377–93.

——. 1995c. "'My Mercedes Has Four Legs!' 'Traditional' as an Attribute of

African Equestrian 'Culture.'" In *Horsemen of Africa: History, Iconography, Symbolism,* ed. Gigi Pezzoli, 49–64. Milan: Centro Studi Archeologia Africana.

———. 1996a. "Analytic Philosophy and Traditional Thought: A Critique of Robin Horton." In *African Philosophy: A Classical Approach,* ed. P. English and K. M. Kalumba, 216–28. Englewood Cliffs, N.J.: Prentice Hall.

———. 1996b. "Does It Matter Whether Linguistic Philosophy Intersects Ethnophilosophy?" *APA Newsletter on International Cooperation* 96, no. 1: 136–40.

———. 1996c. "What's It Mean? 'Analytic' African Philosophy." *Quest: Philosophical Discussions* 10, no. 2: 67–77.

———. 1997. "African Meanings, Western Words." *African Studies Review* 40, no. 1: 1–11.

———. 1998a. "Moral Epistemology: When Propositions Come Out of Mouths." *International Philosophical Quarterly* 38, no. 2: 187–204.

———. 1998b. "Academic Philosophy and African Intellectual Liberation." *African Philosophy* 11, no. 2: 93–97.

———. 2000a. "Variations on a Theme: Ritual, Performance, Intellect." In *Insight and Artistry: A Cross-Cultural Study of Art and Divination in Central and West Africa,* ed. John Pemberton, 168–74. Washington, D.C.: Smithsonian Institution Press.

———. 2000b. *The Good, the Bad, and the Beautiful: Discourse about Values in Yoruba Culture.* Bloomington: Indiana University Press.

———. 2001. "'Witches' as Superior Intellects: Challenging a Cross-Cultural Superstition." In *Dialogues of Witchcraft: Anthropology, Philosophy, and the Possibilities of Discovery,* ed. Diane Ciekawy and George C. Bond, 80–100. Athens: Ohio University Press.

———. 2002. "Modes of Thought, Ordinary Language, and Cognitive Diversity." In *Perspectives in African Philosophy,* ed. Claude Sumner and Samuel Wolde Yohannes, 214–22. Addis Ababa: Addis Ababa University Press.

———. 2003. "Not a House Divided." *Journal on African Philosophy* 2: 1–15. www.africanphilosophy.com/issue2/hallen.html.

———. 2004a. "Yoruba Moral Epistemology." In *A Companion to African Philosophy,* ed. Kwasi Wiredu, 296–303. Malden, Mass.: Blackwell.

———. 2004b. "Contemporary Anglophone African Philosophy: A Survey." In *A Companion to African Philosophy,* ed. Kwasi Wiredu, 99–148. Malden, Mass.: Blackwell.

———. 2004c. "Cosmology: African Cosmologies." In *Encyclopedia of Religion,* 2nd ed., ed. Lindsay Jones. New York: MacMillan Reference.

———. 2005a. "African Ethics." In *A Companion to Religious Ethics,* ed. W. Schweiker, 406–12. Malden, Mass.: Blackwell.

———. 2005b. "Heidegger, Hermeneutics and African Philosophy." *Africa e Mediterraneo* 53 (Dec.): 46–53.

———. 2006. *African Philosophy: The Analytic Approach.* Trenton, N.J.: Africa World Press.

———. 2008. "Yoruba Moral Epistemology as the Basis for a Cross-Cultural Ethics." In *Orisa Devotion as World Religion: Global Yoruba Religious Culture,* ed. Jacob K. Olupona and Terry Rey, 222–29. Madison: University of Wisconsin Press.

Hallen, Barry, and J. Olubi Sodipo. 1994. "The House of the '*Inu*': Keys to the Structure of a Yoruba Theory of the 'Self.'" *Quest: Philosophical Discussions* 8, no. 1: 3–23.

———. 1997. *Knowledge, Belief, and Witchcraft: Analytic Experiments in African Philosophy.* Rev. ed. Stanford, Calif.: Stanford University Press.

Hamminga, Bert, ed. 2005. *Knowledge Cultures: Comparative Western and African Epistemology.* Amsterdam: Rodopi.

Harding, Sandra. 1998. *Is Science Multicultural? Postcolonialisms, Feminisms, and Epistemologies.* Bloomington: Indiana University Press.

———. 2006. *Science and Social Inequality: Feminist and Postcolonial Issues.* Champaign: University of Illinois Press.

———. 2008. *Sciences from Below: Feminisms, Postcolonialisms, and Modernities.* Durham, N.C.: Duke University Press.

Harding, Sandra, and Uma Narayan, eds. 2000. *Science and Other Cultures: Issues in Philosophies of Science and Technology.* Bloomington: Indiana University Press.

Harris, Leonard, ed. 1983. *Philosophy Born of Struggle: Afro-American Philosophy since 1917.* Dubuque, Iowa: Kendall/Hunt.

Heidegger, Martin. 1962. *Being and Time.* Trans. John Macquarrie and Edward Robinson. New York: Harper and Row.

Henry, Paget. 2000. *Caliban's Reason: Introducing Afro-Caribbean Philosophy.* New York: Routledge.

———. 2002. "Culture, Politics and Writing in Afro-Caribbean Philosophy: A Reply to Critics." *Small Axe: A Caribbean Journal of Criticism* 11 (March): 179–90.

———. 2004. "Between Hume and Cugoano: Race Ethnicity and Philosophical Entrapment." *Journal of Speculative Philosophy* 18, no. 2: 129–48.

Hilliard, Asa G., III, Larry Williams, and Nia Damali, eds. 1987. *The Teachings of Ptahhotep: The Oldest Book in the World.* Atlanta, Ga.: Blackwood.

Hord, Fred Lee (Mzee Lasana Okpara), and Jonathan Scott Lee, eds. 1995. *I Am Because We Are: Readings in Black Philosophy.* Amherst: University of Massachusetts Press.

Horton, Robin. 1960. "A Definition of Religion and Its Uses." *Journal of the Royal Anthropological Institute* 90: 201–26. (Reprinted in Horton 1993, 19–49.)

———. 1961. "Destiny and the Unconscious in West Africa." *Africa* 31, no. 2: 110–17.

————. 1967. "African Traditional Thought and Western Science." *Africa* 37, nos. 1–2: 50–71 and 155–187. (Reprinted in Horton 1993, 197–258.)

————. 1973. "Paradox and Explanation: A Reply to Mr. Skorupski, Parts I & II." *Philosophy of the Social Sciences* 3, nos. 3–4: 231–56 and 289–312. (Reprinted in Horton 1993, 259–300.)

————. 1976. "Professor Winch on Safari." *European Journal of Sociology* 17, no. 1: 157–80. (Reprinted in Horton 1993, 138–60.)

————. 1982. "Tradition and Modernity Revisited." In *Rationality and Relativism,* ed. M. Hollis and S. Lukes, 201–60. Oxford: Blackwell. (Reprinted in Horton 1993, 301–56.)

————. 1983. "Social Psychologies: African and Western." An essay accompanying Meyer Fortes, *Oedipus and Job in West African Religion,* 41–82. Cambridge: Cambridge University Press.

————. 1984. "Judaeo-Christian Spectacles: Boon or Bane to the Study of African Religions?" *Cahiers d'études africaines* 96/24: 391–436.

————. 1993. *Patterns of Thought in Africa and the West: Essays on Magic, Religion and Science.* Cambridge: Cambridge University Press. (The new 15-page introduction and 41-page postscript to this volume are of special interest for Horton's more recent reflections on these subjects.)

————. 1995. *Play and Display: Steel Masquerades from Top to Toe: Sculpture by Sokari Douglas Camp.* London: Museum of Mankind.

————. n.d. "Traditional Thought and the Emerging African Philosophy Department: A Reply to Dr. Hallen." Unpublished manuscript.

Horton, Robin, and Ruth Finnegan, eds. 1973. *Modes of Thought.* London: Faber and Faber.

Hountondji, Paulin. 1967. "Charabia et mauvaise conscience: Psychologie du langage chez les intellectuels colonisés." *Présence Africaine* 61: 11–31.

————. 1970a. "Un philosophe africain dans l'Allemagne du XVIIIe siècle: Antoine Guillaume Amo." *Les études philosophiques* 1: 25–46.

————. 1970b. "Sagesse africaine et philosophie moderne." In *African Humanism—Scandinavian Culture: A Dialogue,* ed. Torben Lundback, 187–97. Copenhagen: DANIDA.

————. 1970c. "Remarques sur la philosophie africaine contemporaine." *Diogene* 71: 120–40.

————. 1971. "Le problème actuel de la philosophie africaine." In *Contemporary Philosophy: A Survey—La philosophie contemporaine: Chroniques VI,* ed. Raymond Klibansky, 613–21. Florence: La Nuova Italia.

————. 1972. "Le mythe de la philosophie spontanée." *Cahiers philosophiques africains* 1: 107–42. (Reprinted as "The Myth of Spontaneous Philosophy," *Consequence* 1 [Jan.–June]: 11–38, 1974.)

————. 1973. "La philosophie et ses révolutions." *Cahiers philosophiques africains* 3–4: 27–40.

————. 1974a. "African Philosophy: Myth and Reality." *Thought and Practice* 1, no. 2: 1–16.

———. 1974b. "Histoire d'un mythe." *Présence Africaine* 91: 3–13.

———. 1975. "De Lenine à Descartes: Le personnage du fou et l'argument du rêve." *Annales du DELLSH* 1: 142–53.

———. 1978. "Recherche théorique africaine et contrat de solidarité." *Travail et Société* 3, nos. 3–4: 353–64.

———. 1980. "Sens du mot 'philosophie' dans l'expression 'philosophie africaine.'" In *African Philosophy—La philosophie africaine*, ed. Claude Sumner, 81–92. Addis Ababa: Chamber Printing House.

———. 1981. "Que peut la philosophie?" *Presence Africaine* 119: 47–71.

———. 1982a. "Occidentalisme, élitisme: réponse à deux critiques." *Recherche, pédagogie et culture* 56: 58–67.

———. 1982b. "Langues africaines et philosophie: L'hypothèse relativiste." *Les études philosophiques* 4: 393–406.

———. 1984a. "Aspects and Problems of Philosophy in Africa." In *Teaching and Research in Philosophy: Africa,* 11–20. Paris: UNESCO.

———. 1984b. "Convergences." In *Teaching and Research in Philosophy: Africa,* 271–84. Paris: UNESCO.

———. 1984c. "La culture scientifique dans les pays de la périphérie." *Culture pour tous les temps,* 65–78. Paris: UNESCO.

———. 1985. "The Pitfalls of Being Different." *Diogenes* 131 (Fall): 46–56.

———. 1987a. "Le particulier et l'universel." *Bulletin de la société française de philosophie* 81, no. 4: 145–89.

———. 1987b. "On the 'Universality' of Science and Technology." *Technik und sozialer Wandel: Verhandlungen des 23. Deutschen Soziologentages in Hamburg 1986,* ed. Burkart Lutz, 382–89. New York: Campus.

———. 1988a. "L'appropriation collective du savoir: Tâches nouvelles pour une politique scientifique." *Genève-Afrique* 26, no. 1: 49–61.

———. 1988b. "Situation de l'anthropologue africain: Note critique sur une forme d'extraversion critique." In *Les nouveaux enjeux de l'anthropologie: Autour de Georges Balandier,* ed. Gabriel Gossin. *Revue de l'Institut de sociologie* 3–4: 99–108.

———. 1990a. "Scientific Dependence in Africa Today." *Research in African Literatures* 21, no. 3: 5–15.

———. 1990b. "Pour une sociologie des représentations collectives." In *La pensée métisse: Croyance africaine et rationalité occidentale en question,* ed. Robin Horton et al., 187–92. Paris: PUF.

———. 1992. "Recapturing." In *The Surreptitious Speech: Présence Africaine and the Politics of Otherness,* ed. V. Y. Mudimbe, 238–48. Chicago: University of Chicago Press.

———. 1995. "Producing Knowledge in Africa Today." *African Studies Review* 38, no. 3: 1–10.

———. 1996a. *African Philosophy: Myth and Reality.* Rev. ed. Bloomington: Indiana University Press.

————. 1996b. "Intellectual Responsibility: Implications for Thought and Action Today." *Proceedings and Addresses of the American Philosophical Association* 70, no. 2: 77–92.

————. 1997a. "Introduction: Recentering Africa." In *Endogenous Knowledge: Research Trails,* ed. Paulin J. Hountondji, 1–39. Dakar: CODESRIA.

————. 1997b. "From the Ethnosciences to Ethnophilosophy: Kwame Nkrumah's Thesis Project." *Research in African Literatures* 28, no. 4 (Winter): 112–20.

————. 2002. *The Struggle for Meaning: Reflections on Philosophy, Culture, and Democracy in Africa.* Athens: Ohio University Center for International Studies.

Husserl, Edmund. 1980. *Ideas Pertaining to a Pure Phenomenology and to a Phenomenological Philosophy,* trans. F. Kersten. The Hague: Nijhoff.

Ierodiakonou, K., ed. 2004. *Byzantine Philosophy and Its Ancient Sources.* New York: Oxford University Press.

Ikuenobe, Polycarp. 2006. *Philosophical Perspectives on Communalism and Morality in African Traditions.* New York: Lexington Books.

Imbo, Samuel Oluoch. 1998. *An Introduction to African Philosophy.* New York: Rowman and Littlefield.

————. 2002. *Oral Traditions as Philosophy: Okot p'Bitek's Legacy for African Philosophy.* New York: Rowman and Littlefield.

Irele, F. Abiola. 2004. "Philosophy and the Postcolonial Condition in Africa." *Research in African Literatures* 35, no. 4 (Winter): 160–70.

Jahn, Janheinz. 1961. *Muntu: An Outline of the New African Culture.* New York: Grove.

James, C. L. R. 1995. *A History of Pan-African Revolt.* Chicago: Charles H. Kerr.

James, George G. M. 1954. *Stolen Legacy: Greek Philosophy Is Stolen Egyptian Philosophy.* New York: Philosophical Library.

Kagame, Alexis. 1956. *La Philosophie Bantou-Rwandaise de l'être.* 8 vols. Brussels: Académie Royale des Sciences Coloniales, n.s. 12, no. 1.

Kalumba, Kibujjo M. 2004. "Sage Philosophy: Its Methodology, Results, Significance, and Future." In *A Companion to African Philosophy,* ed. Kwasi Wiredu, 274–81.

Karp, I., and D. A. Masolo, eds. 2000. *African Philosophy as Cultural Inquiry.* Bloomington: Indiana University Press in association with the International African Institute, London.

Kebede, Messay. 2004. *Africa's Quest for a Philosophy of Decolonization.* Amsterdam: Rodopi.

Kincaid, Jamaica. 1997. *Autobiography of My Mother.* New York: Plume.

Kiros, Teodros. 2004. "Zera Yacob and Traditional Ethiopian Philosophy." In *A Companion to African Philosophy,* ed. Kwasi Wiredu, 183–90.

Kresse, Kai. 2007. *Philosophising in Mombasa: Knowledge, Islam and*

Intellectual Practice on the Swahili Coast. Edinburgh: Edinburgh University Press.

Kuper, Adam. 1988. *The Invention of Primitive Society.* London: Routledge.

——. 1999. *Culture: The Anthropologists' Account.* Cambridge, Mass.: Harvard University Press.

Lefkowitz, Mary. 1996. *Not Out of Africa: How Afrocentrism Became an Excuse To Teach Myth as History.* New York: Basic Books.

Lefkowitz, Mary, and Guy MacLean Rogers, eds. 1996. *Black Athena Revisited.* Chapel Hill: University of North Carolina Press.

Legesse, Asmarom. 1973. *Gada: Three Approaches to the Study of African Society.* New York: Free Press.

Lehman, Cynthia. 1997. "SDM MDW PN M WRT MAAT: A Classical Kemetic Foundation for the Study of African Oratory." Ph.D. diss., Temple University.

Lloyd, Barbara, and John Gay, eds. 1981. *Universals of Human Thought: Some African Evidence.* Cambridge: Cambridge University Press.

Lott, Tommy. 2003. "African Retentions." In *A Companion to African-American Philosophy,* ed. Tommy Lott and John Pittman, 168–89. Malden, Mass.: Blackwell.

Machel, Samora. 1981. *Mozambique: Sowing the Seeds of Revolution.* Harare: Zimbabwe Publishing House.

Makinde, M. Akin. 1977. "Formal Logic and the Paradox of Excluded Middle." *International Logic Review,* no. 15: 40–52.

——. 1984. "An African Concept of Human Personality: The Yoruba Example." *Ultimate Reality and Meaning* 7, no. 3: 189–200.

——. 1985. "A Philosophical Analysis of the Yoruba Concepts of *Ori* and Human Destiny." *International Studies in Philosophy* 17, no. 1: 53–69.

——. 1988a. *African Philosophy, Culture, and Traditional Medicine.* Athens: Ohio University Center for International Studies.

——. 1988b. "African Culture and Moral Systems: A Philosophical Study." *Second Order* 1, no. 2: 1–27.

——. 2002. *Awo as Philosopher.* Ile-Ife, Nigeria: Obafemi Awolowo University Press.

——. 2007. *African Philosophy: The Demise of a Controversy.* Ile-Ife, Nigeria: Obafemi Awolowo University Press.

Mamdani, M. 1996. *Citizen and Subject: Contemporary Africa and the Legacy of Colonialism.* Princeton, N.J.: Princeton University Press.

Mamdani, M., and E. Wamba-dia-Wamba, eds. 1995. *African Studies in Social Movements and Democracy.* Dakar: CODESRIA.

Marx, Karl. 1974 [1867]. *Capital: A Critical Analysis of Capitalist Production,* vol. 1, ed. Frederick Engels. New York: International.

Masolo, D. A. 1980. "Some Aspects and Prospective of African Philosophy Today: Part One." *Africa* 35, nos. 3–4: 414–48.

————. 1981. "Some Aspects and Prospective of African Philosophy Today: Part Two." *Africa* 36, no. 1: 67–88.

————. 1983a. "Political Ideology and Dogmatism." In *The Roots of Dogmatism: Proceedings of the Fourth International Philosophy Conference, 23-26 October 1982,* ed. M. Wahba, 253–68. Cairo: Anglo-Egyptian Bookshop, 1984.

————. 1983b. "Philosophy and Culture: A Critique." In *Philosophy and Cultures,* ed. D. A. Masolo and H. Odera-Oruka, 44–51. Nairobi, Kenya: Bookwise.

————. 1983c. "Alexis Kagame (1912–1981) and 'La philosophie bantu-rwandaise de l'être.'" *Africa* 38, no. 3 (Sept.): 449–54.

————. 1984. "Science in Our Lives: Being or Having as Aim of Development." *Philosophie Africaine et Développement,* Recherches Philosophiques Africaines, no. 9 (Kinshasa): 205–12.

————. 1986a. "Kwame Nkrumah: Socialism for Liberation." *Praxis International* 6, no. 2: 175–89.

————. 1986b. "Methods in Philosophy and African Philosophy." *Problèmes des méthodes en philosophie et sciences humaines en Afrique,* Recherches Philosophiques, no. 9 (Kinshasa): 17–22.

————. 1987a. "Kagame and African Socio-Linguistics." In *Contemporary Philosophy.* Vol. 5, ed. G. Floistad, 181–205. The Hague: M. Nijhoff.

————. 1987b. "Ideological Dogmatism and the Values of Democracy." In *Democratic Theory and Practice in Africa,* ed. W. Oyugi and A. Gitonga, 24–41. Nairobi, Kenya: Heinemann.

————. 1991. "An Archeology of African Knowledge: A Discussion on V. Y. Mudimbe." *Callaloo: A Journal of African-American and African Arts and Letters* 14, no. 4.

————. 1992a. "History and the Modernization of African Philosophy: A Reading of Kwasi Wiredu." In *Postkoloniales Philosophieren: Afrika,* ed. H. Nagl-Docekal and F. M. Wimmer. Vienna: R. Oldenbourg Verlag.

————. 1992b. "Narratives and Moral Perspectives: Conversations with Luo Sages." *SAPINA Bulletin* (Bulletin of the Society for African Philosophy in North America) 4, nos. 2–3 (July–Dec.): 1–9.

————. 1994. *African Philosophy in Search of Identity.* Bloomington: Indiana University Press.

————. 1995. "Rolling Between Realism and Relativism: Ethical Perspectives in Cross-cultural Communication." In *The Conditions of Reciprocal Understanding: Selected Papers and Comments,* ed. James Fernandez and Milton B. Singer, 395–420. Chicago: University of Chicago Press.

————. 1996. "Tradition, Communication and Difference: Coming of Age in African Philosophy." *Research in African Literatures* 27, no. 1 (Spring): 149–54.

————. 1997a. "African Philosophy and the Postcolonial: Some Misleading

Abstractions about 'Identity.'" In *Postcolonial African Philosophy: A Critical Reader,* ed. Emmanuel Eze, 283–300. Oxford: Blackwell.

———. 1997b. "African Philosophy: A Historical Overview." In *A Companion to World Philosophies,* ed. Eliot Deutsch and Ron Bontekoe, 63–77. London: Blackwell.

———. 1997c. "Decentering the Academy: In Memory of a Friend." In *Sagacious Reasoning: Henry Odera Oruka in Memoriam,* ed. Anke Graness and Kai Kresse, 233–40. Frankfurt am Main: Peter Lang.

———. 1999a. "Rethinking Communities in a Global Context." *African Philosophy* 12, no. 1: 51–68.

———. 1999b. "Critical Rationalism and Cultural Traditions in African Philosophy." *New Political Science* 21, no. 1: 59–72. (Reprinted in *Identity, Community, Ethics,* ed. T. Kiros, 81–95. New York: Routledge, 2001.)

———. 2000a. "From Myth to Reality: African Philosophy at Century-End." *Research in African Literatures* 31, no. 1: 149–72.

———. 2000b. "Presencing the Past and Remembering the Present: Social Features of Popular Music in Kenya." In *Music and the Racial Imagination,* ed. Philip Bohlman and Ronald Radano, 349–402. Chicago: University of Chicago Press.

———. 2002a. "From Village to Global Contexts: Ideas, Types, and the Making of Communities." In *Diversity and Community: An Interdisciplinary Reader,* ed. Philip Alperson, 88–115. New York: Blackwell.

———. 2002b. "Rethinking Communities in a Global Context." In *Philosophy from Africa: A Text with Readings,* 2nd ed., ed. P. H. Coetzee and A. P. J. Roux, 558–73. Cape Town: Oxford University Press.

———. 2003. "Philosophy and Indigenous Knowledge: An African Perspective." *Africa Today* 50, no. 2 (Fall–Winter): 21–38.

———. 2004a. "African Philosophers in the Greco-Roman Era." In *A Companion to African Philosophy,* ed. Kwasi Wiredu, 50–65. Malden, Mass.: Blackwell.

———. 2004b. "Western and African Communitarianism: A Comparison." In *A Companion to African Philosophy,* ed. Kwasi Wiredu, 483–98. Malden, Mass.: Blackwell.

———. 2004c. "The Concept of Person in *Luo* Modes of Thought." In *African Philosophy: New and Traditional Perspectives,* ed. Lee M. Brown, 84–106. Oxford: Oxford University Press.

———. 2004d. "Reason and Culture: Debating the Foundations of Morals in a Pluralist World." *Diogenes* 202: 19–31. (Reprinted in *The Encounter of Rationalities,* ed. Paulin Hountondji. London: Sage, 2004.)

———. 2005. "Lessons from African Sage Philosophy." *Africa e Mediterraneo* 53 (Dec.): 46–53.

———. 2007. "Reason and Culture: Debating the Foundations of Morals in a Pluralist World." In *La rationalité, une ou plurielle?* ed. Paulin Hountondji, 220–34. Dakar, Senegal: CODESRIA/UNESCO.

Masolo, D. A., and H. Odera-Oruka, eds. 1983. *Philosophy and Cultures.* Nairobi, Kenya: Bookwise.

Mbiti, John S. 1970a. *African Religions and Philosophy.* New York: Doubleday.

———. 1970b. *Concepts of God in Africa.* New York: Praeger.

Memmi, Albert. 1965. *The Colonizer and the Colonized.* Boston: Beacon.

———. 2000. *Racism.* Minneapolis: University of Minnesota Press.

Momoh, Campbell S. 1985. "African Philosophy . . . Does It Exist?" *Diogenes* 130: 73–104.

———. 2000. *The Substance of African Philosophy,* 2nd ed. Auchi, Nigeria: African Philosophy Projects' Publication.

Mondlane, Eduardo. 1969. *The Struggle for Mozambique.* Baltimore: Penguin Books.

More, Mabogo. 1996. "African Philosophy Revisited." *Alternation* 3, no. 1: 109–29.

———. 2004a. "Philosophy in South Africa under and after Apartheid." In *A Companion to African Philosophy,* ed. Kwasi Wiredu, 149–60. Malden, Mass.: Blackwell.

———. 2004b. "Albert Lithuli, Steve Biko, and Nelson Mandela: The Philosophical Basis of Their Thought and Practice." In *A Companion to African Philosophy,* ed. Kwasi Wiredu, 207–15. Malden, Mass.: Blackwell.

Mosley, Albert G., ed. 1995. *African Philosophy: Selected Readings.* Englewood Cliffs, N.J.: Prentice Hall.

———. 2003. "African Philosophy at the Turn of the Century." In *A Companion to African-American Philosophy,* ed. Tommy Lott and John Pittman, 190–96. Malden, Mass.: Blackwell.

Mudimbe, V. Y. 1967a. "Chronique sur le Marxisme et la religion." *Congo-Afrique* 16: 292–306.

———. 1967b. "Physiologie de la Négritude." *Études Congolaises* 10, no. 5: 1–13.

———. 1968a. "Héritage occidental et conscience nègre." *Congo-Afrique* 8, no. 26: 283–94.

———. 1968b. "Structuralisme, événement, notion, variations et les sciences humaines en Afrique." *Les Cahiers Économiques et Sociaux* 6, no. 1: 3–70.

———. 1970a. "Négritude et politique." *Hommages d'Hommes de Culture,* 276–83. Paris: Présence Africaine.

———. 1970b. "Matérialisme historique et histoire immédiate." *Cahiers Économiques et Sociaux* 8, no. 3: 176–283.

———. 1971. *Initiation au français.* Kinshasa: Celta.

———. 1972a. *Autour de la nation.* Kinshasa: Éditions de Mont Noir.

———. 1972b. *Réflexions sur la vie quotidienne.* Kinshasa: Éditions de Mont Noir.

———. 1973a. *L'Autre face de royaume: Une Introduction à la critique des langages en folie.* Lausanne: L'Age d'homme.

———. 1973b. "Pour une sociologie non-coloniale." *Genève-Afrique* 11, no. 2.

———. 1973c. "Héritage occidental et critique des évidences." *Zaire-Afrique:* 89–99.

———. 1974. "La Sorcellerie comme langage et comme théorie." *Cahiers des Religions Africaines* 8, no. 16: 165–279.

———. 1975. "Interdisciplinarité." *Les Cahiers du Cride.* Kisangani.

———. 1977a. "De la Satire comme témoin historique. Réflexions à propos de l'Apocolonquitose du Divin Claude de Senèque." In *Mélanges offerts à L. S. Senghor,* 315–23. Dakar, Abidjan, Paris: Nouvelles Éditions Africaines.

———. 1977b. "Des Philosophes en mal de développement." *Zaire-Afrique* (May).

———. 1978a. "Les Problèmes de collaboration entre les langues Européennes et les langues africaines en Afrique noire." *Recherche Linguistiques* 1.

———. 1978b. "Le pouvoir politique occidental dans les structures de l'Église en Afrique." In *Civilisation Noire et Église Catholique,* 67–87. Paris: Présence Africaine.

———. 1978c. "Niam M'Paya: Aux Sources de la philosophie Africaine." In *Mélanges Alioune Diop,* 192–201. Paris: Présence Africaine.

———. 1979. *Air: étude semantique.* Vienna: Acta Ethnologica et Linguistica.

———. 1981. *Visage de la Philosophie et de la Théologie Contemporaines au Zaire.* Brussels: CEDAF, Cahiers du CEDAF 1.

———. 1982a. "In Memoriam: l'Abbe Alexis Kagame." *Recherche, Pédagogie et Culture* 56, no. 9: 74–78.

———. 1982b. "Panorama de la pensée africaine contemporaine de langue Française." *Recherche, pédagogie et Culture.*

———. 1982c. *L'Odeur du père: Philosophical essay.* Paris: Présence Africaine.

———. 1983a. "African Philosophy as an Ideological Practice." *African Studies Review* 26, nos. 3–4: 133–54.

———. 1983b. "Révélation et Domination (On F. Eboussi-Boulaga's *Christianisme sans Fétiche*)." *Bulletin of African Theology* (Kinshasa), no. 9.

———. 1983c. "An African Criticism of Christianity." *Geneva-Africa* 21, no. 2: 91–100.

———. 1985a. "Espace exotique, espace refuse dans 'The Anatomy of Melancholy' (1621) de Robert Burton." *Cahiers de Linguistique* 11, no. 1–2: 53–66.

———. 1985b. "African Philosophy: An Existence De Facto." *Canadian Journal of African Studies* 19, no. 2: 453–57.

———. 1985c. "African Gnosis, Philosophy and the Order of Knowledge: An Introduction." *African Studies Review* 28, nos. 2–3: 149–233.

———. 1986a. "Placide Tempels and African Philosophy." *Bulletin des Séances, Académie Royale des Sciences d'Outre-Mer* 32, no. 3.

———. 1986b. "Lemba: A Narrative of Social Order." *Culture, Medicine and Psychiatry* 10: 277–82.

———. 1986c. "African Art as a Question Mark." *African Studies Review* 29, no. 1: 3–4.

———, ed. 1986d. "Africanism." *Canadian Journal of African Studies* (special issue) 20, no. 1.

———. 1987a. "Where Is the Real Thing? Psychoanalysis and African Mythical Narratives." *Cahiers d'Études Africaines* 107/108: 311–27.

———. 1987b. "I as an Other. Sartre and Levi-Strauss or an (Im-)Possible Dialogue on the Cogito." *Les Nouvelles Rationalités Africaines* 2, no. 8: 597–611. (Reprinted in *American Journal of Semiotics* 6, no. 1 (1988–89: 57–68.)

———. 1988a. *The Invention of Africa: Gnosis, Philosophy, and the Order of Knowledge.* Bloomington: Indiana University Press.

———. 1988b. "Debate and Commentary (edited with an Introduction)." *Canadian Journal of African Studies* 22, no. 2: 288–334.

———. 1988c. "African Theology as a Political Praxis: Vincent Mulago and the Catholic Theological Discourse, 1950–80." *Présence Africaine* 145: 86–103.

———. 1989. *Shaba Deux.* Paris: Présence Africaine.

———. 1990. "Which Idea of Africa? Herskovit's Cultural Relativism." *October* 55: 93–104.

———. 1991a. *Parables and Fables: Exegesis, Textuality, and Politics in Central Africa.* Madison: University of Wisconsin Press.

———. 1991b. "Letters of Reference." *Transition* 53: 62–76.

———. 1991c. "Reprendre." In *Africa Explores: 20th Century African Art,* ed. Susan Vogel. New York: Prestel.

———. 1992a. *The Surreptitious Speech: Presence Africaine and the Politics of Otherness 1947–1982.* Chicago: University of Chicago Press.

———. 1992b. "Is God Neutral?" *Transition* 56: 100–12.

———. 1992c. "Saint Paul-Michel Foucault." *Transition* 57.

———. 1993a. "The Power of the Greek Paradigm." *South Atlantic Quarterly* 92, no. 2: 361–85.

———. 1993b. "From 'Primitive' to 'memoriae loci.'" *Human Studies* 16: 101–10.

———. 1994. *The Idea of Africa.* Bloomington: Indiana University Press.

———, ed. 1997a. "An African Practice of Philosophy." *SAPINA Bulletin* (Society for African Philosophy in North America; special issue) 10, no. 2.

———, ed. 1997b. *Nations, Identities, Cultures.* Durham, N.C.: Duke University Press.

———. 1997c. *Tales of Faith: Religion as Political Performance in Central Africa.* London: Athlone.

———. 1998. "What Is Comparative Literature Anyway?" *Stanford Humanities Review* 6, no. 1: 164–71.

———. 2000. "Race, Identity, Politics, and History." *Journal of African History* 41, no. 2: 291–94.

———. 2004. "De la Cosmologie Dogon." *Ponts.*

———. 2005. "An African Practice of Philosophy: A Personal Testimony." *Quest* 19, nos. 1–2: 21–37. (Reprinted in *Africa e Mediterraneo* 53: 12–18.)

———. 2007. "Recovering the Obvious: Race and Mental Health." In *The Normal and Its Orders,* ed. Gode Iwele, Laura Kerr, and V. Y. Mudimbe, 101–51. Ottawa, Canada: Editions Malaika.

Mudimbe, V. Y., and K. Anthony Appiah. 1993. "The Impact of African Studies on Philosophy." In *Africa and the Disciplines: The Contributions of Research in Africa to the Social Sciences and Humanities,* ed. Robert H. Bates, V. Y. Mudimbe, and Jean O'Barr, 113–38. Chicago: University of Chicago Press.

Mudimbe, V. Y., Robert H. Bates, and Jean O'Barr, eds. 1993. *Africa and the Disciplines: The Contributions of Research in Africa to the Social Sciences and Humanities.* Chicago: University of Chicago Press.

Mudimbe, V. Y., with Sabine Engel, eds. 1999. "Diaspora and Immigration." *South Atlantic Quarterly* (Special Issue) 98, nos. 1/2 (Winter/Spring).

Mudimbe, V. Y., Gode Iwele, and Laura Kerr, eds. 2007. *The Normal and Its Orders.* Ottawa, Canada: Éditions Malaika.

Mudimbe, V. Y., and Bogumil Jewsiewicki. 1995. "Meeting the Challenge of Legitimacy." *SAPINA Bulletin* 8, nos. 1–2: 79–102. (Reprinted in *Daedalus* 124, no. 3 [Summer 1995]: 191–207.)

Mudimbe, V. Y., and J. L. Vincke. 1974. *Le Prix de péché. Essai de psychanalyse existentielle des traditions européennes et africaines.* Kinshasa: Éditions Mont Noir.

Mudimbe, V. Y., et al. 1976. *Le Vocabulaire politique zaïrois. Une étude de sociolinguistique.* Lubumbashi: Celta.

Ngugi wa Thiong'o. 1986. *Decolonizing the Mind: The Politics of Language in African Literature.* London: J. Curry; Portsmouth, N.H.: Heinemann.

———. 1998. *Penpoints, Gunpoints, and Dreams: Toward a Critical Theory of the Arts and the State in Africa.* Oxford: Clarendon.

Nkrumah, Kwame. 1961. *I Speak of Freedom: A Statement of African Ideology.* London: Mercury Books.

———. 1962 [1945]. *Towards Colonial Freedom.* London: Heinemann.

———. 1965. *Neo-Colonialism: The Last Stage of Imperialism.* London: Nelson.

———. 1969. *Handbook of Revolutionary Warfare.* London: Panaf.

———. 1970a. *Class Struggle in Africa.* London: Panaf.

———. 1970b. *Africa Must Unite.* New York: International Publishers.

———. 1970c [1964]. *Consciencism: Philosophy and Ideology for Decolonization.* New York: Monthly Review Press.

Nyerere, Julius. 1968a. *Freedom and Unity.* Dar es Salaam: Oxford University Press.

———. 1968b. *Freedom and Socialism.* Dar es Salaam: Oxford University Press.

———. 1968c. *Ujamaa—Essays on Socialism.* Dar es Salaam: Oxford University Press.

———. 1973. *Freedom and Development.* Dar es Salaam: Oxford University Press.

Nzegwu, Nkiru. 1985. "Are Western Aesthetic Theories Relevant for the Understanding of African Art?" In *The Reasons of Art,* ed. Peter J. McCormick, 173–77. Ottawa: University of Ottawa Press.

———. 1994a. "Confronting Racism: Toward the Formation of a Female-Identified Consciousness." *Canadian Journal for Women and the Law* 7, no. 1: 15–33.

———. 1994b. "Gender Equality in a Dual Sex System: The Case of Onitsha." *Canadian Journal of Law and Jurisprudence* 7, no. 1: 73–95.

———. 1996a. "Questions of Identity and Inheritance: A Critical Review of Anthony Appiah's *In My Father's House.*" *Hypatia: A Journal of Feminist Philosophy* 2, no. 1: 176–99.

———. 1996b. "Philosophers' Responsibility to African Females." *American Philosophical Association (APA) Newsletter* (Nov.): 130–35.

———. 1998a. "Chasing Shadows: The Misplaced Search for Matriarchy." *Canadian Journal of African Studies* 32, no. 3: 594–622. (Reprinted in the electronic journal *West African Review* 2, no. 1 [Aug. 2000]: http://www .westafricareview.com/war/vo12.1/nzegwu2.html.)

———. 1998b. "The Africanized Queen: Metonymy in Transformative Art." *African Studies Quarterly* 1, no. 4: http://www.clas.ufl.edu/africa/asq/v1/ 4/4.htm. (Reprinted in *Ijele: Art eJournal of the African World* 1, no. 2 [Nov. 2000]: http://www.africaresource.com/ijele/vo11.2/nzegwu3. html.)

———, ed. 1998c. *Issues in Contemporary African Art.* Binghamton, N.Y.: International Society for the Study of Africa (ISSA).

———. 1999a. "Colonial Racism: Sweeping Out Africa with Europe's Broom." In *Philosophy and Racism,* ed. Susan Babbitt and Sue Campbell, 124– 56. Ithaca, N.Y.: Cornell University Press.

———, ed. 1999b. *Contemporary Textures: Multidimensionality in Nigerian Art.* Binghamton, N.Y.: International Society for the Study of Africa (ISSA).

———. 2000. "Crossing Boundaries: Gender Transmogrification of African Art History." *Ijele: Art eJournal of the African World* 1, no. 1 (Mar.): http:// www.africaresource.com/ijele/vo11.1/nzegwu1.html.

———. 2001. "O Africa: Gender Imperialism in Academia." In *African Women and Feminism: Understanding the Complexity of Sisterhood,* ed. Oyeronke Oyewumi. Trenton, N.J.: Africa World Press.

———. 2004a. "Art and Community: A Social Conception of Beauty and

Individuality." In *A Companion to African Philosophy*, ed. Kwasi Wiredu, 415–24. Malden, Mass.: Blackwell.

———. 2004b. "Feminism and Africa: Impact and Limits of the Metaphysics of Gender." In *A Companion to African Philosophy*, ed. Kwasi Wiredu, 560–69. Malden, Mass.: Blackwell.

———. 2006. *Family Matters: Feminist Concepts in African Philosophy of Culture*. Albany: State University of New York Press.

Obenga, Theophile. 1992. *Ancient Egypt and Black Africa: A Student's Handbook for the Study of Ancient Egypt in Philosophy, Linguistics, and Gender Relations*. London: Karnak House.

———. 1995. *A Lost Tradition: African Philosophy in World History*. Philadelphia: Source Editions.

———. 2004. "Egypt: Ancient History of African Philosophy." In *A Companion to African Philosophy*, ed. Kwasi Wiredu, 31–49. Malden, Mass.: Blackwell.

Ochieng'-Odhiambo, F. 2006. "The Tripartite in Philosophic Sagacity." *Philosophia Africana* 9, no. 1 (Mar.): 17–34.

Oguejiofor, J. Obi, and Godfrey I. Onah, eds. 2005. *African Philosophy and the Hermeneutics of Culture: Essays in Honour of Theophilus Okere*. Munster: Lit Verlag.

Okere, Theophilus. 1983. *African Philosophy: A Historico-Hermeneutical Investigation of the Conditions of Its Possibility*. Lanham, Md.: University Press of America.

———, ed. 1996. *Identity and Change: Nigerian Philosophical Studies I*. Washington, D.C.: Council for Research and Values in Philosophy.

———. 2005. *Philosophy, Culture and Society in Africa*. Nsukka, Nigeria: Afro-Orbis Publications.

Okolo, Okonda. 1991. "Tradition and Destiny: Horizons of an African Philosophical Hermeneutics." In *African Philosophy: The Essential Readings,* ed. T. Serequeberhan. New York: Paragon House.

Oladipo, Olusegun. 1992. *The Idea of African Philosophy: A Critical Study of the Major Orientations in Contemporary African Philosophy*. Ibadan, Nigeria: Molecular Publishers.

———, ed. 2002. *The Third Way in African Philosophy: Essays in Honour of Kwasi Wiredu*. Ibadan, Nigeria: Hope Publications.

Olupona, J. K. 1991. *Kinship, Religion and Rituals in a Nigerian Community*. Stockholm: Almqvist and Wiksell International.

———, ed. 2001. *African Spirituality*. New York: Crossroads Publishing Company.

———, ed. 2007. *Beyond Primitivism*. New York and London: Taylor & Francis.

———, ed. 2008. *Orisa Devotion as World Religion*. Madison: University of Wisconsin Press.

Oluwole, Sophie. 1978. "On the Existence of Witches." *Second Order* 7, nos. 1–2: 20–35. (Reprinted in *African Philosophy: Selected Readings,* ed. Albert G. Mosley, 357–59. Englewood Cliffs, N.J.: Prentice Hall, 1995.)

———. 1984–1985. "The Rational Basis of Yoruba Ethical Thinking." *Nigerian Journal of Philosophy* 4–5, nos. 1–2: 14–25.

———. 1992. *Witchcraft, Reincarnation and the God-Head: Issues in African Philosophy.* Ikeja, Lagos, Nigeria: Excel Publishers.

Oruka, H. Odera. 1972a. "The Meaning of Liberty." *African Philosophical Journal* 1 (Jan.–June): 144–71.

———. 1972b. "Punishment and the Causes of Crimes." *East African Journal* 9, no. 4 (April): 10–13.

———. 1972c. "Mythologies as African Philosophy." *East African Journal* 9, no. 10 (Oct.): 5–11.

———. 1973a. "Black Consciousness." *Joliso: A Journal of Literature and Society* 1: 13–24.

———. 1973b. "Marxism and African History." In *Proceedings of the 15th World Congress of Philosophy* 3. Varna.

———. 1974a. "Mythologies et philosophie africaine: une confusion." *Consequence* 1: 38–55.

———. 1974b. "Philosophy and Other Disciplines." *Thought and Practice* 1, no. 1: 27–36.

———. 1975a. "The Fundamental Principles in the Question of 'African Philosophy,' I." *Second Order* 4, no. 1: 44–55.

———. 1975b. "Values and Philosophy and Social Sciences." *Thought and Practice* 2: 87–100.

———. 1975c. "Truth and Belief." *Universitas* 5, no. 1.

———. 1975d. "The Idea of a High God in Africa." *Thought and Practice* 2, no. 1: 29–37.

———. 1976. *Punishment and Terrorism in Africa.* Nairobi: East African Literature Bureau.

———. 1978. "John Rawls' A Theory of Justice for the Defence of Injustice." *Philosophy and Social Action* 4, no. 4: 51–60.

———. 1978–79. "Philosophy and Humanism in Africa." In *Philosophy and Civilization: Proceedings of the 1st Afro-Asian Philosophy Conference— Philosophy and Social Action,* V, ed. M. Wahba, 7–13.

———. 1980. "On Evil and the Great Fairness Universe." *Hekima: A Journal of the Humanities and Social Sciences:* 121–27.

———. 1981a. "Rawls' Ideological Affinity and Justice as Egalitarian Fairness." In *Justice: Social and Global,* ed. Lars Ericsson. Gotab: Stockholm.

———. 1981b [1978]. "Four Trends in African Philosophy." In *Philosophy in the Present Situation of Africa,* ed. Alwin Diemer. Weisbaden, Germany: Franz Steiner Erlagh.

———. 1982a. "Legal Terrorism and Human Rights." *Praxis International* 1, no. 4: 376–85.

———. 1982b. "Ideology and Culture: The African Experience." *Journal of Eastern African Research and Development* 12, nos. 1–2: 73–82.

———. 1982c. "Deterrence in Retribution." *Thought and Practice* 1, no. 4: 376–85.

———. 1983. "Sagacity in African Philosophy." *International Philosophical Quarterly* 23, no. 4: 383–93.

———. 1984a. "Philosophy in the English Speaking Africa." *Nuova Secondaria* 10.

———. 1984b. "Philosophy in Eastern Africa and the Future of Philosophy in Africa." In *Teaching and Research in Philosophy: Africa.* Paris: UNESCO.

———. 1985. "Ideology and Truth." *Praxis International* 5, no. 1: 35–77.

———. 1987. "African Philosophy: A Brief Personal History and the Current Debate." In *Contemporary Philosophy.* Vol. 5: *African Philosophy,* ed. G. Floistad. The Hague: Martinus Nijhoff.

———. 1988a. "For the Sake of Truth: A Response to Wiredu's Critique of 'Truth and Belief.'" *Quest* 2, no. 2: 3–22.

———. 1988b. "Philosophy and the Future of Humanity." *Journal of the Kenya National Academy of Sciences,* Series C: *The Humanities and Social Sciences,* 1, no. 2: 19–25.

———. 1989a. "Ideology and Ethnicity." In *Bottlenecks to National Identity,* ed. J. J. Ongong'a and K. R. Gray. Nairobi: Masaki Publishers.

———. 1989b. "Traditionalism and Modernization in Kenya: Customs, Spirits and Christianity." In *The S. M. Otieno Case: Death and Burial in Modern Kenya,* ed. J. B. Ljwang and N. N. K. Mugambi. Nairobi: University of Nairobi Press.

———. 1989c. "The Philosophy of Foreign Aid: A Question of the Right to Human Minimum." *Praxis International* 8, no. 4: 465–75.

———. 1990a. "My Strange Way to Philosophy." In *Philosophers on Their Own Works,* 14. Bern: Peter Lang.

———. 1990b. "Cultural Fundamentals in Philosophy: Obstacles in Philosophical Dialogues." *Philosophy and Theology* 5, no. 1 (Fall). (Reprinted in *Quest* 4, no. 2 [Dec. 1990]: 20–37.)

———. 1990c. *Trends in Contemporary African Philosophy.* Nairobi: Shirikon Publishers.

———, ed. 1990d. *Sage Philosophy: Indigenous Thinkers and the Modern Debate on African Philosophy.* Leiden: E. J. Brill.

———. 1997. *Practical Philosophy.* Nairobi and Kampala: East African Educational Publishers.

Oruka, H. O., and D. A. Masolo, eds. 1983. *Philosophy and Cultures.* Nairobi: Bookwise Publishers.

Outlaw, Lucius. 1992–1993. "African, African American, Africana Philosophy." *Philosophical Forum* 24, nos. 1–3: 63–93. (Reprinted in *African-American Perspectives and Philosophical Traditions,* ed. John Pittman, 35–62. New York: Routledge, 1997.)

———. 1996. "African 'Philosophy'? Deconstructive and Reconstructive Challenges." In *On Race and Philosophy.* New York: Routledge.

———. 1997. "African, African American, Africana Philosophy." In *African-American Perspectives and Philosophical Traditions,* ed. John Pittman, 63–93. New York: Routledge.

———. 2003. "'Afrocentricity': Critical Considerations." In *A Companion to African-American Philosophy,* ed. Tommy Lott and John Pittman, 155–67. Malden, Mass.: Blackwell.

Owomoyela, Oyekan. 1987. "Africa and the Imperative of Philosophy: A Skeptical Consideration." *African Studies Review* 30, no. 1: 79–100. (Reprinted in *African Philosophy: Selected Readings,* ed. Albert G. Mosley, 236–62. Englewood Cliffs, N.J.: Prentice Hall, 1995.)

———. 1994. "With Friends Like These: A Critique of Pervasive Anti-Africanisms in Current African Studies Epistemology and Methodology." *African Studies Review* 37–38, no. 3: 77–101.

Oyewumi, Oyeronke. 1997. *The Invention of Women: Making an African Sense of Western Gender Discourses.* Minneapolis: University of Minnesota Press.

———, ed. 2003. *African Women and Feminism: Reflecting on the Politics of Sisterhood.* Trenton, N.J.: Africa World Press.

———, ed. 2005. *African Gender Studies: A Reader.* New York: Palgrave Macmillan.

Padmore, George. 2004. *Africa and World Peace.* New York: Routledge.

p'Bitek, Okot. 1966. *Song of Lawino: A Lament.* Nairobi: East African Publishing House.

———. 1970. *African Religions in Western Scholarship.* Nairobi: East African Literature Bureau.

Pearce, Carol. 1992. "African Philosophy and the Sociological Thesis." *Journal of the Philosophy of the Social Sciences* 22, no. 4: 440–60.

Peterson, Charles F. 2007. *Du Bois, Fanon, Cabral: The Margins of Elite Anti-Colonial Leadership.* Lanham, Md.: Lexington Books.

Pittman, John, ed. 1997. *African-American Perspectives and Philosophical Traditions.* New York: Routledge.

Praeg, Leonhard. 2000. *African Philosophy and the Quest for Autonomy: A Philosophical Investigation.* Amsterdam: Rodopi.

Pratt, Vernon. 1972. "Science and Traditional African Religion." *Second Order* 1, no. 1: 7–20.

Presbey, Gail M. 1998. "Criticism of Multiparty Democracy: Parallels between Wamba-dia-Wamba and Arendt." *New Political Science* 20, no. 1: 35–52.

———. 2007. "Sage Philosophy: Criteria That Distinguish It from Ethnophilosophy and Make It a Unique Approach within African Philosophy." *Philosophia Africana* 10, no. 2: 126–60.

Quine, W. V. O. 1960. *Word and Object.* Cambridge, Mass.: MIT Press.

Ramose, Mogobe. 2003a. "I Doubt, Therefore African Philosophy Exists." *South African Journal of Philosophy* 22, no. 2: 113–27.

———. 2003b. "The Philosophy of *Ubuntu* and *Ubuntu* as a Philosophy." *The*

African Philosophy Reader, 2nd ed., ed. P. H. Coetzee and A. P. J. Roux, 230–38. New York: Routledge.

———. 2003c. "The Ethics of *Ubuntu.*" *The African Philosophy Reader,* 2nd ed., ed. P. H. Coetzee and A. P. J. Roux, 324–30. New York: Routledge.

Rodney, Walter. 1982. *How Europe Underdeveloped Africa.* Washington, D.C.: Howard University.

Rorty, Richard, ed. 1967. *The Linguistic Turn: Recent Essays in Philosophical Method.* Chicago: University of Chicago Press.

Salemohamed, G. 1983. "African Philosophy." *Philosophy* 58, no. 226: 535–38.

Sallis, John. 2002. *On Translation.* Bloomington: Indiana University Press.

Sekyi-Otu, Ato. 1996. *Fanon's Dialectic of Experience.* Cambridge, Mass.: Harvard University Press.

———. 2003. "Fanon and the Possibility of Postcolonial Critical Imagination." *CODESRIA Symposium on Canonical Works and Continuing Innovations in African Arts and Humanities.* www.codesria.org/Links/conference/accra/Sekyi_Otu.pdf .

Senghor, Léopold S. 1956. "The Spirit of Civilization or the Laws of African Negro Culture." *Présence Africaine,* nos. 8–10: 51–65.

———. 1963. "Negritude and African Socialism." *St. Anthony's Papers* 15 (ed. Kenneth Kirkwood): 9–22. (Reprinted in *The African Philosophy Reader,* ed. P. H. Coetzee and A. P. J. Roux, 438–48. London: Routledge, 1998.)

———. 1964. *On African Socialism.* New York: Praeger.

———. 1965. *Prose and Poetry.* Ed. and trans. John Reed and Clive Wake. Oxford: Oxford University Press.

———. 1971. *The Foundations of "Africanité" or "Négritude" and "Arabité."* Paris: Présence Africaine.

Serequeberhan, Tsenay. 1989. "The Idea of Colonialism in Hegel's Philosophy of Right." *International Philosophical Quarterly* 29, no. 3: 301–18.

———. 1991a. "The African Liberation Struggle: A Hermeneutic Exploration of an African Historico-Political Horizon." *Ultimate Reality and Meaning* 14, no. 1: 46–52.

———. 1991b. "African Philosophy: The Point in Question." In *African Philosophy: The Essential Readings,* ed. T. Serequeberhan, 3–28. New York: Paragon House.

———, ed. 1991c. *African Philosophy: The Essential Readings.* New York: Paragon House.

———. 1994. *The Hermeneutics of African Philosophy.* London: Routledge.

———. 1997. "The Critique of Eurocentrism and the Practice of African Philosophy." In *Postcolonial African Philosophy: A Critical Reader,* ed. Emmanuel Eze, 141–61. Oxford: Blackwell.

———. 2000. *Our Heritage: The Past in the Present of African-American and African Existence.* New York: Rowman and Littlefield.

———. 2003. "The African Anti-Colonial Struggle: An Effort at Reclaiming History." *Philosophica Africana* 6, no. 1 (March): 47–58.

———. 2004. "Theory and Actuality of Existence: Fanon and Cabral." In *A Companion to African Philosophy*, ed. Kwasi Wiredu, 225–30. Malden, Mass.: Blackwell.

———. 2007. *Contested Memory: The Icons of the Occidental Tradition.* Trenton, N.J.: Africa World Press.

Sigmund, P., ed. 1963. *The Ideologies of Developing Nations.* New York: Praeger.

Skorupski, John. 1967. *Symbol and Theory.* Cambridge: Cambridge University Press.

Sodipo. J. Olubi. 1972. "Greek Science and Religion." *Second Order* 1, no. 1 (Jan.): 66–76.

———. 1973. "Notes on the Concept of Cause and Chance in Yoruba Traditional Thought." *Second Order* 2, no. 2: 12–20.

———. 1980. "Some Philosophical Aspects of the African Historical Experience." In *African Philosophy: Proceedings of the Seminar on African Philosophy*, ed. Claude Sumner, 379–91. Addis Ababa: Chamber Printing House.

———. 1983. "Philosophy, Science, Technology and Traditional African Thought." In *Philosophy and Cultures,* ed. H. O. Oruka 36–43. Nairobi, Kenya: Bookwise Publishers.

———. 1984. "Philosophy in Pre-Colonial Africa." In *Teaching and Research in Philosophy: Africa.* Paris: UNESCO, 73–80.

———. 1988. "Karl Marx, Albert Camus and Frantz Fanon on the Degradation and Re-creation of Human Personality." In *Die Philosophie in der modernen Welt: Gedenkschrift fur Prof. Dr. med. Dr. phil. Alwin Diemer.* Frankfurt am Main: Peter Lang.

Sogolo, G. S. 1981. "Universal Prescriptivism and Racial Discrimination." *Second Order* 10, nos. 1–2: 80–90.

———. 1990. "Options in African Philosophy." *Philosophy* 65, no. 251: 39–52.

———. 1993. *Foundations of African Philosophy: A Definitive Analysis of Conceptual Issues in African Thought.* Ibadan, Nigeria: University of Ibadan Press.

———. 1998a. "The Concept of Cause in African Thought." In *The African Philosophy Reader*, ed. P. H. Coetzee and A. J. P. Roux, 177–85. London: Routledge.

———. 1998b. "Logic and Rationality." In *The African Philosophy Reader,* ed. P. H. Coetzee and A. J. P. Roux, 217–33. London: Routledge.

Soyinka,'Wole. 1976. *Myth, Literature, and the African World.* Cambridge: Cambridge University Press.

Sumner, Claude. 1976. *Ethiopian Philosophy.* Vol. 2. Addis Ababa, Ethiopia: Addis Ababa University.

———. 1999. *Living Springs of Wisdom and Philosophy*. Addis Ababa: Addis Ababa University.

———. 2004. "The Light and the Shadow: Zera Yacob and Walda Heywat: Two Ethiopian Philosophers of the Seventeenth Century." In *A Companion to African Philosophy*, ed. Kwasi Wiredu, 172–82 . Malden, Mass.: Blackwell.

Taiwo, Olufemi. 1993a. "Colonialism and Its Aftermath: The Crisis of Knowledge Production." *Callaloo* 16, no. 4: 891–908.

———. 1993b. "On Diversifying the Philosophy Curriculum." *Teaching Philosophy* 16, no. 4: 287–99.

———. 1995. "Appropriating Africa: An Essay on New Africanist Schools." *Issue* 23, no. 1: 39–45.

———. 1996a. *Legal Naturalism: A Marxist Theory of Law*. Ithaca, N.Y.: Cornell University Press.

———. 1996b. "On the Misadventures of a National Consciousness: A Retrospect of Frantz Fanon's Gift of Prophecy." In *Fanon: A Critical Reader*, ed. L. Gordon, R. White, and T. Sharpley-Whiting. Oxford: Blackwell.

———. 1997. "Exorcising Hegel's Ghost: Africa's Challenge to Philosophy." *African Studies Quarterly* 1, no. 4.

———. 1999a. "Reading the Colonizer's Mind: Lord Lugard and the Philosophical Foundations of British Colonialism." In *Racism and Philosophy*, ed. Susan Babbitt and Sue Campbell, 157–88. Ithaca, N.Y.: Cornell University Press.

———. 1999b. "The Rule of Law: The New Leviathan?" *Canadian Journal of Law and Jurisprudence* 12, no. 7: 151–68.

———. 2000a. "Law's Promise, Law's Handicap: Race and Law at the Turn of the Century." *Dalhousie Review* 80, no. 1: 21–44.

———. 2000b. "This Prison Called My Skin: On Being Black in America." *Annals of Scholarship: Art Practices and the Human Sciences in a Global Culture* 14, no. 1 (Spring): 136–49. (Reprinted in *Problematizing Blackness: Self-Ethnographies by Black Immigrants to the United States*, ed. Percy C. Hintzen and Jean Muteba Rahier, 35–52. New York: Routledge, 2003.)

———. 2001. "On the Limits of Law at Century's End." In *Social and Political Philosophy: The Proceedings of the 20th World Congress of Philosophy*, vol. 11, ed. David M. Rasmussen, 69–80. Charlottesville: Philosophy Documentation Center.

———. 2002. "Prophets without Honour: African Apostles of Modernity in the Nineteenth and Twentieth Centuries." *West African Review:* http://www.westafricareview.com.

———. 2003. "Feminism and Africa: Some Reflections on the Poverty of Theory." In *African Women and Feminism: Reflections on the Politics of Sisterhood*, ed. Oyeronke Oyewumi, 45–66. Trenton, N.J.: Africa World.

———. 2004a. "Post-Independence African Political Philosophy." In *A

Companion to African Philosophy, ed. Kwasi Wiredu, 243–59. Malden, Mass.: Blackwell.

———. 2004b. "*Ifa:* An Account of a Divination System and Some Concluding Epistemological Questions." In *A Companion to African Philosophy,* ed. Kwasi Wiredu, 304–12. Malden, Mass.: Blackwell.

———. 2004c. "Of Citizens and Citizenship." In *Constitutionalism and Society in Africa,* ed. Okon Akiba, 55–78. Burlington, Vt.: Ashgate.

———. 2006. "The Legal Subject in Modern African Law: A Nigerian Report." *Human Rights Review* 7, no. 2 (Jan.–March): 17–34.

———. 2009. *How Colonialism Preempted Modernity in Africa.* Bloomington: Indiana University Press.

Teffo, Joe. 2004. "Democracy, Kingship and Consensus: A South African Perspective." In *A Companion to African Philosophy,* ed. Kwasi Wiredu, 443–49. Malden, Mass.: Blackwell.

Tempels, Placide. 1949. *La Philosophie bantoue.* Paris: Présence Africaine.

———. 1959. *Bantu Philosophy.* Paris: Présence Africaine.

Venable, Vernon. 1946. *Human Nature: The Marxian View.* London: D. Dobson Ltd.

Verharen, Charles. 2003. "Always Something New Out of Africa: In Philosophy Too. Review of *A Short History of African Philosophy.*" H-Africa@h-net.msu.edu.

Verran, Helen. 2001. *Science and an African Logic.* Chicago: University of Chicago Press.

Walcott, Derek. 1992. *Omeros.* New York: Farrar, Straus and Giroux.

Wamba-dia-Wamba, Ernest. 1984. "History of Neo-Colonialism or Neo-Colonialist History? Self-Determination and History in Africa." In *Working Paper No. 5,* 1–20. Trenton, N.J.: African Research and Publications Project.

———. 1991. "Philosophy in Africa: Challenges of the African Philosopher." In *African Philosophy: The Essential Readings,* ed. T. Serequeberhan, 211–46. New York: Paragon House.

———. 1994. "Africa in Search of a New Mode of Politics." In *African Perspectives on Development,* ed. Ulf Himmelstrand, Kabiru Kinyanjui, and Edward Mburugu, 249–61. London: James Currey.

Wang, Xinli. 2007. *Incommensurability and Cross-Language Communication.* Burlington, Vt.: Ashgate.

West, Harry G. 2007. *Ethnographic Sorcery.* Chicago: University of Chicago Press.

Wilson, Bryan. 1974. *Rationality.* Oxford: Blackwell.

Wiredu, Kwasi. 1970. "Kant's Synthetic Apriori in Geometry and the Rise of Non-Euclidean Geometries." *Kant-Studien* 61, nos. 1–4: 5–27.

———. 1972a. "Truth as Opinion." *Universitas* (March).

———. 1972b. "A Note on Modal Quantification, Ontology and the Indenumerably Infinite." *Analysis* (June).

———. 1972c. "On an African Orientation in Philosophy." *Second Order* 1, no. 2: 3–13.

———. 1972d. "Material Implication and 'If-Then.'" *International Logic Review* (Dec.).

———. 1973a. "Deducibility and Inferability." *Mind* n.s. 82, no. 325: 31–55.

———. 1973b. "Logic and Ontology, Part 1." *Second Order* 2, no. 1: 71–82.

———. 1973c. "Philosophy, Mysticism and Rationality." *Universitas* (Mar.).

———. 1973d. "On the Real Logical Structure of Lewis' 'Independent Proof.'" *Notre Dame Journal of Formal Logic* 14, no. 4 (Oct.): 543–46.

———. 1973e. "Logic and Ontology, Part 2." *Second Order* 2, no. 2: 21–38.

———. 1974a. "To Be Is to Be Known." *Legon Journal of the Humanities* 1.

———. 1974b. "What Is Philosophy?" *Universitas* 3, no. 2 (Mar.).

———. 1974c. "Carnap on Iterated Modalities." *Philosophy and Phenomenological Research* 35, no. 2: 240–45.

———. 1974d. "Classes and Sets." *Logique et Analyse* (Jan.).

———. 1974e. "A Remark on a Certain Consequence of Connexive Logic for Zermelo's Set Theory." *Studia Logica* 33, no. 2.

———. 1974f. "Logic and Ontology, Part 3." *Second Order* 3, no. 2.

———. 1975a. "In Praise of Utopianism." *Thought and Practice* 2, no. 2.

———. 1975b. "Logic and Ontology, Part 4." *Second Order* 4, no. 1: 25–43.

———. 1975c. "Truth as a Logical Constant, with an Application to the Principle of Excluded Middle." *Philosophical Quarterly* 25, no. 101: 305–17.

———. 1976a. "Predication and Abstract Entities." *Legon Journal of the Humanities* 2.

———. 1976b. "On the Formal Character of Logic." *Ghana Social Science Journal* (May).

———. 1976c. "On *Reductio ad Absurdum* Proofs." *International Logic Review* (June).

———. 1976d. "Paradoxes." *Second Order* 5, no. 2: 3–26.

———. 1976e. "In Behalf of Opinion." *Universitas* (Nov.).

———. 1976f. "How Not to Compare African Thought with Western Thought." *Ch'Indaba* no. 2 (July–Dec.): 4–8. (Reprinted in *African Philosophy: An Introduction*, ed. R. Wright, 159–71. Washington, D.C.: University Press of America, 1977; and in *African Philosophy: Selected Readings,* ed. Albert G. Mosley. Englewood Cliffs, N.J.: Prentice Hall, 1995.)

———. 1980a. "Philosophy and Our Culture." *Proceedings of the Ghana Academy of Arts and Sciences.*

———. 1980b. *Philosophy and an African Culture.* Cambridge: Cambridge University Press.

———. 1981. "Philosophy in Africa Today." In *Into the 80's: The Proceedings of the Eleventh Annual Conference of the Canadian Association of African Studies,* ed. D. Ray, P. Shinnie, and D. Williams. Calgary: University of Calgary, Tantalus Research.

———. 1983a. "The Akan Concept of Mind." *Ibadan Journal of Humanistic Studies.* (Reprinted in *African Philosophy.* Vol. 5 of *Contemporary Philosophy: A New Survey,* ed. G. Floistad. Dodrecht: Martinus Nijhoff Publishers, 1987.)

———. 1983b. "Morality and Religion in Akan Thought." In *Philosophy and Cultures,* ed. H. Odera Oruka and D. Masolo, 6–13. Nairobi, Kenya: Bookwise. (Reprinted in *African-American Humanism: An Anthology,* ed. Norm Allen Jr. New York: Prometheus Books, 1991.)

———. 1984a. "Philosophical Research and Teaching in Africa: Some Suggestions." In *Teaching and Research in Philosophy: Africa.* Paris: UNESCO.

———. 1984b. "Survey: Philosophy Teaching and Research in English-Speaking Africa." In *Teaching and Research in Philosophy: Africa.* Paris: UNESCO.

———. 1984c. "Some Issues in Philosophy in Africa Today." In *Teaching and Research in Philosophy: Africa.* Paris: UNESCO.

———. 1985a. "The Concept of Truth in the Akan Language." In *Philosophy in Africa: Trends and Perspectives,* ed. P. Bodunrin, 43–54. Ife, Nigeria: University of Ife Press.

———. 1985b. "Replies to Critics." In *Philosophy in Africa: Trends and Perspectives,* ed. P. Bodunrin, 91–102. Ife, Nigeria: University of Ife Press.

———. 1985c. "Problems in Africa's Self-Identification in the Contemporary World." In *Africa and the Problem of Its Identity,* ed. A. Diemer and P. Hountondji. New York: Verlag Peter Lang.

———. 1989. "Death and the Afterlife in African Culture." In *Death and Dying: Cross-Cultural and Multi-Disciplinary Views,* ed. A. Berger et al. Philadelphia: Charles Press.

———. 1990a. "On the Question of the Right to Die: An African View." In *To Die or Not to Die? Cross-Disciplinary, Cultural, and Legal Perspectives on the Right to Choose Death,* ed. Arthur S. Berger and Joyce Berger. New York: Praeger.

———. 1990b. "An Akan Perspective on Human Rights." In *Human Rights in Africa: Cross-Cultural Perspectives,* ed. A. Ahmed An-Na'im and F. Deng. Washington, D.C.: Brookings Institution.

———. 1990c. "Universalism and Particularism in Religion from an African Perspective." *Journal of Humanism and Ethical Religion* 3, no. 1. (Reprinted in *Self, Cosmos, God,* ed. D. Kolak and R. Martin. New York: Harcourt Brace Jovanovich College Publishers, 1992.)

———. 1991. "On Defining African Philosophy." In *African Philosophy: The Essential Readings,* ed. T. Serequeberhan, 87–110. New York: Paragon House. (Reprinted in *Postkoloniales Philosophieren: Afrika,* edited by

H. Nagl-Docekal and F. M. Wimmer, 40–62. Vienna: R. Oldenbourg Verlag, 1992.)

———. 1992a. "Formulating Modern Thought in African Languages: Some Theoretical Considerations." In *The Surreptitious Speech: Presence Africaine and the Politics of Otherness 1947–1987*, ed. V. Y. Mudimbe, 301–32. Chicago: University of Chicago Press.

———. 1992b. "Moral Foundations of African Culture." In *African-American Perspectives on Biomedical Ethics*, ed. H. E. Flack and E. D. Pellegrino. Washington, D.C.: Georgetown University Press. (Reprinted in *Person and Community*, ed. Kwasi Wiredu and Kwame Gyekye, 193–206. Washington, D.C.: Council for Research in Values and Philosophy, 1992.)

———. 1992c. "The African Concept of Personhood." In *African-American Perspectives on Biomedical Ethics*, ed. H. E. Flack and E. D. Pellegrino. Washington, D.C.: Georgetown University Press.

———. 1992d. "Science, Technology and Humane Values." In *Paths to Human Flourishing: Philosophical Perspectives*. Seoul: Korean Philosophical Association.

———. 1992–1993. "African Philosophical Tradition: A Case Study of the Akan." *Philosophical Forum* 24, nos. 1–3: 35–62.

———. 1993. "Canons of Conceptualization." *Monist* 76, no. 4: 450–76.

———. 1995a. "Are There Cultural Universals?" *Monist* 78, no. 1: 52–64. (An earlier version of this paper was published in 1990 in *Quest: Philosophical Discussions* 4, no. 2: 5–19.)

———. 1995b. *Conceptual Decolonization in African Philosophy: Four Essays by Kwasi Wiredu*. Introd. and ed. Olusegun Oladipo. Ibadan, Nigeria: Hope Publications.

———. 1995c. "Knowledge, Truth and Fallibility." In *The Concept of Knowledge*, ed. I. Kucuradi and R. S. Cohen. Boston: Kluwer Academic.

———. 1995d. "Metaphysics in Africa." In *A Companion to Metaphysics*, ed. J. Kim and E. Sosa. Oxford: Blackwell.

———. 1995e. "Democracy and Consensus in Traditional African Politics: A Plea for a Non-Party Polity." *Centennial Review* 39, no. 1 (Winter).

———. 1995f. "Custom and Morality: A Comparative Analysis of Some African and Western Conceptions of Morals." In *African Philosophy: Selected Readings*, ed. Albert G. Mosley. Englewood Cliffs, N.J.: Prentice Hall.

———. 1995g. "On Decolonizing African Religions." In *Decolonizing the Mind: Proceedings of the Colloquium Held at Unisa, October 1995*, ed. J. Malherbe. Pretoria: Research Unit for African Philosophy.

———. 1995h. "Philosophy, Humankind and the Environment." In *Philosophy of Nature and Environmental Ethics*. Vol. 1 of *Philosophy, Humanity and Ecology*, ed. H. Odera Oruka. Nairobi, Kenya: African Center for Technology Studies Press.

———. 1995i. "Philosophy and the Political Problem of Human Rights." In

The Idea and the Documents of Human Rights, ed. I. Kucuradi. Ankara, Turkey: Philosophical Society of Turkey.

———. 1995j. "Particularistic Studies of African Philosophies as an Aid to Decolonization." In *Decolonizing the Mind: Proceedings of the Colloquium Held at Unisa, October 1995,* ed. J. Malherbe. Pretoria: Research Unit for African Philosophy.

———. 1995k. "On Decolonizing African Religions." In *Decolonizing the Mind: Proceedings of the Colloquium Held at Unisa, October 1995,* ed. J. Malherbe. Pretoria: Research Unit for African Philosophy.

———. 1996a. "Time and African Thought." In *Time and Temporality in Intercultural Perspectives,* ed. D. Tiemersma and A. F. Oosterling. Amsterdam: Rodopi.

———. 1996b. *Cultural Universals and Particulars: An African Perspective.* Bloomington: Indiana University Press.

———. 1997a. "Democracy and Consensus in African Traditional Politics: A Plea for a Non-Party Polity." In *Postcolonial African Philosophy: A Critical Reader,* ed. Emmanuel Eze, 303–12. Oxford: Blackwell.

———. 1997b. "African Philosophy and Intercultural Dialogue." *Quest: Philosophical Discussions* 11, nos. 1–2: 29–42.

———. 1998. "Can Philosophy Be Intercultural? An African Viewpoint." *Diogenes* 46, no. 4: 147–67.

———. 2000. "Our Problem of Knowledge: Brief Reflections on Knowledge and Development in Africa." In *African Philosophy as Cultural Inquiry,* ed. I. Karp and D. A. Masolo, 181–86. Bloomington: Indiana University Press.

———. 2004a. "Amo's Critique of Descartes' Philosophy of Mind." In *A Companion to African Philosophy,* ed. Kwasi Wiredu, 200–206. Malden, Mass.: Blackwell.

———. 2004b. "Truth and an African Language." *African Philosophy: New and Traditional Perspectives,* ed. Lee M. Brown, 33–50. Oxford: Oxford University Press.

———, ed. 2004c. *A Companion to African Philosophy.* Malden, Mass.: Blackwell.

———. 2007. "Social Philosophy in Postcolonial Studies: Some Preliminaries Concerning Communalism and Communitarianism." Keynote Address at Rhodes University, South Africa (unpublished paper).

Wiredu, Kwasi, and Kwame Gyekye, eds. 1992. *Person and Community: Ghanaian Philosophical Studies, 1.* New York: Council for Research in Values and Philosophy.

Wright, Richard A., ed. 1984. *African Philosophy: An Introduction.* 3rd ed. Lanham, Md.: University Press of America.

Wynter, Sylvia. 1984. "The Ceremony Must Be Found: After Humanism." *Boundary 2* 12, no. 3, and 13, no. 1 (Spring/Fall): 19–70.

———. 1994. "But What Does Wonder Do? Meanings, Canons, Too? On

Literary Texts, Cultural Contexts, and What It's Like to Be One/Not One of Us." *Stanford Humanities Review* 4, no. 1 (Spring): 124–29.

———. 2001. "Towards the Sociogenic Principle: Fanon, Identity, the Puzzle of Conscious Experience." In *National Identities and Socio-Political Changes in Latin America,* ed. Mercedes F. Duran-Cogan and Antonio Gomez-Moriana, 30–66. New York: Routledge.

Index

BARRY HALLEN has taught philosophy at the Obafemi Awolowo University in Nigeria. He is an Associate in the W. E. B. Du Bois Institute for African and African American Research at Harvard University, and Professor of Philosophy in the Department of Philosophy and Religion at Morehouse College. He is author of *The Good, the Bad, and the Beautiful: Discourse about Values in Yoruba Culture*; *African Philosophy: The Analytic Approach*; and (with J. Olubi Sodipo) *Knowledge, Belief, and Witchcraft: Analytic Experiments in African Philosophy*.